DATE DUE

THE SOCIAL SPIRIT

IN AMERICA

THE SOCIAL SPIRIT

IN AMERICA

BY
CHARLES R. HENDERSON

 BOOKS FOR LIBRARIES PRESS
FREEPORT, NEW YORK

First Published 1897
Reprinted 1972

Library of Congress Cataloging in Publication Data

Henderson, Charles Richmond, 1848-1915.
  The social spirit in America.

  (BCL/select bibliographies index reprint series)
  Reprint of the 1897 ed.
  Bibliography: p.
  1. Social problems. 2. Labor and laboring classes
--U. S. 3. U. S.--Social conditions--1865-1918.
I. Title.
HN57.H48 1972   309.1'73   77-39378
ISBN 0-8369-9911-8

PRINTED IN THE UNITED STATES OF AMERICA
BY
NEW WORLD BOOK MANUFACTURING CO., INC.
HALLANDALE, FLORIDA 33009

TO MY WIFE,

WHOSE COUNSELS AND ENCOURAGEMENT HAVE
MADE STUDY AND WORK A JOY;

AND

TO MANY FRIENDS IN TERRE HAUTE
AND DETROIT,

WHOSE GENEROUS COÖPERATION THROUGH TWENTY
YEARS OF SOCIAL SERVICE HAS TURNED
HOPES INTO REALITIES.

CONTENTS.

Chapter		Page
I.	Introduction	9
II.	Home-Making as a Social Art	23
III.	Friendly Circles of Women Wage-Earners	44
IV.	Better Houses for the People	59
V.	Public Health	72
VI.	Good Roads and Communication	88
VII.	The First Factor of Industrial Reform: The Socialized Citizen	100
VIII.	What Good Employers are Doing	117
IX.	Organizations of Wage-Earners	137
X.	Economic Coöperation of the Community	159
XI.	Political Reforms	174
XII.	The Social Spirit in the State School System	191
XIII.	Voluntary Organization of Education	217
XIV.	Socialized Beauty and Recreation	240
XV.	Charity and Correction	260
XVI.	The Social Spirit in Conflict with Anti-Social Institutions	280
XVII.	The Institutions of Ideals: The Ancient Confederacy of Virtue	304
	Appendix	331

THE SOCIAL SPIRIT IN AMERICA.

CHAPTER I.

INTRODUCTION.

"A POOR and cowardly spirit is every servant of social science who does not labor in the service of promoting civic life," says master Schäffle, a leader of the system-makers. His English peer, the cautious advocate of individual enterprise, says in his last volume: "It may fairly be said that the study of sociology is useless if, from an account of what has been, we cannot infer what is to be—that there is no such thing as a science of society unless its generalizations concerning past days yield enlightenment to our thoughts concerning days to come, and consequent guidance to our acts." The description and explanation of past conditions, especially of the remote past, deal with simple matters of fact. But enterprises of thought and effort which look toward the future must ever have a large element of personal belief and hope which cannot claim so absolute a scientific justification. For us the world is will before it is exact knowledge, for no one can ever know what is possible until the untried is attempted through faith. *Theory and conduct.*

Religious beliefs are social facts quite apart from our personal acceptance of them. When they are our own we cannot conceal them. Honesty and humanity require us to express our best hopes if we really consider them of value. Most of us regard this world, spite of *Religious beliefs.*

many apparent contradictions and enigmas, as the creation of that Father whose character and disposition are most perfectly manifested in the deeds, words, and sacrifices of Jesus Christ. There is much of wrong, cruelty, oppression, of unspeakable and inexplicable wickedness, but the universe has not escaped from infinite goodness. Nature and life show his creative, indwelling energy. History interprets his purpose and his moral order. Social evolution is the unfolding of his mind and will. Evil itself will be found subordinate and subservient to his holiness and love. All who are working for goodness are coöperating with, not contending against, almighty power. Goethe gives us a charming parable : "We hear of a singular custom in the English marine service. All ropes of the royal navy, from the strongest to the weakest, are woven in such a manner that a red thread runs through the whole, which no one can unwind without destroying all; and thus the smallest part may be recognized as belonging to the crown." So the charity of God runs through all the works of human justice and kindness which we here call "the social spirit," a fruit of the Holy Spirit.

Such is our belief. This is not the place for any attempts at proof of such convictions. They have grown up in each of us from inherited and instinctive impulses, traditional teachings, social customs and sentiments, laws, literature, parental influence, historical study, philosophical reflection. Each person must win and test his own view of the universe. Force is out of the question. Bare argument has little weight. Religious beliefs are purified and strengthened by ethical living more than by logical processes. "He that is willing to do His will shall know." Obedience to the good we know is the organ of deeper insight. In the mind of religious men the "social spirit" is a stream from the divine fountain of all being.

It is true that a social history could be written which did not assume the truth of this belief. History alone does not prove that infinite righteousness is at the heart of life. Sociology is not theology. Social science may treat religious convictions as social forces, just as it treats hunger, love, or æsthetic taste, as causes actually at work. It is for theology and philosophy to construct arguments about the reality of God's existence, while sociology finds the belief in divine goodness a phenomenon in life and shows how it acts. Religious belief, however, resembles æsthetic and moral sentiments in this, that it is most adequately appreciated by those who have inward experience of its quality. One born deaf could not be expected to write an edifying treatise on sound, nor one born blind on colors. External effects may be observed by any impartial student, but inner quality and tension can be estimated only by those who live the life. *Attitude of sociology.*

Enthusiasm for humanity, hope of progress, confidence in man may not profess to be religious, but they really assume and imply a divine foundation of happiness through morality. This is precisely the essence of the religious view.

While our moral and religious beliefs are highly personal they are by no means mere private affairs. They must be tested by nature and life. If beliefs do not help welfare, if they weaken human beings in body or mind, if they unfit us for struggle with hunger, cold, and want, they must disappear with the people who cling to them. Hence the very struggle for existence which presses upon us is an external test, independent of our private notions and choices. A false faith can *Test of beliefs.*

no more survive than an inferior plow or an antiquated engine, after competition has had a chance to sift and test.

Elements of motive.

We cannot here follow the long history of the enlargement of thought and the refinement of sentiments. The moral forces are progressive and change with the entire life of man. They are relatively less occupied with mere escape from misery and fear; they are increasingly directed to heightening happiness, delight, service, knowledge. We are passing from a "pain economy" to a "pleasure economy." .By reflection on our own conduct and by observing the actions of our fellow-men we discover the feelings which lead people to produce social institutions.

The world is first moved by hunger and love. Many human beings go little beyond this. Hunger and love conduct men to marriage, hold parents and children in the family, induce men to till and travel, to organize banks, railroad companies, and all commercial enterprises.

Variety of interests.

But in all ages and lands other motives have always acted upon conduct. There is delight in amusement, ornament, and decoration. The play instincts unite with the æsthetic. Many ancient men painted their bodies before they wore clothes. Even in our enlightened times we know of fine barbarians, lingering late in civilized surroundings, who expend their income on ostrich feathers while they shiver without woolen underwear. Rude hunters drew pictures on their weapons and tents, and modern merchants will pay a fortune for a Meissonier or a Bouguereau. The wealth of a kingdom goes into a city art museum. Diamonds are sought at frightful hazard and cost, although a million of them would not feed one beggar. Beauty befits holiness, and so churches are made splendid with fine architecture to please the taste as well as to honor the Creator.

The eager questions of lisping children, the boy's curious search for cocoons, shells, and beetles, the long and costly experiments of Palissy and Faraday, the astronomical and exploring expeditions, the erection of colleges and universities, the publication of books and papers, are all witnesses to the deep and universal and increasing desire of man to discover, to know. Nature, human beings, and the Source of life are objects of intellectual interest, and many men have laid down their lives as the martyrs of science. *Scientific curiosity.*

How eager we are to be in company! Without any definite purpose human beings drift into fellowships and enjoy the simple delights of sociability. Isolation, if it is prolonged, is torture to all healthy persons; the insane are sometimes improved merely by giving them companions; and even criminals beg to sit down, if only in silence, with persons of their kind. *Fellowship.*

Then there is conscience, the profound and inextinguishable sense of the right and the just. To what noble deeds does this moral feeling give birth. How essential it is to social security. What institutions of custom and law and instruction it creates.

Crowning all is the belief in God, the spring of trust, hope, and benevolence. Religion seems to be universal and instinctive. It often takes strange and monstrous forms. It may be made hurtful when it is uninstructed, ignorant, and perverted by selfish men. But it is a primary social force, capable of being made a mighty lever of human welfare. *Religion.*

"Self-interest," the cynic asserts, is the sole motive of human action. But what is this "self" whose

Self-interest.

interest is so powerful? No two selfs are alike or of equal grade. One finds delight in cruelty and low pleasures. Another secures satisfaction in useful service, in heroic enterprise, in noble sacrifices. Such forms of higher self-interest look remarkably like sympathy, love, altruism. A self is a social product, and our interests are in our children, our friends, our neighborhood, our country, our church. It is just as well to call these larger and more generous impulses by higher titles. It does not assist clearness of thought to ascribe selfishness to the patriotic soldier who dies with his eyes turned toward his flag.

The social spirit creates institutions.

"Soul is form and doth the body make." We begin life, without our own selection, in the first institution of history, the family, and for a long time we are content without further alliances. Food, protection, companionship, answers to questions of curiosity, play, work, prayer are all found in this little world. But as he travels further the boy discovers, perhaps with pain, the necessity of going to school. Father and mother are too busy to give their time to teaching, and one learns more rapidly with trained teachers and in the rivalry of a class. At school or on the street the child makes acquaintances and is invited to a party. Life offers fresh attractions and novelties to surprise and please the voyager new to earth and sky. At length the boy, urged by example and necessity, conscious of growing wants, becomes himself a farmer, a manufacturer, or a merchant, or earns his living by industrial service for wages.

The policeman, brilliant with brass buttons, monarch of his beat, attracts attention to the dignities and terrors of government and law. The office of a justice, the grim walls and grated windows of a jail, the solemn forms of a court, are outward signs of the state.

Once in seven days the doors of shops are closed, the doors of churches are open, the bells are rung, the dress is changed, the organ calls the people to sacred song. The same people who yesterday were drudges, toiling with grimy hands, are now worshipers. Their beliefs have made a church and a Sunday, just as hunger made a flour-mill or a slaughter-house. Institutions are social clothes which grow upon us so as to fit our movements and wants.

If we could trace these institutions backward, as we might follow a river to its source, we should find them changing and growing. And if we have knowledge and insight we can detect order, law, method in this growth. We soon find that population grows but that the earth does not stretch. There are more people in the same space than formerly, and they are all hungry, they wear out clothes and houses, and are always wanting better things and have an ambition to get on. This condition leads to foresight, invention, greater industry, more intensive cultivation of the soil, and self-control. The men of science talk of a "struggle for existence." The retail shop-keeper, who is growing gray and bald with worry over competition, knows what that struggle means. Every one on a salary fears that some other person may get his place. This word "competition" expresses a very real and terrible fact. Dislike it as we may when it pinches unusually hard, it can show some good results. It makes people industrious. It helps to transform savages into barbarians and barbarians into civilized men.

It has been said that every man is as lazy as he dares to be. One of the fathers thought that laziness was the original sin, it is so common. But as nature

Institutions grow.

Value of struggle.

Competition. sets an empty plate before the idler at life's banquet, and gives more to the energetic and efficient worker, the tendency of competition is to starve out the feeble, the slow, the indolent, and to give the world and its soil to the healthy, the vigorous, the cunning, the inventive. Some go up as others go down, but the race moves on to finer achievements. Competition itself is softened and sweetened by the sympathies which began in the family, extended to the family stock, and finally expanded into the feeling of humanity, universal philanthropy. There is a struggle for others as well as for self, and our century is very rich in examples of this "social spirit." As we proceed we shall come upon many forms of this broad and powerful force of human benevolence. "All things proceed out of this same spirit, which is differently named love, justice, temperance, in its different applications, just as the ocean receives different names on the several shores which it washes" (Emerson).

Customs. Social beliefs and feelings tend to produce customs and criticism. If many people dislike a disagreeable or injurious habit they are likely to show it, either by soft missiles of words or hard projectiles and blows. Often the blow comes first. Society has an instinct of reaction against anything which hurts. Customs are very strong, as we see in the case of fashions. It is very painful to wear a hat or dress of last year's style. Some men suffer less from a shoe that pinches or has not been paid for than from one which has a peculiar shape. People look at tailors' plates of Paris modes to discover how they can be happy. Yet fashion never appeals to courts and jails. Custom is a governing agency stronger than law.

Special sciences have grown out of the intellectual

efforts of men to comprehend social life in its various aspects. Industries, trades, banks, taxation, have been studied together because they all have to do with those goods and services which minister on the material side to human wants. Carlyle speaks of the "preliminary item" of wealth which makes high thoughts and fine arts possible. The systematized knowledge of the general laws of this field is called economics, or political economy. The study of the forms and methods of governments of townships, cities, counties, states, and nations is the field of the political sciences, of which there are many branches. The systematic study of the church and school has produced a special literature. Sociology has attempted to organize the general results of these special investigations into such a complete and harmonious view that the relative place and value of each may be determined.

Special sciences.

The foregoing paragraphs introduce the particular subject of this book. The word "reform" is often applied to this subject, but it is not wide enough for our purpose and it has suggestions of a different method of regarding the facts. We are to study movements of life and products natural to human society as grass is natural in meadows. In all progressive communities we find people trying to correct abuses and to increase the sum of human happiness. Associated efforts of this kind, if they are destructive of evil, are usually called reforms. But the title "social movements" seems to be more appropriate for the more positive endeavors to augment the means of welfare. Both are ways of doing good.

Movements of the social spirit.

There are three fairly distinct types of voluntary organizations which embody this progressive and creative

Types.

activity of the spirit of human kinship. Sometimes we find groups of persons united by common interests, as desire to secure material wealth, or insurance against loss, or some high forms of æsthetic and recreative satisfaction; and these we call mutual benefit societies. There is a second class of associations whose purpose of good extends beyond their own membership to the entire community; and these are societies of public spirit. The third class of societies is called charitable, and they are composed of persons strong and willing to bear the burdens of the weak. They devote strength and help to the defective, the unfortunate, the criminal.

How improvements begin.

Inventions of machinery or of social schemes are rarely the work of a single mind. Slight changes are introduced unobserved by obscure persons, the improvements are copied by others, and the additions grow insensibly. In other instances a seer, a person of genius, discovers a social need and invents a method of betterment. These men, if they are well disciplined, test their discoveries by careful observation and cautious experiment. They make proselytes and secure adjutants; they inspire propagandists; they form societies, start newspapers, publish tracts, articles, and books; they encourage each other by meetings, conferences, and conventions. It is a fine help if they can induce some unwary enemy to egg or stone them or to put them in jail. They educate the public and make the cause popular, if it have vitality and worth; and finally demagogues and politicians of all colors trample the heels of each other to secure the honor of carrying their banner. Imitators beg permission to whitewash the martyrs' tombs and renew the fading names of the eponyms on the monuments. Thus Howard, Pestalozzi, Wichern, Channing, Garrison, and other leaders of men gain ground and plant their flags on conquered territory.

The chief functions of voluntary associations in such forward movements are : to investigate the subject of social need, and to discover the pain and loss ; to study all that has hitherto been attempted in the right direction, and lay the experience of mankind under tribute ; to encourage the pioneers ; to inform the workers ; to develop plans and secure means ; to agitate and create public opinion ; to send lobbies to councils and legislatures ; to watch the administration of their measures and see to it that they are not mutilated and defeated by ignorance or selfishness ; to improve and guide the work until it has been assimilated in the life of the community; and to undertake any work not suitable for the state or other stable form of society.

Functions of voluntary associations.

It is common to speak of "problems," and the word expresses a fact. Where an innovation has become general and customary there is no dispute, there is no problem. Where all agree no one asks a social question. The sociologist then simply describes and explains a system of industry, government, or recreation as a biologist might describe and explain the structure and life of a crab. But when a minority of the community become satisfied that the majority are moving in a wrong path or are moving too slowly in the right direction, then arises a burning social question. The abolition of slavery may be taken as an illustration. The great majority of our people before the Civil War had come to think of slavery as the " peculiar institution " which properly belonged to the South, natural and suitable there as the wage system was natural and suitable to the North. But a large number of earnest and gifted persons felt that this system tended to poverty, to spiritual degradation, and to injustice. These persons sought

Debatable questions.

to make their view dominate the thought, the feeling, and the conduct of the nation. They came into collision with the interests and beliefs of the majority. This led to dispute and finally to war. In the ensuing struggle the views of the minority prevailed and the fittest survived. Slavery was no longer a problem.

<small>Our purpose and limits.</small>

These pages may be read by the electric light of a city parlor or under the shaded lamp of a farmer's isolated home. City and farm are organic parts of a common country. In some places there is a surplus of wants, and in others there is a surplus of resources. Here let us study how to bring wants and resources together. One may find little here upon the duties of the great. The author does not pretend to dictate policies to experts in business and statecraft. And yet the things here discussed are the supreme interests of millions of our fellows. The national happiness depends on many small satisfactions which senators at Washington seldom think worthy of notice. The real terminus of every great railroad is a threshold. Empires find their reason for being in the family circle.

<small>Nature of civilization.</small>

Lord Russell, lord chief justice of England, said in 1896, before the American Bar Association :

> Civilization is not a veneer ; it must penetrate to the very heart and core of societies of men. Its true signs are thoughts for the poor and suffering, chivalrous regard and respect for woman, the frank recognition of human brotherhood, irrespective of race, or color, or nation, or religion, the narrowing of the domain of mere force as a governing factor in the world, the love of ordered freedom, abhorrence of what is mean and cruel and vile, ceaseless devotion to the claims of justice.

<small>Variety of service.</small>

Many ways of doing good are brought to light. The reader must select from the menu the dish which agrees with his taste and constitution. It is not expected that each dish will suit all. It is not probable that any of these schemes will be copied exactly. But we are at least dealing with facts and actual works more than with castles in the air. The example of a real work of goodness is a candle which casts its beams far over the troubled waves of life.

It is a day of specialization and the tendency to take up and develop particular branches of social service is as necessary in philanthropy as it is in science or in business. Some provision is made for this in the references to special treatises which may be found in the appendix. But there is also need for integration and unification. Before there can be unity, harmony, and good-will in philanthropy there must be a general understanding of the system of special parts which make up the whole. Each worker should seek to discover the relations of his own little fragment with the separate fragments connected with the life of the same community. Dr. Hale says that philanthropists hate each other. It is too true, but it is not necessary. The cavalry, the artillery, and the infantry support each other in the evolutions of an army and in the conduct of battle. So in the peaceful enterprises of justice and goodness the various societies are related and complementary. Such a survey as is here attempted may assist active workers in limited fields to appreciate the kindred labors of others; may increase the feeling of fellowship; may lead to rational coöperation; may enable those who are prone to regard with suspicion if not contempt the efforts of neighbors to hold them in honor and esteem. The most conspicuous sociologist among the Germans has placed on the title page of both editions of his great work a quotation from Paul's letter to the Corinthians, twelfth chapter: "Now there are diversities of gifts, but the

Specialization in philanthropy.

Members of one body.

Body and members. same Spirit. . . . The body is one and has many members." This figure drawn from human physiology had been used in a critical period of Roman history and is employed by Shakespeare. In the New Testament passage the biological analogies of diversity and unity lead onward to the sublime Psalm of Charity which follows. In the one chapter all gifts are recognized, in the other all virtues and duties are traced to one root. The analogy suggests an explanation and serves as an argument. By this better understanding wasteful methods may be brought under the regulative control of enlightened public opinion. The mob may become an army.

> The old order changeth, yielding place to new,
> And God fulfills himself in many ways,
> Lest one good custom should corrupt the world.
> Comfort thyself; what comfort is in me?
> I have lived my life, and that which I have done
> May He within himself make pure.
> —*Tennyson.*

CHAPTER II.

HOME—MAKING AS A SOCIAL ART.

A FAMILY in our time and land means a group of persons united by the bond of near relationship. A larger word is household, since this may include not only parents and children, but also aged relatives, dependent friends in the house, domestic servants, boarders, and even guests. The word home means the family and its residence, with a thousand objects and memories which surround the word with sentiments beautiful and tender. Family members.

Society grows in bulk from the additions by births to each home. The married couple becomes a group. The children must be nourished and brought up to maturity by the toils and fostering care of the parents. If for any reason parental duty remains neglected then the neighborhood, the church, the state must supply the defect; and that means that certain persons, perhaps in addition to their own duties, must carry part of the duty of others. Thus we see that all society is interested in the conduct and welfare of each family. If the children are poorly fed and scantily clothed in winter, or set to exhausting labor too early; or if the house is unhealthy; if cleanliness is a lost art; if food gives dyspepsia instead of strength; if fuel fails when frost bites hard—then society finds upon its hands a heavier tax for cripples, insane, feeble-minded, and paupers. Social functions.

It is in the home that children learn the national

language, receive their first and most enduring impressions about industry, nature, morality, religion, their country. It is in the family, if anywhere, that all citizens learn the first lessons of obedience, thrift, usefulness, order, self-sacrifice, coöperation, which are essential virtues in the general life of mankind, and the essential preparation for the society of the heavenly world.

Forms and development. The household has passed through many forms in the past ages. Savages and barbarians have been accustomed to modes of existence which would be intolerable and immoral with us. Almost every possible experiment has been tried with this institution in the course of history—polyandry, promiscuous intercourse without regular marriage, polygamy, monogamy. Many of the lauded recommendations of professed reformers in our age are merely proposals to go back to obsolete and rejected customs of lower stages of civilization. Many changes may be expected in the domestic relations, but the claim of the Christian form of marriage to be permanent and universal has been vindicated by the sad results of all departures from that type and by the consensus of the moral judgments of the most advanced peoples. All modern states have sought to mold, by custom, sentiment, and legislation, the form of the family to correspond to the demands of the general welfare. For marriage is not a mere private affair to be left to individual caprice, to lawless passion, to selfish individualism.

Social interests at stake. There is an immense social interest at stake and the community is obliged to regulate this relation so as to promote the common welfare. Thus the state has taken away from the father his ancient right to put his son to death, from the husband his right to whip his wife into obedience, and from both parents the right to dispose of their property without regard to the happiness of dependent members.

Each community has a rule by which it judges what is conducive to the common happiness, and it insists, by force if necessary, upon the observance of that rule. If parents or children choose to act contrary to the ordinary belief they will soon feel the stinging shafts of hostile criticism; they may be suspected, detested, shunned. If they go too far in their defiance of public opinion they are liable to arrest and punishment. The social standard is expressed not only in state laws, but also in church discipline, in maxims, and customs. In communities where the Christian creed is dominant the usual standard requires that every marriage should be free and voluntary, without force or constraint; that no one marry under a suitable age; that very near relatives shall not marry; that a man shall have but one living wife, and a wife but one living husband; that life-long fidelity shall be kept sacred; and that divorce shall be granted only for urgent and serious reasons and after mature deliberation. Our usages and laws require parents to fulfill the duties of support and education for citizenship; demand that children care for parents in the helplessness of old age; and exacts purity, modesty, and chastity of all. These rules are by no means exactly alike in all Christian states, and they are only too frequently violated; but the ideal of conduct is held aloft, is constantly made more pure, and is enforced with greater care. The present apparent relaxation of morals is only an eddy in the great current of history and by no means represents the spirit of the age at its best.

Standards of conduct.

Christian law.

If we seek to apply these criteria to actual conditions we discover many pathetic consequences of the lawless-

Defects.

ness or the misfortunes which represent a departure from the ideals. In some homes we merely notice a stagnation or inferior level of refinement, intelligence, or spiritual life ; in other instances there is positive misery. Only those who have surveyed and explored the habitations of the poor in great cities, and who have studied the oriental barbarism of luxurious vice in many fashionable circles, can conceive the misery and the cruelty, the baseness and the pain, the tragic issues and the discouraging products of family life where the finer nature is corrupted by external circumstances or from inward depravity. Follow the city missionary, charity visitor, or sanitary policeman into the crowded flats of any large city. There is insufficient breathing space ; people are crowded so closely that the danger of collision and dispute is ever present ; the entire horde may be huddled together in one room — men, women, children, and boarders—where modesty must be a stranger. Ventilation is so defective that the lungs are ever full of noxious exhalations. Many of the interior rooms are never once brightened with a direct ray of light. When the last basket of coal is gone the cold rushes in to give the mortal stroke to human patience and hope. In the summer those who have toiled all day in a sweat-shop lie gasping for air on the roofs or curb, or in alleys.

Think of the inadequate cooking apparatus of the poor ; of the burnt and spoiled food, bought in markets where no one buys unless his money is low, where deception is rife, where adulteration is unchecked. Is it any great wonder that men take to alcoholic drinks when such meals leave them with indefinable cravings and demonic gnawings? What furniture! The very look of it makes the soul ugly. The books, the papers, are poison to the spirit. Instruments of music are unknown. We are speaking of extreme cases, but the pity is that there are multitudes of extreme cases in this rich land. The wages of the father do not always support the family even when he is employed, and the possibility of being out of work hovers over him always. He may be a vagabond or drunkard, but he may have become all that through the vicissitudes of trade and manufactures which trained him to reason like a gambler and often left him in despair. It is no answer to this plea that the average of wages shows prosperity. Long ago Charles Dickens exposed in "Hard Times" the fallacy of soothing consciences by studying tables of averages. No one who has not become familiar with the concrete facts of life has a right to a judgment.

Low wages.

Look at some of the fruits of such home life, under such accursed conditions. Study the reports of factory inspectors and labor bureaus, or visit great department stores and shops where child-labor can be used and where rigid law has not counteracted the merciless progress of machine industry, and you will be distressed to find that many children who ought to be in school are fixed in the unpitying mills of manufacture and trade. Their pittance of earnings is necessary to sustain the family. One may often find a child tending a machine while his father is seeking in vain for occupation—the babe the successful competitor for a place against his natural supporter. That is cheap labor at war with the home. Such homes turn out thieves, tramps, and abandoned girls. They fill insane asylums and prisons. The coroner's list of suicides is full of horrors, and reveals the tragedies of our imperfect industrial arrangements.

Results of defects in the dwelling.

And what happens to the home when the mother is compelled to work in a modern factory ten hours, per-

Mothers in factories.

haps a long distance from home? There is less of this evil in America than abroad, but there is too much. Most of us think that a mother needs all her time and strength for young children, even when she has cook, nurse, and governess. But try to imagine a mother walking a mile to the shop, toiling the long day at a machine speeded to the American rate, a machine that never feels nerves and never shows pity. Think of her coming back after dark to her children, weary, jaded, fretful, desperate. Tidiness, cleanliness, happiness are impossible. Existence is on the animal plane. The husband has no chance to cultivate a human quality and the saloon seems to him a paradise. Such men move in a fatal circle: their drink habits impoverish the homes, and the squalor and suffering of the home drive them to the saloon.

When girls brought up in such homes seek employment as cooks, housemaids, nurses of children, they are often found to be coarse, rude, insolent, incompetent, vexatious. Why should we be surprised at this? Is it not entirely natural? The splendid mansion is made miserable because it has neglected the education of the poor. Society is a body whose nerves of sensation form a single system, and when one member suffers all suffer together. If, says one, the tooth is aching, the rest of the body must stay awake all night to keep it company.

Temptations of youth.

Family life is disgraced and darkened by the indescribable and unspeakable vices which enfeeble and corrupt youth. These same evils of licentiousness are found in villages and rural communities. Young boys and girls are permitted to roam the streets after school and even after dark, exposed to temptation and to the influence of hardened offenders. We remember an evening in a Swiss village when the church bell summoned all children to their homes, their prayers, and their beds at nightfall. There is some hope that the same civilizing curfew bell, or some substitute for it, may be heard in all this great land. Rebellious, disorderly, selfish, undisciplined children grow up to be annoyances or pests of society. The Sixteenth Year-Book of the New York State Reformatory gives the antecedents of the prisoners. According to the returns 2,550, or 52.6 per cent, of the inmates came from homes that were positively bad, and only 373, or 7.6 per cent, came from homes that were positively good. In England we discover similar conditions. Out of 1,085 juveniles committed to reformatory schools in 1892, only 425 were living under the control of both parents. All the others had only one parent, or had one or both parents in prison, or had been deserted by their parents altogether. (Morrison.) *Bad boys from bad homes.*

The family cannot be absolutely self-sufficing. Each group of human beings must have help of the neighborhood, the church, the school, the legal organization. But all the elements of a complete and happy life should be found in the domestic circle. Not only should the physical wants be supplied, food, clothing, shelter, and comfort, but the intellectual atmosphere should be charged with high thoughts and inspiring interests, and the mental growth should be assisted by papers, books, maps, and other instruments of knowledge. The sense of beauty should be satisfied and improved by pictures, music, verse. The interchange of ideas and sentiments should refine and stimulate the sociable impulses, while the virtue of hospitality will constantly import into the sacred circle fresh materials from without. A joyful obedience to the principles of common welfare should shape conduct, while the religious life of home becomes *Essential elements.*

the supreme element of joy, peace, good-will, and hope. Especially is it necessary in the lonely and isolated country home, unfortunately too common in America, that all the essential elements of a complete life should be provided. Patriotic piety cannot render a higher service than to devise ways of enriching and elevating the existence of these primary social units.

Here is the point to notice the evils of alcoholism and kindred vices. The fight against the saloon and its black allies is a contest on behalf of the home and all it represents for civilization. Perhaps Max Nordau[1] has exaggerated the symptoms of degeneration and has misdirected some of his shafts of criticism of men, books, and works of art; but he may be regarded as an impartial witness in respect to the perils of intemperance. "Morel, the great investigator of degeneracy, traces this chiefly to poisoning. A race which is regularly addicted, even without excess, to narcotics and stimulants, in any form (such as fermented alcoholic drinks, tobacco, opium, hashish, arsenic), which partakes of tainted foods (bread made of bad corn), which absorbs organic poisons (marsh fever, syphilis, tuberculosis, goitre), begets degenerate descendants who, if they remain exposed to the same influences, rapidly descend to the lowest degrees of degeneracy, to idiocy, to dwarfishness, etc." Other causes contribute to the production of inferior, feeble, idiotic, and insane persons: as the crowded life of cities; rapid movement of travel; jars and noises; multiplication of impressions; keen competition; haste to be rich; uncertainty of employment; hunger for sensational pleasures. But the poisonous drinks and drugs which are consumed by modern peoples destroy vitality, arouse and stimulate the selfish passions, let loose the

The ravages of intemperance in the family.

Other causes of degeneration.

---

[1] "Degeneration," page 34. Morel, "Traité des Dégénerescences."

dangerous beasts that make their lair in every human being, and turn home into purgatory.

The culmination and publication of domestic failure is divorce. It is the advertisement of family misery, and lifts the curtain which hides individual wrong-doing. There are acts worse than divorce itself, fearful as are its social disgrace and consequences. Selfishness, unkindness, impurity, and brutality are the deep disease of which divorce is the symptom. Such evils exist where divorce is almost unknown. We cannot judge absolutely of the morality of a people by statistics of decrees of separation. At a later point we shall notice the social movement to counteract the tendency to divorce. But, after all, the family must defend itself. All that makes the homes of our country pure, happy, contented, religious, is a preventive measure against divorce. The best remedies are prophylactic, those which keep the peril not only at arm's length, but entirely out of sight, hearing, and thought.

Divorce.

Our quest for ways of doing good begins where life and charity begin—at home. Each human being starts out in life with hungry cries for nourishment. We may set down in our survey improved methods of housekeeping. Since most of the income of the family usually comes from social service of bread-winners we may defer the discussion of better wages to a subsequent chapter. The original meaning of economics was the law of the house, and we here return to that primitive idea. In the country it is possible to produce upon the premises much of the food and fuel for home consumption. In cities almost nothing is produced, save articles of household use for immediate consumption. Spinning, weaving, tanning skins, manufacture of clothing, preparation of flour, building of houses, making of harness

Amelioration.

and vehicles, of implements and utensils, are carried on in great factories provided with powerful and efficient machinery.

Household accounts.

When once the goods are ready for consumption the economic activity of the household begins. In many parts of Germany thrifty housewives have long had the laudable custom of keeping accounts of receipts and expenditures. There are many advantages in this custom. It fosters thrift, makes possible a wiser distribution of resources, enables social students to make accurate statistical calculations as to real wages, the cost of living, and the actual effects of our industrial system on the people. The Le Play societies in France have been collecting such information for many years and such studies should be prosecuted in this country. (See appendix.)

Instruction in cooking.

Bread is the staff of life, and bread sustains us all the better if it is well cooked and is accompanied by other foods and condiments. A newsboy in a mission meeting joined in the Lord's Prayer until they came to the petition, "Give us this day our daily bread," and then broke in with the irreverent gloss, "and butter on it." Only a very poor boy would have thought of adding that phrase, even in mirth, since most of us take our dainties as a matter of course. Cooking is a fine art—where the food is fine. Ignorance does much damage in the kitchen and in the stomach. Where the mother is an artist she can instruct her daughters. Church sewing circles and ordinary visiting calls are schools of housekeepers. Talk about recipes for nice dishes is not gossip; it is professional discussion. We may speak of household art and science as a branch of education when we come to consider improvements of our schools.

The great industry is crowding out the small industry.

Consolidation has so many advantages that it is adopted everywhere. Little shoe shops yield to huge factories. Small stores succumb to vast department magazines. We must not think that the industry of housekeeping will escape this universal tendency. In crowded cities even millionaires seldom have a front yard. The magnates of Fifth Avenue, New York, build their palaces up to the sidewalk. The occupants of a solid block of flats are numbered by the hundreds. Clothing and utensils are already bought in the market. Food supplies are not heaped up in the cellar, for there is no cellar to a flat. And now the tendency is to form a partnership of families in a common kitchen, sometimes with a common table. Many families rent rooms and take their meals at restaurants. But this is felt to be objectionable because it disturbs family privacy and introduces alien elements. It is not agreeable to chastise a youngster before all the neighbors, and the youngster has the wit to take advantake of parental reluctance. There are good reasons for the movement to build a large number of dwellings about a common kitchen, with a common heating apparatus and janitor service, while the family itself is able to retain its own living rooms separate from all others. Experiments have been tried with this plan, and the difficulty of securing and retaining competent cooks has hastened the change. But the traditions and sentiments of the ages are not easily and quickly broken, and the advantages of privacy ought not to be surrendered so long as it is possible to avoid the sacrifice. There is room for invention and experiment in this field for architects as well as for associations and corporations. Coöperative housekeeping in cities.

Next to food our clothing is a necessity of existence. Suitable dress is a necessity of a beautiful life. Rich Dress.

people may be able to afford waste, but hard-working men ought not to be compelled to lose the results of toil in expenditures on ill-fitting and shoddy garments. The wife of a mechanic who has been taught in girlhood to sew and mend and darn is able to multiply the purchasing power of her husband's wages. Philanthropy has found a field in the schools for teaching women how to make the most of their materials of dress.

Care of the domicile. To the mother is intrusted the domicile. She needs to be a sanitary engineer. She ought to be taught what the microscope has revealed in the realm of bacteriology. She ought to know the mysteries of actinism, the physiological value of oxygen, the significance of smells, the perils of decay, the lurking dangers of pipes and sewers. Every modern science contributes to the health and happiness of home, but only those who have eyes opened by instruction are able to see. In dark and unclean homes diphtheria and typhus, scourges of filth, often take their rise, and thence they spread to afflict the refined and the rich and instruct us all in social solidarity. Fevers begin where ignorance permits accumulation of decaying matter, and strong workmen are reduced to weakness, poverty, and despair. Milk and water, necessaries of life, are the media of deadly germs, unless science has made itself literally at home with the housemother. And who shall teach the mothers? We shall see.

Homes of luxury. It is a mistake to imagine that houses of poverty are the only fields which require the inspiring, cleansing, and renovating energies of the social spirit. Social progress ought to begin with those who have the wealth to command the finest privileges. Dr. Hale's inventive genius has suggested that we need a society for giving occupation to the rich. We may add that many of the busiest people are not busy with work that is socially useful. Idleness, extravagance, waste, anti-social destruction of wealth, coarse and insolent parade, and barbaric ostentation are sins of luxury. Under the powerful law of social imitation these hurtful habits are carried outward in widening circles and copied by those whose narrow means make extravagance ruinous. Ostentation arouses envy, exasperates class feeling, increases bitterness of contrasts, and imperils order. In delightful contrast with the absurd and coarse conduct of the new rich is the elegant simplicity of those who have grown within as their wealth increased without; who know how to use their means under the severe laws of refined taste, and how to socialize their expenditure by providing public grounds, galleries, libraries, means of recreation and culture. Poverty of the rich.

We are not making a plea for a return to the simplicity of the savage with his objectionable costume and his miserable hut. There is a wise and economical expenditure which actually enriches the owner and helps him to multiply the joys of others. If it cost a million dollars a year to support a Shakespeare or a Beethoven it would be a low price for the product. Unfortunately many of the people who spend the most money on themselves do not belong in the same rank with those worthies. Plain living, high thinking, and generous recognition of the democracy are natural companions. Money honestly earned and carefully spent for real and wholesome satisfactions is not wasted. Those who have the widest range of rational pleasures are best fitted to diffuse light and hope about them. Meaning of luxury.

Octavia Hill, whose eminent services in a life devoted to the poor give her words the weight of gold, says: Octavia Hill.

Much has been written of late on the subject of sisterhoods

and of "homes," where those who wish to devote themselves to the services of the poor can live together, consecrating their whole life to the work. I must here express my conviction that we want very much more influence that emanates not from a "home," but from homes. One looks with reverence on the devotion of those who, leaving domestic life, are ready to sacrifice all in the cause of the poor, and give up time, health, and strength in the effort to diminish the great mass of sin and sorrow that is in the world. I have seen faces shining like St. Stephen's with sight of heaven beyond the pain and sin. I have seen shoulders bent as St. Christopher's might have been—better in angels' sight than upright ones. I have seen hair turned gray by sorrow shared with others. And before such one bends with reverence.

Consecration of cheerfulness.

But I am sure we ought to desire to have as workers joyful, strong, many-sided natures ; and that the poor, tenderly as they may cling to those who, as it were, cast in their lots amongst them, are better for the bright visits of those who are strong, happy, and sympathetic.

"Send me," said one day a poor woman, who did not even know the visitor's name, "the lady with the sweet smile and the bright golden hair."

The smile cure.

The work among the poor is, in short, better done by those who do less of it, or rather, who gain strength and brightness in other ways. I hope for a return to the old fellowship between rich and poor ; to a solemn sense of relationship; to quiet life side by side ; to men and women coming out from bright, good, simple homes, to see, teach, and learn from the poor ; returning to gather fresh strength from home-warmth and love, and seeing in their own homes something of the spirit which should pervade all.

I believe that educated people would come forward if once they saw how they could be really useful, and without neglecting nearer claims. Let us reflect that hundreds of workers are wanted ; that if they are to preserve their vigor they must not be overworked ; and that each of us who might help, and holds back, not only leaves work undone, but injures to a certain extent the work of others. Let each of us not attempt too much, but take some one little bit of work, and, doing it simply, thoroughly, and lovingly, wait patiently for the gradual spread of good, and leave professional workers to deal for the present with the great mass of evil around.

We make our houses and they turn upon us the image of our own taste and permanently fix it in our very nature. Our works and our surroundings corrupt or refine our souls. The dwelling, the walls, the windows, the roof, the furniture, the pictures, the ornaments, the dress, the fence or hedge—all act constantly upon the imagination and determine its contents. If a family realizes this truth it will seek to beautify the objects which are silently and unceasingly writing their nature upon the man within the breast. When the families of a community give no heed to this truth there is missionary ground. *Æsthetic element in the house.*

Let us imagine a progressive woman in a village or town where the houses are bare, untidy, and ugly. What can she do to communicate her higher ideals? First of all she can create about her, with the wisest economy of available resources, a home which shall serve as a model. Then she can invite some of her neighbors to sit with her occasionally while all discuss the art of making beautiful homes. One such woman saw in the homes of her acquaintance who had abundant means but defective taste that many incongruous and unsuitable objects were tolerated. Gaudy chromos disfigured the walls of rooms which were in other respects well furnished. A cotton table cover came close to silk plush. Unbearable flames of tissue paper flowers were set in a fine vase. She was determined to remove them without direct and offensive criticism. Thus a circle was formed where each lady contributed a beautiful piece of work and all studied and discussed papers and technical journals which taught the art of decorating homes. An artistic tea closed the meetings. Many homes were improved in appearance. *Example and discussion.* *A Decorative Art Society.*

Every county fair might furnish a school of artistic

arrangement of the household, from kitchen to parlor. Furniture dealers from cities would be willing to send artists to present a model of desirable interiors. Architects would supply plans and views of charming homes. But the managers must be very careful in selecting the tradesmen who are to make the exhibit and the judges who are to assign the awards. At this point it would be wise to secure the advice of teachers of art in responsible schools.

County fairs.

The domestic miseries which reach their climax in wrangling and divorce are often due to the narrow, meager, starved, sterile mental life of the family. The house is a mere place to sleep and eat. The attractions of literature, history, and science are not an organic part of the bond. We can discuss the value of home reading clubs and the C. L. S. C. in succeeding pages, but here we may point out the occasion for some method of turning the rich currents of the higher life in the direction of family interests. Thousands of women spend much time in the kitchen. Occasionally they can sit down to wait or rest. Why should there not be at hand a little shelf with a few good books, so that the domestic or the busy mother might have just a minute with a poet or essayist, and so fill the drudgery of the day with the breath of a noble world?

The intellectual life of home.

There are some things which only women ought to say. Therefore on one aspect of home life we may introduce a lady who will tell us about "The Unsocial Club of Women."[1]

The Unsocial Club of Women.

Did you ever hear of the Society of Unsocial Women? In this club a group of women who have tasted social life until it has palled upon them have agreed to be glad they have a home to stay in, and to stay there and be contented. The members

[1] By Louise Markscheffel, in *The Ladies' Home Journal.*

of the club believe that people can be friends and yet not be perpetually together. They believe that man, the bread-winner and wage-earner of the house (if he is), has rights, and of these is the right to be comfortable, to have some things as he wants them, some things cooked to his taste, a comfortable lounge or chair in a favorite corner, his bed by the east window, if he likes it thus, his coffee hot on winter mornings, the house quiet when he is weary and worried and sleeps lightly. This is one of the cardinal beliefs of the Club of Unsocial Women. The members do not often go visiting, and actually enjoy their homes. Friend knows that friend is true, so she is not fussy about such trifles as visits; but sickness or sorrow brings her promptly.

The members of the Unsocial Club used to have endless and unwieldy calling lists. All of this living for the outside they now eschew as unworthy their time and strength. There was once a fashionable woman who said she only kept up a lengthy calling list so that she would be assured of a large funeral. The women of the Unsocial Club don't care whether they have large funerals or not; in fact, they are so entirely well informed and *au fait* that they know large funerals to be considered the prerogative of genius or of the parvenu. Not that all of their time is spent in the home, for they know they must get into the world a little, lest they lose all sympathy with other than their own immediate interests. *Calling lists burned.*

But going is not the emphasis. They read, keep themselves apace with the movements of the world, are agreeable companions to their husbands, by whom they are valued as treasures most rare, and sometimes travel, visit art galleries and libraries when opportunity offers, read to the sick, invent amusement for the children, and enjoy other pleasures according to their individual tastes.

The members of the Unsocial Club believe that heartsease only comes when social ambitions have ceased, and they know from experience and observation that the woman who has social ambitions finds never peace on earth, by night or day; that she stoops to petty, unwomanly acts to achieve that which she loathes when once attained. And so they voted all this as unworthy. It is not necessary to add that the members of the Unsocial Club forego the alleged pleasure of gossip. *Heartsease.*

Charming club. You would know the members were serene,

to see their faces. They know the right relations of things, and every one of them believes that the art of homekeeping is profession enough, unless necessity casts woman out upon her own industrial resources, in which case they believe she must go bravely forth.

<small>Mrs. Grubb, the busybody.</small>

The need for such an unsocial club is set forth by another woman, Mrs. Wiggin, in her picture of Mrs. Grubb. This lady, Mrs. Grubb, had a chart on her wall to remind herself of her engagements with a long list of societies, in which the society of three children left in her charge was not included. Her expansive but somewhat shallow mind spread over the subjects of temperance, single tax, cremation, abolition of war, vegetarianism, hypnotism, dress reform, social purity, theosophy, religious liberty, and emancipation of women.

Her residence appeared to be a perfect hot-bed of world-saving ideas, and was surrounded by such a halo of spots that it would have struck the unregenerate observer as an undesirable place in which to live, unless he wished to be broken daily on the rack of social progress. Her family circle was not a circle at all, it was a polygon. It was four ones, not one four. The fertility of her mind was such that it put forth new explanations of the universe every day, like a strawberry plant that devotes itself so exclusively to runners that it has little vigor left for producing fruits. She had soft brown eyes, eyes that never saw practical duties straight in front of them—liquid, stargazing, vison-seeing eyes, that could never be focused on any near object, such as a twin or a cooking-stove. Individuals never interested her; she cared for nothing but humanity. Her body might occasionally be in her home, but her soul was always in a hired hall.

<small>Life without a clue.</small>

There was, of course, no unanimity of belief running through all these clubs, classes, circles, societies, orders, leagues, chapters, and unions; but there was one bond of aversion, and that was domestic service of any kind. That no woman could develop or soar properly, and cook, scrub, sweep, dust, wash dishes, mend, or take care of babies at the same time—to defend this proposition they would cheerfully have gone to the stake. They were willing to concede all these sordid tasks as an honorable department of woman's work, but each wanted them to be done by some other woman. Neither had she any sane and healthy interest in good works of any kind; she simply had a sort of philanthropic hysteria, and her most successful speeches were so many spasms.

Granting that this is caricature, we have excellent feminine authority for fearing that it is caricature which comes dangerously near an occasional portrait. The truth is that both men and women of a certain temperament are overborne by craving for notoriety and publicity, and spend their distracted lives in fragmentary talk and work which have no mastery of any subject as a basis. This charlatanism can be corrected only by creating a public sentiment absolutely intolerant of sham reformers who begin to make speeches before they have studied the matter in hand. Reformers must be taught that no individual is responsible for every good cause and that there must be a division of labor in philanthropy as in scientific research and in business or industry. If all could learn that certain persons are fitted by natural and acquired gifts for leadership in definite and restricted lines, and that the duty of others is appreciation and assistance, we should have much less waste of effort and more steady and assured progress. *Broken lives.*

The only "leisure class" in America are well-to-do women. Men are usually too busy to deal with social service at first hand. They pay in their checks and buy out of responsibility. They ought to have some small credit, however, for what their wives and daughters accomplish. It is a sign and proof of a savage plane of non-culture when the men loaf and smoke while the women build the huts and hoe the maize. It is an evidence of civilization when men sizzle in summer *Our leisure class.*

offices while their wives and daughters are off at the seashore resting and recuperating after charity balls and reform committees, world without end.

Religion in the home.

Why not have a sanctuary all the year round and dwell in the house of the Lord forever? The public temple is indispensable, but first the home. Schools supported by public money cannot teach religion. That is pretty well settled for us by our historical condition. This leaves the field and the responsibility for domestic religion. It is upon this point that religious people ought to concentrate associated effort during the next generation. The Sunday-school system is fairly rooted and has already produced magnificent results. But that great institution has definite limits. There are some signs that parents have come to depend on Sunday-school teachers to perform a duty which can never be delegated. This is a sore evil. When the holy flame expires at the altar of home it is likely to be dim everywhere. The old family worship, which Burns has so beautifully praised, must be revived.

The Mothers' Union.

As a hint of what may be done let us cite the English society called "The Mothers' Union."[1] It was formed in 1876 in the Winchester diocese. Its objects are to uphold the sanctity of marriage; to awaken in mothers a sense of their great responsibility as mothers in the training of their boys and girls; to organize in every place a band of mothers who will unite in prayer, and seek by their own example to lead their families in purity and holiness of life. Mothers of all classes and ranks have joined this union. A card is given each mother, on which is a prayer for her daily use. Rules are printed on the card and definite ideas of the purpose are thus kept before their minds. They agree to bring up

[1] "Woman's Mission," page 68.

their children in habits of obedience, truth, purity, and self-control; to watch over their conversation, companionships, and amusements; to be careful as to the literature placed in their hands, the books and newspapers they read; and to inculcate temperance. The union has two organs which have a wide circulation. The society is worked by a diocesan organizing committee, and they have a central fund for the circulation of information and the printing of annual reports. Here is a hint for mothers. But have the fathers no duty?

The ideal of mothers.

CHAPTER III.

FRIENDLY CIRCLES OF WOMEN WAGE-EARNERS.

New problems. THE question of the relation of the family to external associations has many sides. It is obvious that the craze for organizing something has frequently driven good people to excesses. And yet there is a proper place for associated effort. In earlier days our grandmothers prepared the food, clothing, soap, and candles in the house. But steam-power and machinery have drawn into the factory many of those industries in which women were formerly engaged. Consider some of the results of this change. Girls and women have simply followed their natural employments to the places where they could use effective machines which are too costly for private houses and too heavy for hand or foot-power. They seek employment in huge spinning-mills, seed warehouses, tobacco factories, tailor shops, canning factories, cheese factories, print works, bicycle establishments, millinery houses.

Industrial situation of women. The goods thus made must be sold, transported, distributed. This cannot be done at home, and so we have a growing army of girls and women in offices, stores, and mills, employed in almost all kinds of trades and professions. They are separated from their families, work under uncongenial conditions, and have new dangers to confront. On the whole, they have, as Mr. C. D. Wright's inquiry showed, proved themselves superior to the demoralizing temptations of their surroundings. The fact that crime increases among women as they engage in industry was to be expected. But that tendency will not dominate the movement to give women a larger opportunity. Perhaps most of these women and girls live at their own homes or in private families. But many of them have no home at any time and all feel the absence of family surroundings during the hours of public toil. It would be the height of folly and injustice to throw the least obstacle in the way of women who wish to earn an honorable and independent living. Rather should we assist them to make the best of their difficult position. At the best the peril and the suffering are very great. It was to meet some of the difficulties of this situation that clubs for wage-earning women were formed, sometimes by the working women themselves, sometimes by their friends who had good-will, wealth, power, and leisure.

It is evident that variety of method is demanded by the variety of conditions. In some situations the girls and working women are too much isolated from each other, or too little accustomed to initiative, to undertake organization without help from others. In city life there are many thousands who have no certain dwelling-place, form few permanent ties, and require temporary homes until they can safely make other adjustments for themselves. Very young girls have no experience with organization and do not know how to coöperate. Under such conditions the service of women of leisure is indispensable, although it ought to aim at making the girls self-supporting and self-governing as far as possible and as quickly as possible. *The method of patronage.*

The Young Woman's Christian Association is an organization whose branches are spreading over Christendom. The local society is often founded and supported by women of means who see the trials and perils of their homeless sisters and desire to surround them with relig- *The Y.W. C. A.*

ious influences and aids of the higher life. Young women in factories, offices, and stores, weary of the din and dirt and toil of the daily battle for bread, need a safe lodging-place at night and on Sunday. Or even if they dwell with parents, a cozy clean room, where lunch may be spread and warm drinks provided at noon near the place of work, is welcome and good. Health may be prolonged and energy restored by a quiet hour. Recreations and entertainments in the common residence or in a special hall add brightness and attraction to life and prevent that deadly emptiness and vague craving for excitement which only too often lure to ruin. Classes are formed for teaching languages, music, and the arts, by which earning power may be increased and the spiritual life enriched. All these outward appliances furnish a medium through which the pervasive influence of kind matrons may be felt.

A homeless girl.

The boarding-house of a city is not seldom a dreary place, furnishing room and meals as a mere business transaction without any of those elements of companionship which make up our idea of home. Many young women are too much scattered over the city to form any permanent union for coöperation, and strangers coming to a city ignorant of the perils which beset the unwary and innocent, are in danger of making a fatal choice of lodgings. In railroad stations in American cities a woman may find notices directing her to some such home, Catholic, Protestant, or other. The Young Woman's Christian Association, with its permanent board of lady managers, offers advantages which are not otherwise furnished and it meets a real social need.

Boarding-houses.

Groups of King's Daughters or other circles of Christian girls have found a beautiful opportunity in providing rooms for noon rest in the center of a busy town

Noon rest.

where thousands of young women are employed. It does not require much capital or machinery. A room is rented in a convenient locality. This place is provided with lavatory, tables, furniture for rest, and is made dainty and beautiful with decorations and pictures. Some of the young ladies in turn are present to receive their friends, converse, read, sing, play, and in various ways make the hour cheerful. Acquaintance with the girls furnishes a medium of helping them in a hundred ways. As soon as possible the girls should form a club and make it as nearly self-supporting and self-governing as can be. This is one way by which the unhappy divisions of society may be crossed by human kindness. *Fellowship.*

"Poor little 'Marm Lisa,' as the neighbors called her. She had all the sorrows and cares of maternity with none of its compensating joys" (Mrs. Wiggin). "Marm Lisa" is a type of thousands in these days when the mother must go abroad to earn a living and the oldest daughter, herself needing a mother's care, must bend her young frame and untaught mind to the severest and most exacting tasks of child-care and culture. Good women have seen this social call and have endeavored in various ways to divide the burden of the little mothers. The establishment of a crêche, or day nursery, is one method, and this involves the employment of a hired nurse for the task. In other places young women who had no money to give but could offer a certain amount of time and work have devised ways of gathering the little mothers into a room, helping them with the infants, and have taken advantage of the meeting to impart such useful knowledge and training as the poor girls require. *The Little Mothers' Aid Association.*

An English institution of wide range of usefulness, called the Girls' Friendly Society, has found its way

The Girls' Friendly Society.

into the United States. It is a guild for mutual aid rather than for charity, although it is managed by women of leisure. The main features are thus stated by Miss Edith Sellers in "Woman's Mission":

> The society was founded in 1875 by Mrs. Townsend, for the purpose of uniting in one great fellowship women and girls of all ranks. The associates are as a rule ladies of culture; the members are of all sorts, from trained teachers to workhouse helps; for the only condition the society imposes on those who join it is that they shall be of good character and be striving to do their work in life honestly. Each associate undertakes to help a certain number of members by all the means in her power, but especially by treating them as her personal friends. The members in their turn are bound to act as friends to each other. . . . England and Wales, Scotland, Ireland, the colonies, America, and North Central Europe, have each a separate, autonomous society, the only connecting link amongst them being the Central Council in London. . . . The English society stands in close relations to the Established Church, of which it is a powerful auxiliary. . . . The secretaries of all the branches in a diocese form a diocesan council; the presidents of the diocesan councils, together with the colonial and foreign presidents, the heads of departments, and ten elected members, form the Central Council.

The work is divided into ten departments. Each of these departments has a special task, as: caring for the interests of educated persons, factory girls, domestic servants, workhouse girls, free registries, lodges, recreation rooms, emigration, schools and homes for industrial training, cheap and wholesome literature, and charge of members when they are ill.

Protective agencies.

The people of our country intend to make public law minister to the most humble citizen. But this intention is often thwarted through the cruelty and coarseness of base men. There is a field, especially in cities, for a society whose mission it is to secure legal protection for friendless women and helpless children. These societies are supported by voluntary contributions of interested friends. They employ a firm of lawyers for presenting cases in court and giving legal advice. "There is a constantly increasing tendency toward the quiet and thoughtful adjustment of difficulties. The advisory features are considered the most helpful and hopeful indications." Through this agency money withheld by dishonest employers is secured; the complaints of wives against cruel husbands are investigated; men guilty of criminal assault are prosecuted; chattel mortgage usurers are brought to reasonable terms; seducers are compelled to assist their victims; sewing-machine frauds are brought to light and punishment; and in general the forsaken and desperate are made to feel that the powers that be are on their side in the contest with misery and neglect. One poor mother, left by a worthless husband to care for five small children, was helped until she could support herself in a comfortable house; and she gratefully said: "It's you folks did it, putting heart in me so often when I could not go on alone." *Legal protection.*

The founders of another useful association have thus stated their object : *The Consumers' League.*

Recognizing the fact that the majority of employers are virtually helpless to improve conditions as to hours and wages, unless sustained by public opinion, by law, and by the action of consumers, the Consumers' League declares its object to be to ameliorate the condition of the women and children employed in the retail mercantile houses of New York City, by patronizing, so far as practicable, only such houses as approach in their conditions to the standard of a fair house, as adopted by the league, and by other methods.

By a "fair house" they mean one in which equal pay is given for work of equal value, irrespective of sex. In the departments where women only are employed the minimum wages should be six dollars per week for experienced adult workers, and should fall in few instances below eight dollars. Wages are paid by the week. Fines, if imposed, are paid into a fund for the benefit of the employees. The minimum wages for cash girls are two dollars per week. The hours are from 8 a. m. to 6 p. m., with three quarters of an hour for lunch, and a general half-holiday is given on one day of each week during at least two summer months. A vacation of not less than one week is given with pay during the summer season. All over-time is compensated. The rooms are so arranged that work, lunch, and retiring rooms are apart from each other and conform to the sanitary ordinances. Seats are provided and their use is permitted. Humane and considerate behavior toward employees is the rule. Fidelity and length of service meet with due consideration. No children under fourteen years of age are employed.

A "fair house."

This league investigates retail establishments, learns whether they conform to the minimum standards just outlined, and then publishes a "White List" which recommends the more humane houses to public patronage. It is practically a form of boycott without objectionable features. The tendency is to bring all salesrooms under the rules which secure humane treatment of employees. There seems to be no doubt that these women and girls need such protection. They are usually timid and unaccustomed to associated action; they are young and therefore without the wisdom and experience which would enable them to act on their own behalf; if they sink down under their burden their places are easily filled from a throng of eager and hungry applicants; competition to them means death or degradation unless they have the help of others. Dr. W. S. Rainsford tells of a

A just boycott.

girl who for ten days before Christmas worked until 10:30 every night of the week and from 9 a. m. to 5 p. m. on Sunday. No food was provided while she endured this strain. Her wages were four dollars per week. When she got home on Christmas Eve she fainted from exhaustion.

Shoppers are advised to shop during reasonable hours, in the morning if possible; and to avoid Saturday afternoon, so as to build up a custom favorable to a half-holiday. Holiday purchases should be made early, so as to diminish the strain on employees. Customers can help the girls by inquiring if seats are provided and used, and by treating them with patience and consideration. On the other hand, the saleswomen must help themselves. They cannot be simply carried by outsiders. Reforms are always based on improved character and are fruitless without that inner quality. "Our efforts to secure for all the women and girls who work in retail shops in this city the same conditions which exist in the shops on the 'White List' of the Consumers' League are hampered by the fact that the service is often better in the shops which are not on the 'White List.' The saleswomen in the shop which of all others in New York gives its employees the greatest number of privileges have been so notoriously rude in their treatment of the public that ladies have given that reason for not patronizing it, and thus a very strong moral as well as business argument can be made in favor of fines and severity of discipline."

Advice to shoppers.

The name of Miss Grace H. Dodge is identified with a movement which deserves particular study, as it seems to have a genuine root in the life of European and American peoples. Enlargement of economic opportunity has brought with it a new sense of independence

Working Girls' Societies.

and personal responsibility. Fewer women expect or desire to be in absolute subjection as a condition of support. Women who have caught the spirit of the new era despise charity as a source of living, and they are sensitively suspicious of anything which has a taint of pauperism. They are willing to work long hours at hard work, and with miserably inadequate wages, in order to maintain their self-respect and keep "the glorious privilege of being independent." They are drawn together by the fact of a common calling, and this not only gives them a feeling of sympathy for each other but it creates class distinctions which are as keenly felt as those which fill the circles of the upper "four hundred" with envy, spite, and all uncharitableness. The seamy side of solidarity is exclusiveness. As industrial association has brought them together, without regard to denominational lines, any method of combining them must scrupulously and delicately keep to what is common and avoid the discussion of controversial matters. For these reasons there is a field for organization quite different from that of the Young Woman's Christian Association and the Woman's Christian Temperance Union. This field is occupied by the Working Girls' Societies, whose methods may be illustrated by the following suggestions.

Any one who is interested, whether wage-worker or woman of leisure, may make the beginning. It is prudent to start with young women, since the work is chiefly for girls. The earlier meetings for consultation should be held in one of the homes of the girls or in some secular place which will not give offense to denominational prejudices. One of the first steps will be to raise about $150 for furnishing the club rooms and paying rent for the first month. This money may be borrowed and gradually repaid from the dues. About two hundred girls of various occupations should be invited to the first meeting for organization, and if a sufficient number respond the constitution and rules may be discussed and adopted. Forms may be procured from the Association of Working Girls' Societies in New York or from some particular society, and these forms should be ready for the first meeting. *Constitution.*

The officers elected should include working women and women of leisure, and these officers may constitute a council or executive committee for administration. But all important matters should be brought before the entire association for discussion and decision. The committee on rooms is asked to look out a quiet place on a retired street where rents are not excessively high. The committee on furnishing should be assisted by all the members in making the rooms beautiful. It is very desirable to have a piano, and this can be rented. When the rooms are ready an opening reception should be held, and at this time explanations should be carefully made to the newspapers and to the neighboring clergy, so as to prevent all misunderstandings. Up to the time of the reception publicity should be avoided. Very early in its history the club will provide for class instruction. It is stated that in a large city the expenses are about $40 to $50 per month : rent, $25 ; coal, $4 ; gas, $3 ; cleaning, $4 ; piano, $4. The fees for expenses are about twenty to twenty-five cents per month. *Rules.*

"Volunteer teachers, books for the library, even money, when unsolicited, may, by vote of the club, be accepted with pleasure unmixed with the dread of patronage." Public educational and art institutions, open to all, may be used. But these clubs ought not to solicit help nor in any way become dependent on out- *Independence.*

siders. Self-government and self-support are inseparable. The members seek to secure higher wages and claim a fair reward for their industry, and they wish to pay for all which they enjoy. The fundamental principles of their organizations are coöperation, self-support, self-government.

From reports of the clubs we discover the range of their activities and advantages. They employ a woman physician, who is paid out of the funds. Teachers are paid from special fees for instruction in dressmaking, sewing, embroidery, fancy work, crocheting, knitting, cooking, millinery, bookkeeping, and various English studies. A library with reading-room is provided and æsthetic culture is promoted by pictures, photographs, musical entertainments, and readings. "Practical talks" have formed an important part of the work from the beginning. They are not lectures, but just what their name implies; and, as the rooms are not large, the greatest freedom of conversation is enjoyed. Certain common interests are set forward by various devices of thrift and coöperation. The club room becomes a station for the Penny Provident Fund and is thus connected with a savings bank. A mutual benefit fund is sometimes started, which is a protection when work is slack, when sickness or other misfortune befalls. An employment bureau for the members mobilizes their industrial force. During the summer the club is able to secure very inexpensive outings in the country for girls on vacation. A Domestic Circle, composed of young married women, is formed, and has contributed to the preparation of young mothers for the important duties of motherhood and housekeeping. An inner band called the Three P's Circle (from their motto, "Purity, Perseverance, Pleasantness"), develops more earnest womanhood and devises ways of making homes more bright and pleasant. Classes are formed to learn the art of "first aid to the injured." Lectures on health and on legal relations give the girls a more accurate notion of the conditions of physical well-being and of their social environment.

While the members dread to receive they find it truly blessed to give. There is but a single step from mutual benefit to disinterested kindness. "We have such a good time, what can we do for others?" That is the note of a woman's voice. So we naturally find the clubs of self-reliant girls forming Lend a Hand Clubs and visiting committees for the sick. The members arrange to go to hospitals and to carry to sick children fancy scrap-books, full of pictures, to make dull days tolerable. They supply beef tea, flowers, fresh eggs to the sick poor. These gracious, delicate, personal ministries do not appear in the lists of rich contributors to institutional charity, but there is One who sees. *Benevolent work.*

The Working Women's Social Club, of New York, is an illustration of the coöperative method of providing a home for unmarried women. Any woman engaged in household service may become a member. The plan includes the establishment of a home where women of this calling may find board and comfortable surroundings when unemployed or in need of rest, and the establishment of a training school for the instruction of women in household work. By the payment of small regular dues provision is made for care in case of sickness or lack of employment. The wages of women engaged in domestic employment are usually sufficient to provide moderate fees for this kind of sick insurance. It renders it unnecessary for them to go to a charity ward of a hos- *Working Women's Social Club.*

pital when they are too ill to work. By the payment of a small sum each month into a common treasury, and by making a contract with hospitals, the right to board, nursing, and medical attendance can be enjoyed without a thought of dependence or humiliation. Such an arrangement can be made where a large Bible class of working women is connected with a church. There is no better proof of the weakness of selfishness and the power of coöperation than the success of these plans of mutual help.

Bible Class Clubs.

The "Jane Club," one of the fruits of the Hull House, Chicago, may serve to illustrate another method of coöperative housekeeping for homeless women. Any self-supporting unmarried woman, or widow without dependent children, between the ages of eighteen and forty-five, who is of good moral character, is eligible for membership. Members who attain the age of forty-five and who have previously belonged to the club are not affected by this provision. The home provided is very attractive, and all the members share benefits, expenses, and losses.

The "Jane Club."

It is easy to see that such associations may be abused. But the general and normal tendency must be to fit girls for domestic life. In these clubs girls learn all the arts which make women more useful in the household. They learn to cut and fit dresses; to prepare food daintily, and to set a table so that it will have a refining influence; they learn the structure and functions of the body and the laws of hygiene, the principles of modesty, purity, and dignity, and the way to that higher self which is awakened by consciousness of the help of the Divine Father. The practical talks and the class instruction assist the formation of womanly character and secure adaptation to domestic life.

Influence of clubs.

Miss Grace H. Dodge is a competent witness:

A live working club is felt in many directions, and homes, factories, shops, neighborhoods, towns, and villages should feel the good of the organization.

One aim of the first society was that by association together, wives, mothers, and home-makers should be developed, that the tone of womanhood should be raised, and earnest lives developed in girls who, perhaps, without bright, helpful association would have been content to remain in narrow circles of selfishness or frivolity. This desire has been realized, and many homes have been created or made beautiful by club members. Dozens of girls have had hidden talent cultivated, and have shown by brave, true living and working what the society has done for them. This is a possibility in every club, and the officers must see that the importance of the home life and the beauty of earnest living are recognized, and that the influence of bright womanhood is appreciated.

A society opens fields of usefulness for many young women of greater or less culture, leisure, and education, and those many, who are busy during the day but who have talent and brains, are needed to help the girls who have not the same natural advantages.

Miss Dodge's testimony.

It is impossible to separate that part of social service which belongs to women and to distinguish their specific share. The unit of the nation is the home and there the mother is queen by divine right. This century of the purest literature would not be so pure or so rich if the contributions of women were omitted. The public school system is in the hands of women, and the same thing is largely true of the Sunday-school. In charities and churches, in missions to the heathen at home and abroad, American women have a high place and commanding influence. All professions, trades, and arts are open to them and occupied by them with honor. Therefore in all our succeeding chapters we shall be studying woman's work, even when the fact is not specifically stated. And this union of service is highly

Union of man and woman for service.

desirable. Julia Ward Howe's name gives high sanction to the thought : "Every enlargement of freedom brings with it an extension of moral responsibility. . . . To see the best men move in sympathy and harmony with the best women, and to see both linked together by zeal and service to all ranks of their fellow creatures, this is what my heart desires, this is what American men and women owe to their country." And Marion Harland : "Woman should by now have ceased to be a specialty. There should be no need of 'movements' in her behalf, and agitations for her advancement and development apart from the general good."

Freedom brings responsibility.

CHAPTER IV.

BETTER HOUSES FOR THE PEOPLE.

The external system which serves society affects human character and happiness very closely at many points. The places in which we dwell and work, the paths by which we walk, the means of transport and communication, are all related to each other and to community welfare.

Our study of the family has shown us the meaning of the social movements to secure more suitable external accommodations, especially in the crowded and congested centers of population. In the open country a man may build almost any kind of a house without much danger to his neighbors. But in large towns a private dwelling is not a mere private interest. If the house is too high it casts upon all neighbors a depressing and unwholesome shadow. Brightness is turned into gloom. If one builds a chimney so that it develops cracks the entire block is in danger of conflagration. If the air is foul in one dwelling of a tenement it may poison twenty families who live under the same roof. The single family is helpless without associated action. Frequently the better people of a whole district lack the knowledge, courage, or power to defend themselves from filth, disorder, and demoralizing influences of bold and shameless characters. They are sometimes crowded into quarters for which they pay high rentals but which do not furnish decent accommodations for the development of worthy human qualities. Take some examples

Dwellings.

Helplessness of the individual.

60   *The Social Spirit in America.*

from reports of inspectors of a certain city, and remember that many of these houses are owned by highly respectable and even eminent landlords.

<small>Examples of "how not to do it."</small>

No. —. One-story frame house, built on rear of lot, below grade; two feet lower than alley. Poorly ventilated. Dark and damp. Ceiling low. Floor on ground. Three feet of refuse, consisting of dead dogs, cats, and other matter piled against west side of house. No. —. Two-story frame house, occupied by two families. First floor store, three living rooms, and stable. Thin boards between kitchen and stable. Two horses in stable. Kitchen door opens into stable. Horses not two feet from kitchen door. Stable not clean and foul odor from same. House unfit for human habitation. No. —. Plumbing and drains in bad condition. Yard filled with rubbish. Filthy and foul-smelling vault in rear. No. —. Building in last stages of decay, floors rotten, walls open to the air, ceiling broken, no water or sewer connections, corners filled with decaying rubbish. Character of the whole place beggars description. No. —. On an alley; formerly a stable, or shed for horses; four feet below grade. Floors and wall damp; no sewer connections. Corners filled with decaying rubbish. In this eight people stay. Two are sick children. No. —. Small house, low ceilings, no ventilation, below grade, vaults uncleaned, no sewer connection, stable adjoining where apples, bananas, and vegetables in various stages of preservation are kept. In these premises ten Greeks, two horses, and one goat all live in a confused mass with the fruit to be sold in the streets. No.—. Similar vile conditions. Eight Greeks live here with their fruit. From this place last winter a case of diphtheria was taken. At that time a horse was stabled in the same room with the men.

A volume of such descriptions might be copied here. It is well known that the death-rate in such quarters is much higher than in the parts of the city where order and cleanliness are maintained.

<small>Death-rate.</small>

In New York City, in a population of 255,033 persons, only 306 had access to a bathroom in the houses in which they lived. In the old, dilapidated, filth-soaked, dark, unventilated buildings the death-rate among children under five years of age ran up to 254.4 in a thousand, while under wholesome conditions it might be reduced to thirty in a thousand. Christendom still shudders when it reads of Herod's "slaughter of the innocents," but that butchery was insignificant in proportions when compared with the murderous effects of city tenement life. The general death-rate for such a crowded quarter is 61.97, while that of the city at large is only 20.03.

<small>Murder of the innocents.</small>

Why do these people not leave such miserable houses? The question betrays the ignorance of the questioner in respect to the income of such people and the possibility of securing better accommodations for what they are able to pay. Why do not the landlords put the houses into a sanitary condition? Perhaps they are non-residents and leave the collection of rents to hired agents who think of commissions and not of the interests of the occupants. Perhaps the landlord would not make a change which cost him much even if he had gone with the inspectors. Perhaps the owner is himself an ignorant immigrant or native who is "saving" a fortune and, seeing that a dirty house brings as much rent as a healthy house, compels his tenant to help him in his scheme of thrift. Perhaps it is because the alderman from that ward is so busy seeking booty and boodle from giving away franchises that he cannot find time, even if he had the knowledge, to protect his fellow-citizens from the ravages of greed and pestilence. It is well said that before we can disinfect our tenements and alleys we must disinfect our city councils. Moral character and external conditions of health are in reciprocal relations, they act and react upon each other as causes.

<small>Neglect.</small>

This social misery has been felt in all civilized lands since the rise of modern sanitary science made dull resignation to disease a crime, and since the beginning of the rapid growth of large towns under the pressure of machine industry. The problem has been studied by highly competent engineers, statisticians, accountants, municipal administrators, physicians, philanthropists, and business men. Vigorous efforts have been put forth to provide adequate housing for the poor of cities; but there is still room for the heroic virtues of citizenship in this field. Let us see what can be done.

Investigation. First of all, we must study local conditions and place the results of investigation before the public. Light is a very effective moral disinfectant. Information about abuses is often the only remedy that is required. Owners of houses which are unfit for human habitation become very sensitive to public criticism when the publications are confined strictly to facts set forth by photographs and measurements and descriptions by eye witnesses. Landlords may sometimes be persuaded to correct the conditions which increase disease without the penalty of publicity. For such investigation a course in bacteriology, chemistry, sanitary science, and microscopy is an excellent preparation; but any experienced housekeeper equipped with a tape measure, with normal standards of propriety, and with a healthy olfactory organ, can soon detect enough causes of pestilence to supply nightmares for a whole ward. People who tolerate such abuses have no right to sleep soundly of nights until they have tried to remedy the wrong.

Landlord missionaries. Octavia Hill's noble name is connected with a movement of great and increasing significance. With the help of John Ruskin she secured control of some houses whose inhabitants had an unsavory record for untidiness and other unneighborly qualities. Without any pretense of philanthropy she went among them as a rent collector. One of her first principles was to require prompt payment of rent. This established natural business relations between her and the customers. The power to eject a disobedient tenant was in the background of her friendly counsels of perfection; but she soon proved that it would not often be necessary to employ this legal coercion. She found ways of rewarding those who took superior care of her property, and hope was a more reliable motive than fear. The heedless and awkward were obliged to wait for improvements and conveniences which their more skilful and tidy neighbors enjoyed first. Thus she transformed the houses and the people at the same time.

Business and philanthropy.

This method of social service has been taken up in the United States. One philanthropic lady of leisure and wealth who was looking about for a career worthy of her station and opportunities found it in collecting rents in the tenements owned by her husband. After a time she reported that she had lost some interest in philanthropy but had increased the interest on her investment. It is no reflection on a mode of philanthropy that it turns out to be wise economy and brings five per cent. Indeed a great idea never becomes catching till it shows well in a trial balance.

One form of this rent-collecting plan (tried in Cincinnati by Mr. C. G. Fairchild) deserves more particular notice. In this instance the philanthropist in disguise of a hard-hearted collector went to live in the same house with the people. He was not regarded by them as an outsider but as a sort of chief janitor or caretaker of the building. His family, whose culture was of the highest

An example.

order, went with him and aided materially in the task of renovation. On this point he says :

<small>A model rent collector.</small>

In this discussion drop out of mind the thought of sacrifices. Life in the tenements of our cities can be just as wholesome physically and with more of a tonic morally even for our children than in the more sensuous and sheltered suburbs. . . . The scope of our activity is bounded by the one thought : how can we in the long run promote the value of this property. This may seem narrow and mercenary, but as a matter of fact it has brought us in helpful contact with nearly every branch of the city government and the main charitable organizations of the city. It has brought us into exigencies of individual and family life where . . . we were called to exercise the most delicate and accurate judgment touching the most complex and important questions of character and human welfare.

This gentleman took a house which had a bad reputation. Charity visitors dreaded to go there.

The place was lonely, the house forbidding, the halls cold and cave-like, the reputation was of the worst, and the next streets poured in their disorderly elements.

He took possession of this property with very little improvement by the owners.

<small>Rising standards.</small>

This living upon the premises is the most vital thing connected with the whole work. We found some good people, people who merit and receive our admiration and our love. Here is a woman, the mother of ten children born in rapid succession, who has carried and is still carrying the burden of her drinking and inefficient, not to say lazy, husband ; who is working all night at a restaurant, half the hours at washing dishes and the other half at scrubbing floors, for fifty cents a night and a basket of broken victuals. In times past charitable hands have helped her, but as her children have grown to help this aid has ceased and she pays her rent promptly and preserves a wholesome family life. . . . In a little home of two rooms once or twice a week we would find the kitchen floor spotlessly clean, though it was the living room and sleeping room of four small children. One day in praising the appearance of the portion of the outside hall which it fell to this family to care for the father pointed to a little girl of eight who had done this work.

Other aspects of the problem were more discouraging. Some of the people were guilty of carousing and making disturbance. Neighbors or strangers would sometimes fill the streets with confusion. But a firm and intelligent use of the legal authority of a landlord brought order and quiet in place of chaos and conflict. The necessity of protecting one's own family gives such a worker a moral force which could never be gained by a casual visitor or pastor. This is a form of service which cannot be delegated. Many rent collectors have made utter failure of the method because they let it out to contract while they went to Europe or to a seaside resort. *Absenteeism.*

Miss Clare Graffenried says :

The chief cause of bad conditions in manufacturing towns, more visible in them than in large cities, is absenteeism. The manufacturer of to-day seldom lives at the central source of industry from which he draws his wealth. He lives away from it, and when he does that the model industrial settlements do not grow up. . . . I was talking lately with a Connecticut manufacturer who has surrounded himself with conditions that are almost ideal. I could not help praising him for many things he had done. There was practically no poverty there. "Why," he said, " do you suppose I should do all this if I did not live here myself?"

The problem of housing the people is closely connected with that of cheap and convenient transit from center to circumference. With the increased provision of rapid and cheap electric trains it will be possible for many to live in little homes of their own far from the congested regions. This will have a tendency to lower rents and improve conditions at the center. Where the hours of labor are very long, or where they are irregular *Suburban homes.*

and include much night work, or where the wages are excessively low and uncertain, the wage-earner cannot go any distance. Thus one reform waits on another and all must be carried forward at the same time.

Towns made to order.

In some instances important manufacturing establishments have been placed near a water-power or on lands selected on account of nearness to a great commercial city. The famous town of Pullman is a conspicuous illustration. There is a town where the contaminating influences which curse a city are kept at a distance. Beautiful buildings and grounds, model workshops, charming lodge rooms, library, reading-room, church, theater, playgrounds, flower beds, ornamental shade trees, hotel, are all so arranged as to present a satisfactory vista at every step and to bring elevating agencies near to all. This is not the place to analyze the economic basis of the plan or to follow out the effects of the industrial contracts. Unquestionably a generous public spirit and a high appreciation of the æsthetic values in industry have been a part of the inspiration of this enterprise. Much as we may dislike centralized control, it is difficult to see how such results could be accomplished without a design of superior intelligence carried out by a single executive will. In time a way

Pullman.

may be found to reconcile these advantages with a plan of industry which agrees with the democratic tendency of our age. But that will be when democracy itself has improved both in taste and coöperative spirit far beyond anything yet known. Meantime capitalistic leadership has shown the way to build a town where nothing gives serious offense to the eye.

Modern manufacturers are already beginning to discover advantages in assisting their employees to secure homes of their own, while themselves shaping the plan of the town as a whole with a view to health, convenience, and beauty. Associations of wage-earners have succeeded in building small homes at greatly reduced cost, and the future will certainly bring forth many more such enterprises. But after making ample provision in such schemes for well-paid mechanics, clerks, and salesmen, there remains a multitude of people whose low wages and uncertain occupation render the purchase of homes an unrealizable dream. They will remain renters. They must be near their task. They cannot command capital or credit.

It is not enough to prosecute recreant landlords and eject poor people from untidy houses. They must have a place of shelter. It has been found that stock companies can build excellent tenements, entirely suitable for human habitation, rent them at a rate which competes with the miserable dens now offered to the poor, and still return a moderate interest on the investment, the property being good security for the capital. *Private building companies.*

The City and Suburban Homes Company of New York has begun its work under such favorable auspices, with such competent leadership, and with such complete assimilation of the world's experience, that we may venture to give its essential features particular notice. It has a capital stock of $1,000,000, assured by the purchases of wealthy men, but open to the public in shares of ten dollars each. It offers interest at five per cent, the surplus over that being reserved for extending operations. This company will facilitate proprietorship among the better paid members of the wage-earning population. To this end it will purchase areas of land where good transit facilities are afforded. The intending purchaser can have some voice in selecting the style of his home, as plans of small houses *Example of a building association.*

costing from $1,000 to $2,000 will be offered for choice. Twenty or thirty houses will be built at one time, so that the purchaser can reap the advantages of coöperative methods. The client will pay down ten per cent of the purchase price of the house and lot, with option of either a ten, fifteen, or twenty years' period in which to repay the remainder in monthly installments. These monthly payments will also cover the cost of a life insurance policy. All this will cost purchasers little more than rentals in the city.

For rent.

This company also turns to the congested districts with plans of building model apartment houses for wage-earners who cannot escape from the city and cannot command capital for the purchase of homes of their own. The plans for these houses have been made by architects who have become experts in this branch of their art. Every room will be open to air and light. Every apartment will have its private water closets, laundry tubs, etc. No bedroom will have less than 70 square feet of floor area and the smallest living room will have 144 square feet. Laundries, steam drying-rooms, baths, gas stoves, and other conveniences will be supplied. For the same rentals now paid in slum dwellings which are infested with vermin, foul with disease, dark and noisome, a poor family can secure twenty-five to thirty per cent more room. It is not supposed that a few corporations can supply the overwhelming needs of a metropolis; but by the influence of competition and example they hope to compel other landlords to come up toward their standard.

Municipal action.

Voluntary associations of private citizens have not the power to do all that needs to be done for the housing of the poor. We must invoke the help of legislature and city government before we can overtake the need. Such is the bad power of ignorance, selfishness, and greed that the community must use its supreme authority in order to protect community interests. Enlightened self-interest has not been found in experience an adequate motive. If the public is defended it must arm and rule its own troops. Every city must frame and enforce ordinances which require builders to submit their plans to public engineers and sanitarians for approval in advance. These building regulations must prescribe minutely and specifically the qualifications of plumbers, the cubic feet of space for rooms, the height of ceiling, the window space for admission of light, the number of stories, the quality of materials in walls and roof, the method of ventilation, the amount of space which may be covered by the house and the amount which must be left free, the kind and position of drain pipes, the fire escapes, the thickness and materials and structure of chimneys, and every other condition of health and safety. The ordinances of the larger cities contain in themselves a sanitary code which all citizens should study. *Public self-protection.*

At the risk of being regarded utterly visionary we may venture to suggest that the future American will not live as our contemporaries live, in isolated dwellings. It is not good for families nor for men to dwell alone. In our cities people hurt each other by crowding; in the country they wither and pine in solitude. When the rich merchant can get out of his office he flies from the noisy throng as from a plague, and when it is possible he buys a summer residence in the country. The city enfeebles vitality and dwarfs child life. Its fret and bustle file away the nerves. In rural regions the opposite evils are seen. Our great system of individual landownership has some disadvantages. Aside from the fact that farm- *Arrangement of farmhouses.*

ing has become a competitive art in which large capital and unusual qualities of administrative ability are demanded, there are other considerations which point to some other system of ownership and control which will secure higher degrees of coöperation, a wiser use of materials and machinery, and more genial arrangement for residence in groups. Ultimately that method will prevail which most nearly corresponds to the economic interest of the nation, but a transition may be rendered more easy and pleasant if the situation is more thoroughly understood and if a tendency to sociability is fostered in sentiment and action.

After all, the suggestion here made is not at all without precedents in experience. In Europe the tillers of the soil generally live in villages around schools and churches. But in America the family lives in a vast and unbroken silence. There are too few opportunities for reciprocal services and intellectual interchange. Medical care and nursing are too difficult to obtain in extremity and emergency. Common interests are discovered too slowly and the farmers are defrauded by those who are in a position to respond more quickly to the swift changes in the commercial world. No doubt many difficulties are in the way of an adoption of the European custom. But there are already instances of the successful application of the ancient method in this country. As men set higher value on social joys; as they outgrow the extreme individualism which made our pioneers so brave and hardy but also so rude; as the refined pleasures of music, literature, and science come to be more valued, we may hope to see the village increase and the isolated and lonely farmhouse become more rare. When that movement has made progress would it not be possible to secure better fire protection and so reduce the

Forms of ownership.

Beginnings made.

risks and cost of insurance? Would it not be possible to have graded schools where now the country teacher is made head of a pedagogical menagerie? Would it not be reasonable to expect that many of the best youth would have a warmer attachment to the wholesome life of the country and not be drained off in excessive numbers to swell the army of miserable people who worry through life in the narrow quarters of crowded cities?

Real sociability.

CHAPTER V.

PUBLIC HEALTH.

Social cost of disease.

EVERY adult citizen represents a large expenditure for his rearing and education. A witty friend says that it requires twenty years and two thousand dollars to transfer the center of gravity from the stomach to the brain. The expense is borne chiefly by the parents and by the community; a long investment before appreciable dividends are returned by the individual. The death of a strong man is the loss of all that he has cost. His sickness is a serious injury to the productive forces of the community; it disarranges the order of business and hinders the action of his associates.

In Boston, in 1892, the average loss of time for sickness was twenty-four days in the year; in Berkshire fourteen days; in Massachusetts at large the average was seventeen days. The estimated loss from sickness among wage-earners was $15,000,000, and for the whole population $40,000,000. Much of this loss was preventable by good sanitation; perhaps $3,190,916 for the working people, which is equivalent to the interest on $50,000,000. The state could well afford to spend a good deal of money on means of limiting this waste of life.

War less destructive than disease.

Preventable diseases cause more loss of life than war with all its horrors. England, in twenty-two years of continuous war, lost 79,700 lives; in one year of cholera she lost 144,860 lives. It is said that for every human being dying twenty fall sick, and every case of sickness is equal, on the average, to a loss of $50. Some years ago over one fourth of the deaths in England were from preventable diseases. Sanitary improvements reduced the typhoid rate in twelve small towns 47⅔ per cent. Two hundred years ago the death-rate in London was eighty in one thousand ; now it is 21½, in spite of greater crowding. A comparison of the statistics of 1861–70 with those of 1871–80 shows that deaths from phthisis decreased 359 per million. These figures give hope and they condemn neglect as criminal.

"Mr. Wadly—described as a stout, robust gentleman—could not understand all the fuss made nowadays about the water question. Mr. Cooper cut the knot. He said that sin had brought disease into the world, and the Almighty permitted the outbreak of diarrhœa in their midst ; neither doctors nor any one else could prevent it. Mr. Cooper is not far wrong. Sin has much to do with diarrhœa, especially municipal sin, which permits a population to drink sewage, and then coolly satisfies itself with referring the judgment to the Almighty." (Quoted by Mr. Waring.) Mr. Cooper was wide of the truth in saying that the doctors could not prevent such diseases; for the doctors have made great advance in spite of bad theology, gross ignorance, and immoral politics. *A case of libel.*

The economic value of good customs may be felt in this way. Many thousands of our citizens belong to mutual benefit societies, lodges, and insurance companies. The rate of premium depends on the average health and longevity of the shareholders or members. Those who live longest and who are most careful of their health must pay higher rates because of the carelessness, stupidity, awkwardness, gluttony, unchastity, lechery, wine-bibbing, and beer-guzzling of others. *Disease and insurance.*

Manufactories are hindered by the feebleness and irregularity of sick men.

Sanitation is the interest of all. Fevers which start in a pauper's cellar travel along drain systems and rise up into the sumptuous bathrooms of marble mansions. Deadly gas, the product of ferment in the lower town, finds vent in the palace which crowns the hill. Enfeebled people, victims of defective drains and filthy streets, become paupers and transmit to posterity a burden of taxation. Depressed by the enervating influence of dark rooms and foul air, many weak persons easily become addicted to alcoholism, seeking in artificial stimulants a momentary elevation above the feeling of exhaustion, at the expense of prolonged misery and multiplied wrongs.

Causes of disease. The foes of health creep out of the ground, sail in the atmosphere, swim in the drinking water, and swarm in the food. For a complete discussion of the subject we refer to the systematic works, and here summarize some of the results of scientific investigations.

Heredity. Generations dead have bequeathed to us in imperfect constitutions and unwholesome environments a sad legacy of disease. Millions of the present race are liable to sickness in consequence of the ignorance of their ancestors, of their vices, their self-indulgence, their superstition, their neglect.

Soil. In towns our streets and alleys, whose natural function is to facilitate communication and cleanliness, have often become the agencies of destruction. The earth, the pavements, the gutters are frequently covered with a mud which embalms the bacteria in frosty weather and lets them loose when the sun of spring warms them into life. This mud is a composition of organic matters which would be very useful as fertilizer in the gardens but becomes deadly when it is out of place. This slush and paste of the street is tracked into houses and brings with it untidiness, debasement of æsthetic and moral feeling, germs of disease, and consequent illness.

Beneath the houses, unless science and law flash their vigilant lamps into the corners, the cellars are only too often heaped with all kinds of decaying matters, vegetables, cloth, rags, wood. Perhaps the walls are moist and covered with mold. There fevers originate, rise ghostlike through doors and floor, and fill the houses with terror, gloom, and mourning. Near city, town, and village may be seen the damp morass, the vile-smelling pond, the stagnant pools, where the microscopic foes of energy and longevity thrive and organize for invasions of human habitations. *Hidden enemies.*

The privies which still linger in many towns and among fairly intelligent people are terrible sources of contamination of the soil, of water, of air. No degree of culture in the parlor can clear a family of the charge of barbarism when it tolerates these disgraceful and anti-social instruments of disease and death. There is no longer any excuse for reading people who permit the organic wastes of the body to accumulate in the execrable, offensive, and disgusting pits which our half-culture permits to exist.

In country places and villages there is a great peril in the sources of drinking water. The filth of barnyard, valuable fertilizing fluids, is drained into the well to poison the family and the cattle. The surface wells are especially dangerous, for they take the organic matter from the surface and while the water may be perfectly clear and sparkling it is deadly as a drink to man and beast. The water supply must be severely questioned in the interest of health. Typhoid fever is com- *Water supply.*

76   *The Social Spirit in America.*

Typhoid fever.

municated by this agency. In 1894 twenty-five of the principal cities of the United States had an average mortality from typhoid of 39.6 per 100,000 of population. The cities which had the largest mortality from this disease were supplied with a highly suspicious quality of drinking water (Dr. G. H. Rohe). In Chicago, the extraordinary outbreak of typhoid in 1889 to 1893 led to the extension of the intake pipe in Lake Michigan to a distance of four miles from the shore; typhoid mortality fell from 159.7 per 100,000 in 1891 to 31.4 per 100,000 in 1894.

Duty of temperance people.

Temperance people are engaged in a noble enterprise. Their holy creed of pure cold water ought to be lived up to. But there are communities where abstinence from alcohol is a sacred custom, and where a colorless liquid more dangerous than beer or light wine is the only beverage of children. Great cities send hundreds of thousands of children to school while their boards of education quarrel over defective filters and succumb to the blandishments of corrupt agents. Meantime the death-rate of school children indicates the mortal effects of intrigue, and mental incapacity of officials charged with a high task.

Food.

Food and milk, necessaries of life, become the vehicles of unfriendly bacteria. The intelligent people of our towns and cities are unable to protect themselves against the ignorance and neglect of dairymen, farmers, and railroad officials. Every town must provide a large force of inspectors and detectives who are under orders to visit all the dairies, milk establishments, groceries, and commission houses which supply the food of the population. Often the fever travels a long distance from an infected house in the country. The cans which contain the milk are lined with disease germs.

Vigilance must never close its eyes. The causes of death are hidden in the means of life.

In addition to the sources of contamination already mentioned we must give heed to the other means by which air is poisoned. Public buildings, as court-houses, concert halls, theaters, where multitudes find entertainment or pursue public business, are frequently so ill ventilated as to be destructive of health. Churches are great sinners in this respect. The thrice-breathed air, robbed of oxygen, left full of the waste products of a thousand lungs, is shut up tightly from the close of Sunday service to the next Sunday morning. The sanctuary smells like a sepulcher. Blessed is the janitor who knows oxygen when he inhales it. Would not the sweet and heavenly flowers of piety thrive more finely in a purer air and a brighter light? The minister's sore throat would not so often annoy the hearers and bring the messenger of glad tidings to an untimely end of service, if the church were kept full of pure air as well as of pure doctrine. *Foul air.*

Then in going to church, school, shop, and office we must use the street-cars. When ungentlemanly men are permitted by law to expectorate upon the floors we may be sure the air will be loaded with flying microbes. Medical authorities warn us against this aggravation of the perils of consumption. The dried sputa of diseased lungs communicate the dreadful malady to unsuspecting travelers where the germs are driven about in the dust of the air. *Street-car floors.*

In country schoolhouses one may only too frequently see a single room into which all the children come with wet and streaming clothing. The schoolroom should not be a drying room but a place for teaching. Open closets for airing outer garments should be provided.

Cleanliness of the body must be insisted on by the teachers, because the exhalations from the skin enter the lungs with the polluted air. For this reason a spray bath is an important adjutant of ventilation in quarters of a city where habits of bathing are almost unknown.

Economic causes. Public health is affected by all that affects the material income of persons and families. We seldom hear of a case of starvation; but all charity visitors and physicians are familiar with starvation diseases. Insanity is sometimes the consequence of imperfect food supply, uncertainty of employment, commercial crises and depressions, class antagonisms, trade disputes.

Social selection of the unfit. As long as society favors the feebles, gives them the means of existence without insisting on limitation of a feeble posterity, so long it must pay the penalty of having an accumulating population of degenerates. Some day we shall learn that it is not only a social duty to keep alive those who already exist, however bad or defective, but also to see that disease dies in the death of those thus humanely sheltered. So long as people are self-supporting social law can do little; but as soon as a family claims a "right to labor and support," the society has a right to determine on what terms the support shall be given. The high rate of morbidity and mortality in a particular business is sometimes due, not merely to the fact that it is dangerous to health, but to the fact that it is conducted by a class of persons who have low vitality and are peculiarly liable to disease. Such are some of the problems for the social spirit. This brief chapter is not a treatise on public hygiene, but a series of illustrations of the need of studying such a treatise and applying its teaching. The people perish from lack of knowledge, and they will not seek the knowledge unless they come to set a higher estimate on the dignity of the body. When we regard our bodies, as Paul did, as the "temples of the Holy Spirit," we shall discover that sanitary art is a kind of worship. *Dignity of the body.*

A forest of green trees will not appear red to a sober man. The habits of individuals are the customs of society. Take an example of the dependence of public health on family customs: the reduction of the typhoid plague by boiling drinking water. The board of health discovers bacteria of a malignant and fiendish variety in the water supply. For the time being no other general source is available. The board issues a ukase commanding all housewives, in the name of science, to boil the drinking water. In the localities where the people read the newspapers the water is boiled and typhoid disappears, and the reputation of that city as a health resort rises many degrees. But there are people who do not know that these impish foes of human health lurk sleepily in ice, and such persons pay the penalty of ignorance after they have melted a colony of hibernating bacteria in gallons of pure water and come down sick in consequence. In the palatial dining-cars they are at pains to advertise the pure spring water, but the pedigree of the ice is seldom shown on the card. It may be taken for granted that it is always bad, since it is usually employed to chill and poison the drinking water. *Influence of customs and habits.*

Public health means health of the people. If the people do not care for health no benevolent despot will step from the clouds to force the luxury upon them. Professor Gould's admirable report shows that voluntary associations of citizens are important agents in sanitary reform and he illustrates methods by the experience of the civilized world. He tells us: "Some of the most prominent witnesses before the English Royal *Sanitary aid societies.*

Commission on the housing of the working classes, of 1885, stated their belief that the existing laws were ample for dealing with all sanitary questions if they were properly enforced." No law works automatically and mechanically. The benefits of government are not enjoyed at so cheap a price. Administration depends upon the state of public knowledge, of popular taste and customs. When men are in the habit of expectorating on the floor of street-cars and on sidewalks, and so long as they insist on using a smoking-car as swine use a sty, and so long as people throw fruit, paper, and cigar stumps in every direction where we must walk and look, just so long will it be impossible to have a clean city. Where cleanliness is popular, as in Berlin or Dresden, a comparatively small force of sweepers can maintain a tidy appearance and a purer atmosphere.

Custom.

Mr. Gould's summary of the functions of sanitary aid associations is as follows: To organize and mold popular sentiment in favor of wise sanitary legislation. . . . To assist boards of health by bringing to their knowledge the existence of insalubrious conditions. . . . To encourage sanitary authorities by support of public sentiment when they need it, and to spur them to action when they are inclined to relax effort. To assist in the education of the poor on sanitary questions; teaching them that there is an authority to appeal to against nuisances, instructing them in procedure; leaving in their homes a printed list of elementary hygienic observances, giving suggestions on the care of infants, and the conditions to be observed in the treatment of persons in the cases of infectious diseases. To publish facts gleaned from official sources which show certain neighborhoods to be unhealthy. Education lies back of reform. In sanitary matters eternal vigilance is the price of safety.

Functions of sanitary aid associations.

Church visitors and charity workers who move about among the poor and become acquainted with them ought to study books on hygiene and sanitation and they should distribute tracts and sell books on the divine laws of health as well as on the cure of souls. Associated charities through their visitors have frequently discovered and exposed the violations of sanitary laws by landlords and tenants. Such unofficial inspectors should be careful not to become mere peevish faultfinders, but should take able physicians and lawyers into their counsel and make complaints only on well-ascertained facts of a nature too serious to pass over in silence. No permanent success can be gained without hearty coöperation with the constituted authorities.

Charity visitors.

Now that psychologists are emphasizing psychophysics and physiological psychology, and universities are measuring the physical and mental capacity of students by means of mathematically accurate instruments of precision, and the correlation of physical and mental processes is established and estimated in terms of foot-pounds and calories, even the finest idealists and spiritualists are insisting on community care of health. The individual cannot protect himself, and is safe only as all are defended from egoistic microbes and deadly dust. In a sparsely settled district the traveler may drink with impunity from any wayside spring. The pure and sparkling stream does not mock his thirst with poison in solution and with millions of microscopic foes lying in the ambush of a drop. But our cities contaminate their water supplies. The very earth becomes saturated and charged with deadly elements. The death-rate rises, and, thermometer-like, tells how the wells are becoming impure. The poor people cannot afford to import water from distant springs and they

Public water supply and drainage.

City soil.

suffer first and most. At last a cry of distress goes up, as when the angel of death passed over Egypt, smote the first-born in palace and hovel, and filled the land with mourning and terror. Led by the physicians, that guild of benefactors who prefer public health to private gain, the city begins to consider the serious problems of securing pure water, of disposing of sewage, of destroying or utilizing garbage. "Free as water and air" means nothing in a city, for everything costs heavily.

The physicians foremost.

Here again there is work for the social spirit. The evils that accompany defective water supply and drainage are not like those self-limiting diseases of childhood which all must have and which soon run their course. These evils grow steadily worse until the more intelligent citizens consider, unite, and agitate for improvement. In the United States it is even more important than in Europe because we have few permanent and well-trained officials. Our abominable spoils system often turns men out of office as soon as they have begun to learn the best methods. Men who employ their time in bargaining away franchises to corrupting corporations have no time left for such trivial matters as the health of citizens. The only redeeming feature of the spoils system is that it occasionally ejects hopelessly bad officials and gives the public a momentary rest of expectation. When the social spirit has driven out the mere private spirit from city legislatures we may hope for Edenic conditions. Meantime societies of citizens should publish health maps of their towns, discover with expert aid of health officers the exact location of plague spots, and arouse the officers to a more conscientious discharge of their duties.

The spoils system kills.

Those comfortable people who have bathrooms and

plenty of living apartments in their houses are hardly able to realize the demoralizing forces operating upon a family of eight who must perform all the functions of daily life in one room and even take in lodgers. It furnishes amusement to talk and write about the "great unwashed," and it must be confessed that the clothing of many working people does smell vilely in street-cars where dainty people come in contact with men who sleep in suffocating rooms and work in fumes and vapors and sweat. And yet poor people will wash if they have a fair chance. Bad surroundings make bad characters. Men who are compelled to be dirty at last become indifferent and forget the luxury of cleanliness. We have medical authority for defending even swine from the charge of the original sin of filth. "The hog is a clean animal. It is certainly a mistaken idea that he desires and needs even any kind of a wallow." *Public means of cleanliness.*

In a certain rescue mission which deals with vagabonds this has been put to a test. A laundry is provided where tramps can wash their own clothing ; and, contrary to the authority of the comic newspapers, this laundry has a large patronage, and a hundred men may be seen waiting for their turn to use the hot water and soap. In New York City a public bath-house has been offered for several years in a locality accessible to the poor. During the years 1891 to 1896 401,652 baths were taken. During the year ending September 30, 1896, the total baths taken were 93,808, of which 68,856 were taken by men, 14,125 by women, 4,301 by boys, 2,265 by girls ; children's free baths, 4,261. A fee of five cents entitles the bather to towels and soap, with the use of the compartment for twenty minutes. In many cities the spray bath is used in place of the old tub or tank bath system. It is to be preferred because there *Tramps will wash.* *Spray baths.*

is no danger of taking contagious diseases as there is when many persons wash in the same small body of water.

It is claimed that the spray bath is less expensive and that it is more tonic in its effects. In a small town a spray bath might be furnished at very low cost and with great advantage to health. Since "cleanliness is next to godliness" there may be a good reason, in benighted, tardy, or otherwise peculiar communities, for providing in connection with churches spray baths for those who need to wash themselves as well as their garments. The ancient priests were not willing to go unclean to serve at the altar, but we have found worshipers and lusty singers who are not so scrupulous.

Public washhouses. In crowded cities there are many families of "cliffdwellers" who must live, sleep, cook, eat, wash, iron in one to three rooms. The noisome steam of wash-tubs fills the air with noxious fumes and detestable odors. The huge tenement on days of laundry work is to a sensitive person unendurable. In hot summer weather the stove transforms the living apartments into purgatory. The social spirit seeks relief in municipal washhouses and laundries, where the poor can take their clothing to wash and iron at a trifling expense. The cost of fuel is very small when many use the tubs and the enhanced comfort and health are a good return for the investment.

Public lavatories. In a city few public lavatories and places of convenience are to be found outside of hotels and saloons. In all European cities a decent provision is made for the public in all parts of the cities. The saloon is always open to men at all hours and its power for evil is augmented by every service it renders. Health and morality suffer from the inexplicable and inexcusable neglect of American cities and towns.

It is a pleasure to record the wise philanthropy of Mr. Nathan Strauss of New York, who could not endure the spectacle of the babies dying all about him because their parents could not secure for them wholesome milk. Science connects with the famous name of Pasteur the wonderful discovery of a process by which the bacteria in milk can be rendered harmless without coagulating the albumen and rendering the milk indigestible. But philanthropy and public sympathy are necessary to make the glorious discovery of use to humanity. Mr. Strauss furnished sterilized milk in tenement homes of the poor, and in those districts the rate of infant mortality instantly fell. Why should not city boards of health supply Pasteurized milk at cost to those who need? Pure milk.

Mr. Baker of Boston found that the grocers in a tenement district were not keeping pure milk. He spent $30,000 on refrigerators and gave them out. Medical men saw the blessed results in the saving of infant life.

It is highly desirable that parents should know the elements of the science and art of school hygiene in order to coöperate with public authorities. In towns where vaccination is universal the once-dreaded scourge of smallpox is no longer feared. In some localities the people are so ignorant and superstitious that they resist compulsory vaccination, and in those localities the disease is likely to break out at any time. And as clothing is frequently made up in such neighborhoods the social peril is very great. School hygiene.

It needs to be widely understood that many skin diseases are communicated from person to person, and that children who have "ring-worm," certain forms of sore eyes, ulcerated throats, erysipelas, consumption, must be excluded from school. The danger from whooping cough, scarlet fever, diphtheria, measles, and mumps is more generally appreciated. But it is highly desirable that parents should be gathered into the schoolhouses and instructed by sanitarians, with the aid of the magic lantern, so that they may more clearly see the necessity for the precautions urged by men of science.

Study of hygiene.

The foundation of national health must be laid in the teaching of physiology and hygiene in the public schools and by extension methods among adults. Already great advance has been made.

After all, public health is at the mercy of public officers. Sanitation on a large scale is the work of experts employed by commonwealth or municipality. The health of the community depends in great part on its political morality and intelligence. No large scheme of drainage, sewage, water supply, food and milk inspection, can be carried out by individuals or voluntary associations. Hence the supreme importance of efficient local government. All heads of households need to know enough of sanitation and hygiene to regulate their own conduct and to realize the necessity of expert service and common coöperation. But for the highest success in resisting disease we must depend on engineers, boards of health, and sanitary police. The connection between public health and political morality is close and vital.

Health and politics.

The social spirit has employed the inventions of science and art in the interest of the public. A century ago only two cities had water works. Diseases due to ignorance of sanitation, to lack of good and abundant water and defective drainage, have retreated before patriotism armed with knowledge. Smallpox is no longer dreaded. Yellow fever, which once raged in New York, Philadelphia, and Baltimore, has crept

Progress.

back to the dismal swamps of undrained districts. Dickens's description of the devastations of malaria in the fertile regions of the Mississippi Valley has long since ceased to be applicable. Mark Tapley would now find no such occasion for the display of his devotion and cheerful courage in a struggle with ague.

Malaria.

CHAPTER VI.

GOOD ROADS AND COMMUNICATION.

Their significance for civilization.

THE power of the Roman Empire depended in great measure on its splendid roads, the traces of which may yet be found not only in Italy but also in the remote parts of Europe which once came under the sway of the Eternal City. Our own civilization could not advance at railroad speed without railroads. The movement to secure better means of transport and communication is supported and urged by many converging interests. The farmers, with growing intelligence, see that with smooth, hard highways they can get their grain to market at much less cost and under more favorable conditions for the market. The capitalists are eagerly looking for employment of their idle funds. The noble army of bicyclers, to whom tacks, broken glass, ruts, mud, and heavy sand seem mortal enemies of joy, are allies of the associations consecrated to improved ways. All social enterprises wait upon this enterprise. Industrial operations are fostered; the circulation of money in remote districts, the interchange of courtesies, the growth of ideas and of fellowship, the prosperity of schools, lodges, churches, sociables, entertainments, spelling-matches, and musical classes are all assisted by good roads. It is said that city people go insane because they feel so much jar and crash and crowding, while country folk become insane because of isolation and loneliness. Good roads favor nervous equilibrium.

Social function of roads.

Military men advocate good roads as a measure of defense and aggression in times of war or riot.

Each person who feels the desire to advance the common welfare can have a share in this reform without joining a club or spending too much time on committees at the county seat. One may build a foot bridge over a stream where many like to cross. A tree which has fallen across the road may be cut into firewood and drawn away. A Good Samaritan may replace a broken plank where a horse might break its leg. Another might give his dominie a point for his sermon on "the highway of holiness" by hinting that more people would come to church if the county road were put in better repair, better drained, and covered with gravel. Almost all can serve their country by agitation and talk. In this country, as in Holland, a deal of good grist is ground out by windmills, and so they are not to be despised. They are useful as well as picturesque.

Every voter counts one.

The very effort to secure better paths of travel has a moralizing influence. Hon. J. M. Rusk said:

Moral influence of effort.

> No one man can improve the highways of a neighborhood. All must act together in behalf of their common interest, and people in yielding something to the common interest will in the end, by intelligent coöperation and systematic methods, be the recipients of benefits far beyond any possible results arising from discordant and uncompromising individual demands. Every person must be brought to see this and be induced to yield his individual interest to a wider range of road improvement and to a single system wider than the horizon as seen from his own doorstep.

Thus a spiritual bond of unselfish devotion to common well-being is the prelude and condition of the material road which facilitates communication between towns. The thing is the outside of an idea and the idea is the inside of a thing.

Economy of good roads.

It is estimated that the total weight of farm products marketed in the United States each year amounts to 313,000,000 tons. It is said that the cost of hauling this may be $946,500,000. It has been estimated, although there may be some exaggeration in the estimate, that $600,000,000 of this could be saved if we had smooth, hard roads. Such figures are largely conjectural, but they help us to realize the vastness of the interest at stake and the possibility of an immense economy through improvements. We have many strong testimonies of practical experts that the improvement of country roads may, by suitable methods, be made to pay, and that without undue financial strain. The problem is not the same for all localities, and experience teaches us to avoid the crushing load of public debt. A moderate debt, however, may indicate a real gain. Hon. Edward Burrough, president of the board of agriculture in New Jersey, is reported as saying that on a new stone road from Merchantville to Camden his teams haul eighty-five to one hundred baskets of potatoes where they formerly hauled twenty-five. "One of our counties issued $450,000 of four per cent bonds and put down sixty miles of stone roads, averaging sixteen feet wide, and though they pay taxes to meet the interest on these bonds, their tax-rate is now lower than it was before the road was built." The increased value of property and the enhanced returns from product at lower expense for marketing make the investment reasonable.

"Mud tax."

The farmer does not escape a heavy road tax even if not one dollar is spent on public highways. The "mud tax" is heavier than that imposed by the authorities, for it is paid "in wearing out his horses, his wagon and harness, in wallowing through the highway with half a load ; in wasting his time waiting for the sun to make it passable in the spring ; in driving to town with a double team when one of the horses might be left at home to do farm work if the road to town was smooth and hard as it should be " (Mr. Otto Dorner).

An interesting and suggestive illustration of our subject comes to light in the report of Mr. R. O. West, attorney of the city of Chicago. On January 1, 1897, there were pending in the courts 684 suits at law against the city with claims for damages amounting to $9,393,-600. The total amount of damages sustained by the city in 1896 for personal injuries was $216,369.50. It cost something over $55 to defend each case. Physical and moral causes are closely linked, for "the large increase of suits was due to the increase of population, the bad condition of the wooden sidewalks, especially in the outlying districts, and the agencies instituted and abetted by certain lawyers for the purpose of collecting all suits of this character and prosecuting them on commission of one half of all money recovered and without any cost or trouble to the clients." The principle illustrated may be applied to cities in all parts of the land. The entire community is responsible for defects in sidewalks, bridges, or roads. The injured members can make their claim good as against all others. It is the common interest that the sidewalks should be sound and safe.

Sidewalks.

The recent enthusiasm for better roads is manifesting itself and seeking means to gain its ends in various directions. Obviously the first step was to employ the old system of "working the roads" where it prevails with more rigid rules and higher efficiency. The difficulty has been to secure real work from those who took this way to pay their road taxes. Much depended on

Methods.

the character of the official in charge. Frequently where there was honest labor with a minimum of shirking the effort was mostly wasted because it was put forth without rational plans. It has sometimes been found that the town officers can secure far better results if the taxes are paid in money and the laborers are hired to perform specific tasks under direction of the overseers. The commutation of money rates for personal service is according to the natural order of society with a developed trade and currency system. "Working out a road tax" belongs to a primitive barter system, and it is especially liable to abuse in large towns with dense population. In some places the assessments have been made according to some scale of benefits received and laid upon the property which gained most from the improvement. When it seems apparent that the wisest method involves a distribution of cost over several years, townships and counties have found it best to borrow money for the early completion of a road and pay interest on bonds. In still other regions the state, as in Massachusetts, has undertaken the direction and development of the scheme on a scale impossible for smaller districts. It is manifest that a commonwealth can command a higher order of engineering talent than is possible for a township or county. And where a drainage system must be completed in order to secure dry road-beds the state must frequently control the construction and adjust levels as between the smaller legal divisions.

Many friends of the cause have strongly advocated the employment of convicts on the public highways. The good roads movement has not always employed sound reason, and many arguments and suggestions born of zeal more than of understanding must be

Cash wages.

Working prisoners.

revised. It is proposed to employ convicts on the highways, the argument being that their labor is cheap and will not compete with the free labor of wage-earners. The fact is that there is no non-competitive work. If the convict is idle the taxpayer must support him. If the convict mends the country road there is one place less for a wage-earner of some kind. But any one who has ever seen a chain gang, and has not been already degraded by the custom, cannot think of tolerating the employment of convicts before the public eye. They are likely to be morally offensive in speech and gesture. To prevent escape they must be guarded by riflemen and a certain number will be shot down every year. The vaunted boast that we are seeking the reformation of the offender and not revenge comes to be a hollow mockery. Some states and countries have thus tried the experiment and such results always follow. The low productive energy of prisoners under such conditions and the high cost of supervision and guarding render the economic argument very weak. It is entirely possible to employ convicts and country vagrants within enclosures at breaking stone. This may be found feasible in some localities. But the chief end of imprisonment is to teach and train the offender, if he is still young, to work at some useful calling. If he is old and hardened the occupation is less important, but he must be treated with humanity. This view has been branded "sentimentalism," but it is based on direct observation of the chain gang and on the almost unanimous consensus of opinion of students of penology. Work in the open air is highly desirable, reformatory, and hygienic, but not work of criminals in contact with the public. *Difficulties.* *How far practicable.*

There are certain advantages and elements of fairness in a state tax for the more important highways. If the state offers a county or township a certain sum on condition that the district thus aided shall complete a certain length of road according to specifications, there is at once a motive for local enterprise and a guarantee of superior workmanship. When it is considered that cities are to receive much of the benefit it seems only just that they should divide the expense with farmers, and this can be adjusted only by a state tax. Where the general interest is far more important than the local interest a state road may justly be constructed on the basis of a state tax.

Zealous advocates of smooth paths, stumbling home after dark and dragging their bicycles, are not always careful to hear the other side. The farmer who must pay for the improvements must be treated with consideration. After all, if he seems slow he is in the majority and reads his newspaper. If he pays taxes rather than shares or money rent he is likely to cool the ardent road-menders with his objections, as follows: dirt roads are not bad all the year, but only a few weeks at a time, and when they are good they are very good indeed; much smoother, softer, and quieter than the harsh gravel. No farmer drives on a gravel road when the noiseless side track is passable. And as to cost: with corn at sixteen cents a bushel and oats at twelve cents a bushel the improvement of roads is too serious an expense to make a present to bicyclers and pleasure-drivers. These conservative landowners recall the craze of railroad and canal construction when counties and states plunged into bankruptcy and repudiation, or pressed the groaning population during a whole generation with heavy interest charges. He desires a solid and even surface for his wagon, but he pauses until the expense can be estimated. He sees that "political" management has so increased the cost of making gravel roads in some places that he sighs for the toll roads which cost much less than his present road tax. It was only fair that this reputable body should be heard, as it must be heeded at the polls.

The inventions of our age are at the service of sociability. The condensation of population has made better means of transport and communication practicable; science and art have supplied the contrivances for convenience; and the spiritual dispositions of men have coöperated with all self-regarding motives to make swift and safe transport desirable. In a country where, as in China, the strongest unit of association is the extended family or clan, and where a national and cosmopolitan feeling is very weak, railroads and telegraphs are regarded as an impertinence. The growth of sociality is not merely the result of improvement, it is also a cause of research, invention, and common use of improvements. It is fraternity as well as drills and dynamite which bores tunnels through granite mountains. *Electric roads.*

It is impossible to set bounds to the use of electric cars. We can already see that the fresh air and green fields of the country are not so far from the city dweller as they were a few years ago. We can already safely prophesy that farmers will soon be carrying grain and vegetables to market and fertilizers back to the soil at the rate of twenty or thirty miles an hour instead of four miles an hour. Even gravel roads will have their rivals. The social influence of this change is beyond present calculation. Life's pulse will beat more rapidly. Let us trust that a more kindly understanding will be fostered when men of city and farm meet each other more frequently to exchange sentiments and ideas, as well as commodities. *Effects of cheap transit.*

Communication.

The transportation of persons and goods is always closely connected with the instruments of intellectual correspondence. No technical treatment of our system of telegraphs and postal service is here attempted. But the value of these agencies to the sense of fellowship and the enlargement of life must be pointed out. The production and exchange of material goods is merely a "preliminary item." The system of communication serves not only the interests of trade but also those of intelligence, art, and religion. The expansion of souls by bartering spiritual goods is the chief concern of humanity. Financial rewards and social fame are prizes sufficient to awaken the talents of inventors. The laboratories of universities prepare the scientific basis for useful machines. Ordinary motives may be trusted to extend lines of telegraphs and telephones among a people eager to learn and capable of moral union. Capitalists all over the civilized world are eager to find a place for lucrative investment. The miser's gold goes begging for some man-serving task in order that it may earn its six per cent, and the most mercenary slave of Mammon is yoked up with philanthropy to do the bidding of the common will.

Social ministry of telegraphs.

It is true that a great nation must be served by great combinations of capital; and these powerful hired hands are not always quickly obedient to that largest wisdom which is akin to justice and goodness. But the nation which found a way, through a bloody and sorrowful road, to abolish slavery, will know how to keep its captains of industry within the bounds fixed by the conditions of universal welfare. In the meantime telegraphs and telephones, while in economic form private monopolies, are really the nerve system of the social body, the material means of welding this nation and all nations into one spiritual community. It is incredible that a system whose social function it is to serve humanity should ever come to be a mere minister of selfishness.

Post-office. The postal system of our government has made familiar and inviting one way by which the people can directly control the machinery of spiritual interchange. There is no large party ready to urge that this department of social service be handed over to private control. All are satisfied with the arrangement. England, France, and Germany have government ownership of these organs of mental traffic. Vast as is the power of concentrated capital and managerial shrewdness, the laws of life are on the side of regulation in the general interest, and the tendency of the ages is against selfish uses of wealth.

Cheap postage. Cheap postage has rendered a great service to human culture, to family affection, to commercial progress, to the growth of a religious kingdom among men. Our legislators have not viewed a moderate "deficit" with alarm, because facility of intercourse pays for its cost in ten thousand ways. Doubtless with completed civil service reform, with a stable force of employees who owe their places to their own efficiency and fidelity and not to the selfish caprices of political "bosses," we shall see progress in the Post-office Department, which already occupies so honorable a place.

Rural delivery. We ought to consider that we are still predominantly an agricultural people; that the majority of our population are farmers; that all are equally entitled as taxpayers to the best advantages of our government; and that rural neighborhoods need the earliest possible information about crops, markets, and social movements. Urban residents can learn much from conversation. Isolated farmers are those who most of all require help from a perfect organization for the diffusion of fresh and accurate knowledge. Private enterprise will never extend an express line, a telegraph, telephone, or an electric service where it does not promise prompt cash dividends; but the post-office sends a letter across the continent at as low a rate as is required for a city delivery. Why should not the mail be collected and distributed at every farm gate every day? Farmers cannot afford to go to town for letters and papers when a much less expensive agency can be furnished without additional machinery. We may confidently look for a gradual and, perhaps, rapid extension of a free daily delivery system in all settled farming districts.

Electric bonds of country and city.

With extended electric communication and transportation, with the telephone ringing at every village, and with electric power carried afar along metal wires, we may look for the extension of manufactures in country places. This tendency may be a serious counterpoise to the present mad rush to the crowded and unhealthy cities. It may come to mean a real cottage and garden, a cow and a poultry yard for millions of wage-workers or small independent mechanics. It may mean that the ideas of Ruskin and Morris are not so wild after all, and that artistic handwork may in some degree replace the monotonous, machine-made, inartistic products of the huge, ugly factories of the towns. It is difficult to foresee the actual course of future events, but the outlook for a saner, finer, healthier life is surely brightened by electric motors and cars and telephones.

World-wide view.

We are led forward to a still wider vision. It will be remembered that in 1896 a message was transmitted around the world in fifty minutes, the words being composed by Mr. Chauncey M. Depew: "God creates, nature treasures, science utilizes electrical power for the grandeur of nations and the peace of the world." The telegraph aids in settling or avoiding disputes, leads to clearer understanding, allays suspicion, puts a speedy end to venomous rumors and rankling memory of injury, terrifies the criminal who flies from justice only to discover that the lightning tracks its prey. The ship captain looks up at the weather bureau signal for a warning of storms. The farmer reaps or journeys according to the knowledge brought from all stations of observers. And thus the network of swift conveying lines, magical as genius, ministers to common utilities and to the cementing of cosmopolitan friendship.

Signal service.

CHAPTER VII.

THE FIRST FACTOR OF INDUSTRIAL REFORM: THE SOCIALIZED CITIZEN.

> Our remedies oft in ourselves do lie,
> Which we ascribe to heaven.

Natural law in the economic world.

OUR first duty in respect to "the present social system" is not to mend it or praise it, but to understand it; not to do something, but to find whether anything can be done; not to fly into a passion and lose our wits, but to concentrate our wits on definite problems. If we find that some knots are too hard to untie we may let them rest while we attempt what is practicable. The immediate field of this book requires us to give undue space and emphasis to change and reconstruction by conscious plan, and this may lead us aside from a point where we see facts in true perspective. Dissent at many vital points need not prevent us from admitting that Mr. Spencer is profoundly right in saying:

Labor already organized.

Blind to the significance of innumerable facts surrounding them, multitudes of men assert the need for the organization of labor. Actually they suppose that at present labor is unorganized. All these marvelous specializations and these endlessly ramifying connections, which have age by age grown up since the time when the members of savage tribes carried on each for himself the same occupations, are non-existent for them; or if they recognize a few of them, they do not perceive that these form but an infinitesimal illustration of the whole. A fly seated on the surface of the body has about as good a conception of its internal structure as one of these schemers has of the social organization in which he is embedded.

This caustic criticism of amateur economic reform is none too severe. It has come to be regarded as a criminal offense for a man to practice the art of surgery or medicine or even pharmacy without having given proof of training. As society becomes more complex and intelligent it becomes more exacting. The medical schools are compelled to lengthen their course from one year of study to five years. A knowledge of industrial history, of economic principles, of political and legal development, is even more necessary to a social adviser than knowledge of embryology and anatomy is to the physician. Tinkering the industrial system is far more serious than setting bones or tying arteries. In both cases a community must get on with such knowledge and leadership as it can command, and the coöperation of laymen is unavoidable. But educated laymen are not nearly so apt as ignorant people to prescribe medicine.

Amateur economists.

It is obviously essential to national welfare both that there should be a body of expert social students and that the people be generally so well informed that they will be discreet in the selection of administrators. All citizens, and even children, may be taught to treat emergency cases with much skill and to give "first aid to the sick and injured" while a physician is coming. So all citizens in a self-governing republic must learn enough of economic principles and history to guide them in business and in voting. It is impossible to delegate all questions of finance, taxation, tariff, and municipal franchises to cliques of benevolent despots who enjoy a monopoly of science. The final jury, after all the learned advocates and judges have spoken, is the common people, who, as Lincoln said, must be favorites of the Creator since he made so many com-

Need of general information.

mon people. If manufacturers and bankers desire the majority to vote intelligently they must come down from their thrones and communicate their knowledge to their political masters at the polls. There is no escape from this responsibility save in bureaucracy and despotism, and the campaign of 1896 made this apparent to the most haughty and obtuse of aristocrats. There is one method open to wealth and that is only too often taken, the thorny path of bribery and corrupt purchase of councils and legislatures. But let us hope that an enlightened social spirit will make this way impassable even for billionaires.

<small>Vitality of the industrial system.</small>

The social body has inexhaustible vitality or it could never have survived the bleeding, purging, and quack economic nostrums which have so long been administered for its health. Great is the healing power of nature, since the nation has outlived not only the drafts of crime and pauperism, the thefts of officials and legislatures, the parasitic robbery of selfish politicians, the jobbery of social wreckers, the depleting effects of famine, pestilence, war, and city aldermen, but even the well-meaning but uninstructed schemes of philanthropic reformers. Mr. Gilman paints these incompetents with accuracy :

> Six or twelve months are quite sufficient time for them to run up a pretty gingerbread work of the walls of their Utopia, to pave the streets with candy, and set fountains of sweetened honey running in all the public squares. The expense of the journey to the pasteboard city is made very low, and every man may command a copy of an infallible guide-book.

<small>The eternal purpose.</small>

There must be in the very structure of the world a wisdom which transmutes error itself into wisdom and crime into progress, or the end of the world would have come with explosion long ago.

The primary wants of men, as hunger and desire for shelter and comfort, and the secondary motives, as love of admiration, praise, decoration, and worship, have stimulated men to labor. Increase of population on a limited territory with limited resources sharpened competition between individuals and between groups. Accidental discoveries with chance division of labor revealed the fact that specialization secured increased product at diminished cost. By insensible gradations, so faint that history has seldom preserved an account of the transitions, the several trades developed. The order of development was noticed and reflected upon only when civilization had already attained a high level. No man planned this order in advance. Each man pursued his own interest, selfish or generous, and the industrial order grew. We can now see, from the height of our century, that there was a plan, but it was not discovered at the dawn of time. Even yet no human being comprehends the system in all its details. *The industrial system a growth.*

But while industrial development has thus proceeded naturally and spontaneously, we must not overlook the fact, as some are prone to do, that this is a human development. The evolution of a planetary system from fire mist, of a tree from a seed, of a bird from the egg, has many points of similarity with that of society. But there are marked differences and contrasts, just because man is something more than earthy ball or bird or tree. Into the process of industrial development man himself enters with all his inherited and acquired powers of intelligence, taste, conscience, religion, will. The savage may be able to plan some simple work, like the making of an arrow-head, a stratagem for trapping deer, or a ruse of jungle warfare; but the civilized man invents a locomotive, a steamship, a trunk railway, an interna- *This growth is in human life.*

tional trade union. The activity of shaping intelligence becomes even a more important factor. A state may project a scheme of forestry whose best results will not be realized for a century. It is characteristic of men that

> We look before and after,
> And pine for what is not.

Intelligence a factor.

Enlarged, multiplied, refined desires quicken ingenuity and give motive to industry. The air is rife with schemes of betterment, many of which, like precocious May blossoms, will perish frost-nipped and wind-shaken. It is a severe law of evolution that millions of germs must die that the species, the type, the race, the persistent truth, the victorious idea, may live and flourish. With increase of intelligence force may be economized and the ratio of wasteful failures be reduced. The higher forms of life are produced and maintained at less cost to parents than is true of lower forms of life.

Individualists and socialists.

Some writers and thinkers dwell too exclusively upon one or other of the aspects of truth, and thus we have two extremes of speculation. The individualists emphasize the truth that personality is the chief end of social action and that a man must not hang with parasitic weakness upon his neighbor. The socialist tends to emphasize the truth that we are members of a community. Optimism and pessimism, as temperaments, are connected with these theories of development in a very odd way: the socialist is optimistic when he is revealing the glories of the state of the future Bellamy paradise, and pessimistic when he harrows our souls with the miseries and cruelties of our "capitalistic system"; the individualist is optimistic in praise of "this best possible world," especially if he has grown rich in it, and he cannot use too black a paint in setting forth the dangers of governmental regulation of business. With this singular and remarkable exception, he thoroughly believes in governmental help and paternal care if he is asking for a valuable franchise or a special tariff rate for which he is quite willing to pay a "reasonable consideration," not to the dear people but to their authorized representatives and robbers. Aristotle long ago recommended the golden mean as nearest the truth, and George Eliot professed a good creed when she declared herself to be neither optimist nor pessimist, but just a meliorist. Our limits oblige us to give scant and inadequate treatment to the natural harmonies of our economic system, since we are in search of the more artificial and positive agencies of human satisfaction and improvement. Meliorism.

Our present business is with modes of amelioration, the correction of abuses, the improvement of methods. No instructed person questions, even in his most sanguine hours, that there is need of improvement. "Something is wrong," is a phrase on all our lips, even when we are bewildered in fixing the responsible author of the wrong or in pointing out the way of escape. Sympathy clouds imagination with the gloom of human sorrow. Those who live constantly among the very poor often come to feel that life has nothing but misery and wrong. A vast literature of fiction, history, social analysis, and statistics has made us familiar with the phenomena of wretched poverty, economic inequality, tragic contrasts. An abundance of cruel and bitter poverty can always be found in cities and even in some rural districts. The satirical story of "Ginx's Baby" could be written anywhere. Ginx was a man with small income and large family, two facts which seem to have elective affinity for each other. He "looked around his Needs and wrongs. "Ginx's Baby."

nest and saw many open mouths about him. His children were not chameleons; yet they were already forced to be content with a proportion of air for food; and even the air was bad. They were pallid and pinched. How they were clad will ever be a mystery, save to the poor woman who strung the limp rags together, and to Him who watched the noble patience and sacrifice of a daily heroism." It is true that "Lord Munnibagge, a great authority in economic matters, . . . had never heard of a case of a baby starving. There was no such widespread distress as was represented. People were always making exaggerated statements about the condition of the poor. He did not credit them." But then Lord Munnibagge had turned the wrong end of his telescope to his eye and the moon seemed to him only a small and distant asteroid. And so "a right honorable gentleman extinguished the subject in his own little brain with his big hat; but everywhere else the sparks are still aglow."

"Lord Munnibagge."

Those who are not blind or deaf at heart can easily find, if they will, tragedies far more terrible than those over which they stir jaded and *blasé* spirits at the theater. Women who spend an income on poodles might have pets enough if they spent a little more time and affection on human beings made in the divine image. There are the toiling mothers who work for a pittance far into the night, faint, weary, despairing. Twenty-nine cents a dozen for sewing shirts and overalls! That means slow death or vice. Hearts break under that sign "plain sewing." Laborers without skill earn in irregular ways ten dollars a week and spend one fourth of this for rent alone. When sickness comes, as it is sure to do, there is no credit, and beggary is only a week off. Few people starve to death outright; but in

Tragedies.

every hard winter our physicians and charity visitors report suicides and death from starvation diseases. Men try to break into prisons to escape cold and hunger. Prison fare is better than that of multitudes of working people and it is more sure.

Every year there are armies of willing men out of employment. The word "unemployed" is an indefinite term which covers several classes of those who are out of work. But among them are found, especially in years of financial depression, a great troop of honest men. The very inventions which are the marks and means of social progress turn into the cold street many men who are too old to learn to use the new machinery. Progress moves forward in its triumphant chariot and crushes its own ministers under its pitiless wheels. Witness the effect of the introduction of the type-setting machines, which have reduced the price of our daily papers but which have brought to many a respectable home of veteran compositors desolation and despair. The period of transition to better things is full of horrors. The cost of general progress is too often borne by a part of society. Is it not strange and pitiful that men with strong arms and stout hearts should go hungry, cold, and ragged, driven to suicide by the cries of hungry children, while wheat is a drug in the market and looms are idle? Is there no "physic for this grief in all the earth and heavens, too"? Among all our great "captains of industry" is there not organizing ability enough to make a more economical distribution of the industrial army? Is it altogether strange that men who suffer much from causes over which they have no control should investigate and question that gigantic system which looms above them and is so unmerciful as well as mysterious?

The unemployed.

Distribute cost of progress.

Mr. E. L. Godkin has said with wisdom :

Betterment.

In examining the ills of our lot, the first question we have to ask is, Are they remediable? Complaints unaccompanied with remedies or suggestions of remedy, are, we all acknowledge, among the most useless forms of human activity. Continual discussion of wrongs or afflictions which cannot be removed is generally held to indicate weakness of character. . . . If I am to speak strongly I should say that the sowing of discontent among the masses, among men in a democratic country in our day, without specifying the evil and laying your finger on the culprit, is very distinctively anti-social work.

But there is a related truth ; he who sees the evils of society is morally bound to seek constitutional and specific remedies, and not give out the impression to toiling and suffering multitudes that their way is blocked and that hope is unreasonable. This drives men to desperation, and it, also, is distinctively anti-social. There is "no escape from death and taxes." But decay may be postponed by suitable hygienic, dietetic, and sanitary measures ; many diseases are preventable ; and even taxes may be more equitably assessed and honestly applied. The sphere of voluntary action is limited but it is large and important.

What the individual can do.

All that is achieved must be the result of personal enterprise and patient toil. Human nature is the primary consideration. Man cannot be blest in spite of himself. There are no social changes for the better which go forward independent of individual action. If a nation lifts a million foot-pounds that weight is the sum of many lifts. Modern sociology has not discovered any royal highroad to competency which the author of the Hebrew Proverbs overlooked. The sluggard's garden is still full of weeds and thistles. The borrower is still slave of the lender. Mr. Spurgeon's John Ploughman sums up homely wisdom in the jingle :

> Once let every man say *Try*,
> Very few on straw would lie,
> Very few of want would die ;
> Pans would all have fish to fry ;
> Pigs would fill the poor man's sty ;
> Want would cease, and need would fly ;
> Wives and children cease to cry ;
> Poor rates would not swell so high ;
> Things wouldn't go so much awry—
> You'd be glad, and so would I.

"Poor Richard's Almanac" needs to be corrected up to date for its tables, but the maxims of industry, thrift, and honesty represent one side of truth which will never be obsolete. There are only a few methods of acquisition, as industry, frugality, economy on the one hand, and theft, fraud, robbery, and beggary on the other. This applies to thieves of all grades, rich and poor. There is no substitute for hard work. But he who mixes thought with brute power serves himself and society better than does one who brings to his task the primitive forces in which oxen, horses, mules, donkeys, iron, and steam surpass stupid and awkward human giants. Man must set his hands to work for his wits as foremen, and must guide his fingers with intelligence. A nation composed of men who like wheelbarrows better than engines can never become rich.

The blacksmith who spends his evenings learning mechanical drawing, the tensile strength of iron and steel, the history of inventions as disclosed in patent office reports, is ever preparing himself to rise, and he is also contributing a larger share to social wealth. Misfortune and accident sometimes lead to misery. Not all the causes of poverty lie within the range of individual will and character or can be removed without the coöperation of the community. But every man can go a certain

[sidenote: Thrift.]

[sidenote: Power of personal will.]

distance on the path of self-education and self-reliance. If the sense of the power and responsibility of the individual decays, if men generally grow into the habit of looking to others or to the government for the initiative, the strength of character and productive force must diminish, and with these personal happiness. Multiplying zeros will not solve the labor problem. A nation of dwarfs is not a great people.

Problems of population.

Economic progress is impossible so long as people think that children are "sent." They are "brought" into existence by a conscious and responsible act of rational beings. There is very general agreement among classic economists that no social readjustment can improve the condition of wage-earners so long as ten men are scrambling for one position. In India, where girls marry at the age of twelve, and where the land swarms with a superabundant population, over 12,000,000 persons died within a few years, of starvation and of famine epidemics. Under such conditions it is not altogether strange that infanticide should be regarded as moral and religious. There is a limit to the earth's surface, a limit to the productive power of an acre of land, a limit to the ability and willingness of men to move to free land. John S. Mill did not sufficiently make account of other elements of the causes of poverty, but he represents a respectable school of economists in saying :

J. S. Mill's view.

Only when, in addition to just institutions, the increase of mankind shall be under the deliberate guidance of judicious foresight, can the conquests made from the powers of nature by the intellect and energy of scientific discoverers become the common property of the species, and the means of improving and elevating the universal lot. . . . Unhappily, sentimentality rather than common sense usually presides over the discussion of these subjects ; and while there is a growing sensitiveness to the hardships of the poor, and a ready disposition to admit their claims upon the good offices of other people, there is all but universal unwillingness to face the real difficulty of their position, or advert at all to the conditions which nature has made indispensable to the improvement of their physical lot. Discussions on the conditions of the laborers, lamentations over its wretchedness, denunciations of all who are supposed to be indifferent to it, projects of one kind or another for improving it, were in no country and in no time of the world so rife as in the present generation ; but there is a tacit agreement to ignore totally the law of wages, or to dismiss it in a parenthesis, with such terms as "hard-hearted Malthusianism" ; as if it were not a thousand times more hard-hearted to tell human beings that they may, than that they may not, call into existence swarms of creatures who are sure to be miserable, and most likely to be depraved ; and forgetting that the conduct which it is reckoned so cruel to disapprove is a degrading slavery to a brute instinct in one of the persons concerned, and most commonly in the other helpless submission to a revolting abuse of power. Poverty, like most social evils, exists because men follow their brute instincts without due consideration. But society is possible precisely because man is not necessarily a brute. Civilization in every one of its aspects is a struggle against the animal instincts.

Misplaced pity.

We read at intervals that the doctrine of Malthus has been discredited by science. In the form in which Malthus himself left his teaching it did require modification. Criticism has corrected the formula but not denied the essential truth of the doctrine that animal instincts must be brought under rational control. Civilized peoples in their more intelligent ranks have accepted the law and reduced it to practice. Among all cultured societies the age of marriage has risen. Trades unions recognize the truth of Malthus's law of population when they restrict the number of competing apprentices or in other ways seek to prevent immigrants and others from interfering with the victories won in strikes. These changes have been accompanied by increasing comforts, a lower

Practical acceptance of the doctrine.

Moral restraints.

infant mortality, and a larger, happier social life for women. Immorality has also accompanied this tendency to smaller families, but it cannot be said that society has so many hopelessly brutal, desperate, cruel, and besotted members as in the early decades of the century. And it is precisely where self-control and prudence are unknown that vice and crime reign supreme. These facts prove that the population problem, serious and perplexing as it is, should not be regarded as insoluble. It is true that those who cause themselves and society most suffering from excessive size of families are the last to adopt the "moral restraints" advised by Malthus. But, on the other hand, many of these low families are precisely those which lose most from excessive mortality, especially among infants, and from confinement in prisons, penal colonies, and asylums for idiots.

Personal character.

Character is the fundamental condition of economic betterment. It would be more accurate to say that a human nature adapted to the conditions of the best life is the essential element. For we are too apt to use the word character as a mere synonym of an amiable disposition. But we must include more in the definition if we are to retain the word. Intelligence and strength are duties. This world has no place, at least of happiness and respect, for the weak. All climates, all markets, all professions weed out the unfit. The only favor that society, mighty as it is, can show to feebles is to let them die out with as little pain as possible. An ignorant man, a savage who has lost his way in modern civilization, fights like a blind man with keen antagonists armed with sharp weapons and obliged to be pitiless. A man who has no skill and energy has no place in a competitive world. It is reported that out of six thousand applicants for employment at the Cooper Union Free

Labor Bureau only eight persons proved to belong to trades unions. This illustrates the law that skill and coöperation are necessary to make men able to stand alone. Among the elements of character required by the modern conditions of existence is the desire to enjoy a variety of goods. A negro plantation hand, debased by slavery, makes an inefficient, unreliable, lazy, factory hand if the earnings of two days in the week are sufficient to buy all he wants. A man who is content with corn, bacon, and a one-roomed cabin has no place in the modern industrial system, which runs by steam and requires every employee to keep up with machinery six days in the week and ten hours in the day. A civilized man wants many things and is willing to work hard to get them. *Desire to enjoy.*

The favored classes owe the first duty. Successful people, especially the heirs of unearned wealth, and parasites who live upon the fruits of common toil, are wont to declaim against the vices of the poor. The vices of the rich look so beautiful in satin robes and evening dress that they charm like virtues. Vulgar variety theaters are often very objectionable and coarse, but then many costly operas on which wealth is lavished sufficient to build many model tenements are frequently mere nasty crime set to fine music, and the only redeeming feature of the libretto is that it is in a foreign tongue. It would be amusing if the thing were not so exasperating and dangerous, to hear a fine gentleman declaim against the extravagance of the poor in periods made eloquent by expensive champagne. There is an immense amount of cant about the wastefulness of the "lower classes" on the part of those who, if they were paid according to the value of their social service, would be clothed in rags and fed on hominy like other paupers. *Social duty of wealth.*

Hypocrisy in advice.

No reasonable person will complain that property has been accumulated in vast and convenient masses so long as the process of acquisition has been honest and the investments are consistent with social welfare. A rich and industrious manufacturer is, so far as he is an investor and manager, a mere trustee of social capital. Nor does a reasonable and instructed person object to very unusual expenditures for personal use so long as those expenditures give leisure for higher forms of service, and bring into the common life finer natures enriched by pictures, travel, and wide intellectual relations. It is the meaningless, barbaric, sensual, depraving, enervating, immoral, debasing, voluptuous, ostentatious use of wealth against which all should protest in every effective way.

Luxury.

Such mad extravagance as flaunts itself at many watering places and on public occasions diverts capital from the production of goods which are within the reach of all industrious men; consumes the products of exhausting toil without any rational return in beauty or knowledge or culture; makes ordinary houses, furniture, and clothes relatively more expensive, and tends to increase the number and intensity of crises and depressions. It arouses bitter feelings among all citizens, and even among the rich themselves. The only enjoyment possible to derive from ostentation comes from the sight of the envy of neighbors, and that pleasure is inhuman. Luxury works by the law of suggestion and imitation upon all men and awakens an ignoble discontent which embitters all existence and brings many into debt and dishonesty. In colleges this meaningless display sets up a materialistic standard of success, lowers the tone of scholarship, discourages the poor student, and drags ideal aims into the dust. It intensifies the mad race

Its law.

for riches, the worship of mere wealth, the temptations of fraud, oppression, and corruption. Let us bring two sober and competent witnesses. Says Mr. Andrew D. White:

It must be confessed that during recent years there have been some conduct of rich men and several careers of rich men's sons fit to breed nihilism and anarchy. Many wild doctrines among the poor may be traced back to senseless ostentation among the rich. Glorification in our press of this woman's "tiara" and that woman's wardrobe; of this young millionaire's genius in driving a four-in-hand, and that young millionaire's talent in cooking terrapin; of some Crœsus buying or begging his way into the society of London or Paris; of social or financial infamy condoned by foreign matrimonial alliances; what wonder that men out of work in tenement houses, or struggling with past-due mortgages on the prairies, should be led by such examples to look at all property as robbery?

Evil example.

And Mr. Goldwin Smith:

Few things in social history are more unlovely or more likely to provoke righteous indignation among the people than the matrimonial alliances of the upstart and sometimes ill-gotten wealth of New York with the needy aristocracy of Europe. What must an American workman feel when he sees the products of American labor to the extent of scores of millions sent across the Atlantic to buy nobility for the daughter of a millionaire! The thing is enhanced by the extravagant splendor of the nuptials. Nor are these marriages merely offenses against feeling and taste. They are an avowal that American wealth is disloyal to the social principles of the republic.

Buying wives with titles.

There is an impression in many quarters that existence on less than ten thousand a year is unworthy of a human being. Any man who has a small income is regarded with ill-concealed contempt. It is true that many very worthy, gracious, and useful citizens spend a good deal more than that on themselves every year. But quite as valuable citizens have served the world at less cost. Socrates, Milton, Shakespeare, Dante, and others of similar rank did not cost as much as many a supercilious dandy has consumed in a few wine parties.

Fallacy of defense of luxury.

One of the most exasperating elements of the case is that these flippant and shallow spendthrifts dress themselves in the feathers of economic virtue and strut about as benefactors of the land. They claim the exalted merit of "circulating money" and "increasing employment of the poor." It is true the economists, from Adam Smith down, have exposed the miserable fallacy of this sophism of vanity which would present a vice for the worship of mankind; but then the weak head which is turned by selfishness could not comprehend the economic doctrine of consumption if it were printed in capital letters. The only correction of such a narrow spirit will probably be found in the taxing power of an educated democracy. But educated people can do something to suppress the sensual vanity of the luxurious by ceasing to pay it homage and begging invitations to its parties.

The best contribution any man can make to the economic welfare of society is himself, as a socialized citizen who finds his habitual satisfactions in ways which are, on the whole, favorable to the well-being of all. By a quotation we may bring the witness of two eminent men to bear on our theme. Mr. Ruskin wrote:

Radical purification.

The only final check must be radical purification of national character. But in this more than in anything, Plato's words . . . are true, that neither drugs, nor charms, nor burnings, will touch a deep-lying political sore any more than a deep bodily one; but only right and utter change of constitution; and that they do but lose their labor who think that by any tricks of law they can get the better of those mischiefs of commerce, and see not that they hew at a hydra.

CHAPTER VIII.

WHAT GOOD EMPLOYERS ARE DOING.

The leaders of industry, if industry ever is to be led, are virtually the captains of the world. If there be no nobleness in them there will never be an aristocracy.
—*Carlyle.*

IT is almost an unpardonable sin for a "mere theorist" to give advice to practical business men on any matter touching the conduct of their business. If the town were in danger of conflagration in consequence of the methods of the manager he would still be inclined to regard all that went on in his factory as a private affair. He hates advice as the worst sort of vice. It is proposed in this chapter to eschew and avoid this fault. We shall give no counsels of perfection for other people to follow at their own expense. We shall confine our discussion to matters of fact which ought to be generally known, and to the judgments of successful business men who have treated their employees as men and not merely as "hands." *{The lowly place of a theorist.}*

This course is legitimate, and it is the only one which an essayist, teacher, preacher, or editor can properly take. Facts must talk. If books do not directly reach a certain class of thick-skinned employers by the direct route, ideas may find the weak joints of their harness by the way of public opinion. Most capitalists care far more for a good name than they do for money, and American business men are not misers. They love power and praise, senatorial seats and reputation for *{Motive of honor.}*

philanthropy, far more than mere possession of millions. Indeed, the books of assessors show that they are very generally exceedingly modest in the publication of their personal property ; and if we did not have Jenkins's account of weddings, banquets, balls, and opera parties, yachts, butlers, and Keeley Cure colonies, we should sometimes be inclined to pity them for their small success in fighting fortune. But even those who evade the assessors are not incapable of wincing under the shafts of literary criticism, especially when it works with universal suffrage as ally. There are few men of this powerful and intelligent class who are not open to appeals to the most generous motives which do honor to our kind. If we are to gain heroes we must praise heroism when it appears. Generosity is contagious. Philanthropy is a bank on which the community can draw very heavy checks — if they are not too heavy. When philanthropy gives reasonable hopes of paying dividends it walks in silver slippers.

<small>All sorts of men.</small>

Managers of industrial establishments have control over the actions and surroundings of their employees. The wage-earner has an apparent freedom of contract, and can offer his services to any employer. But, as Mr. Spencer says, "This liberty amounts in practice to little more than ability to exchange one slavery for another ; since, fit only for his particular occupation, he has rarely an opportunity of doing anything more than decide in what mill he will pass the greater part of his dreary days. The coercion of circumstances often bears more hardly on him than coercion of a master does on one in bondage." Whether a man breathe pure air or expand his lungs in an atmosphere laden with poisonous exhalations and fine dust; whether he work in a crowded room or in a spacious and lofty shop ; whether

<small>Power of employers.</small>

<small>Coercion of circumstances.</small>

he have a clean place to wash his hands and face, and a tidy room for his lunch, or must feed like swine by the gutter or greasy bench, assailed by disagreeable odors; whether he look out from his toils through clear glass to see bright sunshine and flowers, or through obscured panes upon a wilderness of dirty and rusty fragments of machinery; whether he be compelled to endure the villainous profanity and obscenity of an overseer from whom he takes his orders under penalty of discharge, or can receive instructions from a gentleman; whether he be treated as a beast of burden or as a creature compact of nerves and pride, who can suffer and remember; whether he be made to feel every minute that he is a suspected thief who must be watched or a man of honor who can be trusted—all this depends somewhat on himself but much more on the character of the employer. Under the wage system the initiative must always be taken by the man whose employing and discharging power is a whip with a long lash. He who seeks and gains place and power can never escape an unusual share of responsibility. *Sky and landscape.*

It is often asserted, in spite of the discussions of a half century, that the entire duty of an employer is discharged when he has paid the rate of wages for which he has contracted, and that the rate of wages is fixed by the labor market absolutely apart from the will of the employer. The "labor question" according to this philosophy is entirely simple: pay the market rate of wages and there is an end. Any suggestion of further social or moral responsibility is sometimes met with fierce invective and charges of "sentimentalism" and impertinence. It is not strange that business men, sensitive to criticism of honor, should resent any hint of injustice. Nevertheless society cannot release the most *Responsibility of employers.*

powerful class of modern times from their duty. As soon as capitalists are assailed by superior numbers they ask the community to turn out with guns and taxes to drive away the strikers and rioters, and they have a right to such protection. Society cannot afford to let rich men hire their hordes of detectives at personal cost, as did the feudal lords of half-barbarian ages and as some employing corporations have done in recent years. Modern society must control all armed bodies by its own general laws. Therefore society has a right to inquire, in case of social disturbance and call for protection, who is responsible for the cost of armed defense. And as the wage-worker must respond to the legal inquiry so must the employer. Where public opinion is passing judgment outside of courts it must be equally impartial. A successful and humane capitalist, famous for his sharing profits with wage-earners in his employ, says :

Employers dependent on society.

We are told that the strike and the election of labor candidates must be met. Met by what? By force and carnage or by reason and justice? Can a man lay claim to morality, much less to Christian humility, who answers his brother's despair and his sister's degradation with the brutal words of Cain? The *noblesse oblige* of the French, the Golden Rule of all religions . . . declare that we are not for ourselves alone, we are our brother's keeper.

It is not out of a preacher's study or an editorial sanctum, but from business experience that he writes :

Witness of a money-maker.

No man can justly take to himself all that selfishness and power and cunning can bring within his control. Where ignorance and injustice and distress are the deepest, there is his sternest responsibility. (Mr. N. O. Nelson).

He believes that the wage system is itself responsible for piling up a surplus so rapidly, without increasing the purchasing power of the wage-earners, that like a flooded water-wheel it stops the entire productive machinery. Crisis, depression, starvation, ill-will, cruel injustice, he thinks, are inseparable from the traditional wage system.

Mr. Andrew Carnegie voices the common impression of capitalists and economists, and probably of labor leaders themselves, when he declares that the ideal of coöperative production is very far off. It seems certain that for many years, perhaps for generations, the chief control of business must be mainly in the hands of a comparatively few men of great organizing ability. Most men who attempt to direct the immense systems of business which characterize modern life have failed. Only those who have extraordinary endowments have succeeded. This very fact makes it socially imperative that those who direct the management of business during this age of transition from the wage system to the coöperative future should have in high degree that sense of obligation which alone makes power gracious and secure.

Coöperative production far distant.

Happily employers have changed their character during this century in the typical and most advanced industrial countries. The earlier English managers had risen from the ranks of coarse and narrow laborers in the days before free schools had softened the manners of the populace. To a great extent this has been true in this country among the "self-made men who are proud of their makers." But employers tend to become what society admires and praises; they take color from their environment, and yield to the terrors of criticism or the charms of flattery. When society ceases to worship bare wealth, crude lucre, and shows its respect for higher human qualities, it will have still higher, gentler, more humane capitalists. Social selection is already at work. More sons of rich men graduate at college, and the finer, nobler life of college and technological school

Improved character of employers.

is transforming the factory and the wholesale house.

Difficulty of personal relations.

It is true that the day has gone by for those close personal relations between "master and man" which obtained before this age of huge factories, great impersonal corporations, and foreign syndicates. The capitalist employer is to the wage-earner a myth, a soulless thing, a vague and perhaps terrible and remote demigod, who has no concern in the business but to draw dividends, even if they bring the blood of laborers with them. "Corporations have no souls" and classes in society have no backs to smite. And yet individual stockholders, bondholders, and especially directors are not so far removed as at first sight appears. The president of a railroad has no trouble in securing a knowledge of every defective rail, of every broken lamp, of every ounce of oil used by trainmen. The hierarchy of responsibility by which vast enterprises are controlled from a central office is one of the amazing phenomena of our century. It is not impossible to use a detective service to surprise an impolite conductor or a sleepy switchman. The great corporation can set its spies on the most minute actions of its servants. And the encouraging fact is that the members of this service are of a far higher quality than they were some years ago, better in dress, speech, and manners.

Forces of selection.

Now the men who can thus control the very thoughts of their employees are able to affect their fortunes and happiness by personal influence through this same complicated but omnipresent machinery. The most successful managers of great affairs are coming to recognize this responsibility. The time will come when it will be impossible for a corporation which is brutally indifferent to the physical and intellectual well-being of its men to secure helpers. Employers compete with each other

What Good Employers are Doing. 123

for workmen and they compete with each other for public approval. The consumers have the balance of power, and when that fails the democracy has universal suffrage in reserve to bring to terms men who will not heed a hint of humanity.

The power of employers to increase wages is limited but real. The conditions of economic life give the master power to "oppress the hireling in his wages." Economists agree that there is a margin between the maximum and minimum which a business permits to be paid on wages account. Of course if the rate rises too high the manager is bankrupt. But the margin is quite wide enough for some employers to show how mean or how generous they wish to be. Industrial fairness is not absolutely secured by automatic social machinery. Some employers have a reputation for grinding the faces of the poor, while others deserve a good name as doing their best. So that even in this restricted field, where the upper and nether millstones seem to press so hard, there is a space in which the disposition and character of the captain of industry can show themselves. The tendency is for the better workmen to gravitate toward the best employers, those who strive to reach the highest possible levels of wage reward. The process of social selection tends to eliminate the inferior employer by driving his inferior goods out of the market. And where a business falls into the hands of men who are willing to "sweat" the wage-earners, democracy at last finds a way to correct the harshness of greed by legislative measures. Thus the social spirit is a factor when one would least expect it, when it seems that the terms of destiny are hard as fate.

Maximum and minimum wages.

One whom the writer of these pages reveres as a son and pupil, and mentions here with grateful filial memo-

A filial tribute.

ries, was wont to boast in a modest way that all those who worked in his employ for wages after a few years owned their own homes. He paid the highest rate of wages and then lent them his ability as a business man in showing them how to invest their savings. And his example was such that they were won to a nobler use of their powers and means.

Illustrations of the social spirit in a factory.

In a little book accessible in cheap form to all, Mr. D. Pidgeon has told about "Old World Questions and New World Answers." He fills many pages with descriptions of the effects of intelligence, refinement, democratic and Christian feeling in the practical management of New England factories. A few illustrations will show how slovenliness and cruelty of some employers is rebuked by the taste and humanity and by the enlightened self-interest of a superior order of managers.

New England.

The New England manufacturer has no notion of spending the greater part of his day in a dirty, ill-furnished, ill-ventilated room, or, indeed, of asking his bookkeeper to do so. On the contrary, he houses his staff in large, handsome rooms, fitted with many clever devices for facilitating work, from among which the telephone is never absent. Most of his clerks are girls, who also conduct the correspondence, using the typewriter almost universally for this purpose. The offices are kept scrupulously neat and clean, and their occupants are distinguished by an air of briskness very different to that which characterizes their duller brethren of the desk in England. The workshops, again, are so comfortable, and the operatives so like the masters in ideas and manners, that an Englishman is altogether, but agreeably, surprised on his first introduction to a Yankee factory.

He describes the workshops of a watch factory :

These might more appropriately be called saloons, so sightly are they and so beautifully fitted with every appliance for comfort and convenience. Entering at the operatives' door we came, first, upon the dressing-room, where each workman has his ticketed hooks for coat and hat, his own ticketed towel, while the common lavatory is equal to that of an English club. The girls' toilet room is quite dainty in its arrangements, a separate supply of water, for instance, and separate vessels for hand and face-washing being provided. The most exact neatness and scrupulous cleanliness are assured, by the appointment of a special attendant to this usually neglected department. . . . The first requisites of a watch factory are abundance of light, neatness, and cleanliness. No man can do his best when physically uncomfortable, whether from excess of heat or cold, poor light, or, above all, bad air. It is now universally acknowledged, at least in the Naugatuck Valley, that everything which contributes to the comfort and mental benefit of the workman pays good returns on its first cost. Hence the walls of the train-room are all windows, the ceilings are high, the warming and ventilation are perfect. There is no smoke, dust, or bad air, and the operatives are comfortably seated at their respective benches. *Kindness pays.*

And here is a pretty picture of personal relations:

A few moments before six o'clock we stationed ourselves at the factory door to watch the issuing operatives. Of these the greater number are girls, but, girl or man, almost every one had a smile and a nod for the manager, and a smile and nod which were charming because of their eloquence as to the relations between employer and employed. Of one Mr. L. would say, " He is our librarian "; of another, " He teaches in my Sunday-school "; of this girl, " She is the best singer in our church choir "; of that, " She is my wife's right hand at a bee." If there is military discipline inside the works, there is both friendship and equality between employer and employee without the walls. *Picture at the factory door.*

With such delightful examples the theorist has no need to point the moral or preach a sermon; he has only to hold up a mirror. Passing through beautiful gardens of flowers one comes to the library of the factory on whose walls the practical Yankee, a compound of shrewdness and ideality, has caused to be hung this legend, the words of Horace Mann: *Yankee idealism.*

Remember that the learning of the few is despotism, the learning of the multitude is liberty, and that intelligent and principled liberty is fame, wisdom, and power. The well-educated operative does more work, does it better, earns more money, commands more confidence, rises faster and to higher posts in his employment than the uneducated workman can.

Sentiment with money value.

This is sentiment, but sentiment that can be coined into money, sentiment which raises the occupation of a business manager from the despicable position of a slave-driver to the proud elevation of the spiritual leader of his fellow-workmen. Such employers are friends of social peace, guardians of justice, successors of the apostles of piety, wisdom, and humanity.

Sir E. Chadwick furnishes a valuable illustration of the power of a wise and moral employer.

The East India Company instituted an inquiry into the causes of sickness and break-down among their employees: they proved that through influences which they had brought to bear and which had been suggested by the collection of facts of prevention, they had secured from their workingmen in London returns as favorable to health as had been obtained from men living in rural districts. The success was due to the circumstance that the company had learned how to make the health. Selecting their workingmen with care at first, they made provision against sickness. They supplied medical attendance free of expense, so that the moment a man began to fail he could be certified from labor; and as in course of time each man by increasing age lost power to carry out the heavier work, except at serious cost to his health and strength, they reduced his labor, and allowed it to become suitable, stage by stage, to his actual condition for labor.

Help the inspectors.

Employers can coöperate with factory inspectors in the effort to exclude tender children from the exhausting labors fit only for adults, in the protection of workers from accident and disease. It is their plain duty not to resist reasonable factory legislation, as they have too often done, but to assist in it, since it is simply a movement to lift the plane of competition and provide for the future a healthier and stronger race. It is a most unfortunate obstacle to social peace when capitalists secretly or openly combine to obstruct and annoy inspectors instead of fostering reasonable legislation and helping to carry it into effect. It should be understood by this time that factory legislation is the chief means by which honorable and humane employers are enabled to protect their employees without being ruined by heartless and unscrupulous competitors.

One of the great causes of social friction is an unsuitable form of payment, and this is a frequent source of anger apart from the amount of the wages. This is a matter which is largely under the control of the managers. Abuses of power have been so flagrant that legislation had to be invoked to correct them. In mines, lumber camps, saw-mills, and other industries employers have insisted upon paying wages in orders on their own stores. No doubt with honest and liberal employers this arrangement has been the most economical, and frequently it has been a means of great convenience for the isolated workmen. But in the hands of unscrupulous employers the system gives power to rob the workingmen of all beyond a mere existence. They are compelled to pay monopoly prices. It is a pity that the baser employers have thus perverted their power and even fought the legal remedies which have been passed in spite of their protests.

Method of paying wages.

The object of selecting a method of remuneration is on the one side to secure the best quality and highest amount of service, and on the other to promote the health and economic welfare of the wage-earner. Into the technical details of time wage, piece wage, and other current schemes we cannot enter in this place. They are largely determined by the nature of the special forms of industry and no general rule can be laid down for all. But there is one principle of great practical importance and of universal application : that method should be adopted which appeals to the better nature and higher motives of the workmen. All charity and sentiment excluded, this principle is declared by sagacious managers, peers of the strongest, to be practical and imperative. There is a mean and antiquated notion among some employers that it is beneath them to consult wage-earners in making arrangements, and that it weakens discipline. Employers of the better class have already proved that conferences with workmen, and a high degree of confidence shown them, have a reward in good understanding and avoidance of outbursts of unreasoning because uninstructed men.

Consulting workmen.

> Be noble ! and the nobleness that lies
> In other men, sleeping but never dead,
> Will rise in majesty to meet thy own.

It is pitiful to see a real master of the massive engine of business become distrustful of his workmen, cynical and suspicious because they have misunderstood him and returned his kind advances with contempt. It requires a lofty and superior spirit to persist in doing kindness after repulses and insinuations of cowardice and selfishness. And yet this is just the task laid on those who repeatedly remind the world that they belong to the "higher classes." An able and humane superintendent opened a resting and reading-room for his employees. There had been dissatisfaction with wages and the men charged his kind act to fear. It made him angry and he turned them in wrath out into the cold. The milk of human kindness had turned acid

Trials of patience.

in the thunder storm. Why could he not trust the might of mercy just a little further? Had they not some slight cause for their suspicion of sinister motive? Had they always met such friendliness and good faith that confidence must be taken as a matter of course? Surely large endowments and superior social position should call for corresponding display of patience and generosity, and, if need be, pity with those whom a hard and bitter lot has made to feel that they are aliens. Fortunately other men have persisted in kindness until it has won its reward. Perhaps generosity would more frequently succeed if it were not tainted with a lordly feudal spirit which is becoming more and more antiquated and dangerous in a land of political equality.

Many improvements in the lot of our wage-earners can be secured without any new societies, clubs, or guilds. Have we not already churches, pulpits, clubs, parties, homes, newspapers, campaigns, and a hundred other vehicles of expression? If each one of us could discover one particular act which any particular employer might reasonably be expected to perform and tell him so, very sweetly, a score or more of us, he would be likely to do it if he could, and he would be ashamed to put himself in the wrong by getting furiously angry. *Creating public opinion.*

The fears and anxieties of wage-earners are due to real and not imaginary causes. Millions of our fellowmen live close to the margin of their income, and any slight change in their plans must lead to misery. There is a strict limit not only to the possibility but to the wisdom of "saving." There are men who "save" money at the cost of vitality, of the education of their children, and the decent comforts of home. There are millions of honest, industrious, thrifty people who are daily ex- *Provident measures.*

posed to the danger of discharge, to sickness, due to their employment and surroundings, to accident, and to sudden death. They are affrighted and worried by the thought that they may leave wife and children without income. It irks them sore that their children should be in danger of beggary, or be unable to fit themselves for a trade. The process of providing for these emergencies by the savings bank method is very slow and uncertain. In cities unskilled laborers cannot buy costly land for homes. Ordinary life insurance requires premiums which are simply impracticable for men with low wages and family expenses. Some of the "industrial" companies make it easier by collecting the premiums weekly; but this is a costly method and is often abused in practice, especially in connection with the insurance of young children.

Friendly leadership.
It is just here that employers, especially great and permanent corporations, have their opportunity. Scores of establishments are providing various plans of collecting insurance funds against times of sickness, accident, and death. Some of these corporations add a subsidy by way of aid and encouragement. Here is a great firm which provides a bookkeeper to care for the accounts of the society of employees who contribute a small sum each week and govern the entire plan through their own officers. There is a company which collects and manages the funds by its salaried accountants. Experiments are being tried in various parts of the civilized world, and some of the most instructive and hopeful of these are American.

Testimony of a capitalist.
It is a pleasure to quote, not a theorist and preacher, but a railroad president, Mr. O. D. Ashley, on the social obligation of capitalists in relation to employees and the public.

What Good Employers are Doing.   131

If there is social unrest in the civilized world, a fact which will hardly be disputed, we are bound, not only as Christians but as parts of the human brotherhood, to give careful examination to all plans which contemplate man's improvement and elevation in the social scale, and in the United States, especially, where the liberty of the individual is a marked feature of our system of government, we are bound to study plans which may render that personal liberty more precious and enduring.

His little book, "Railways and Their Employees," contains descriptions of various methods by which managers of large industries are assisting their employees in providing against the times of need.

One of the methods most worthy of study is that of Mr. Alfred Dolge, at Dolgeville, New York. The account given by Mr. Paul Monroe is used here. The firm employs about six hundred men. It does not seek to own and control the houses of the village although it assists the workmen in securing ownership of homes. Capital for building is advanced at a low rate of interest. A gymnasium, public hall, library, and reading-room are furnished for the people. A complete system of schools, from kindergarten to academy, is provided. Mr. Dolge does not believe in "profit-sharing," because he thinks it wrong in principle, since it depends on the will of the employer and cannot be made an inseparable part of the wage-earning system. He proceeds upon the fundamental idea that the industry should provide for the depreciation of men as much as for the depreciation of machinery and other plant, and that a business that cannot do this much is not safe for the capitalist or for society. He believes, after twenty years' trial, that one per cent of the wages fund, in his business, will provide for the waste of human life. A life insurance fund is provided by making the

Dolgeville.

Depreciated bodies.

premiums a fixed charge against the profits, making the fat years provide for the lean years according to a definite plan. The pension system takes a part of the same fund and gives payments to faithful employees in case of inability to work on account of sickness, accident, or old age. Each year those who have been five years in the house are entitled to a credit called an endowment account. This fund is payable when the employee has arrived at the age of sixty years or upon his death.

Means of culture. Employers, as influential members of the community, are able to serve wage-earners by promoting the educational agencies of the city or town. It is not always necessary to establish libraries and reading-rooms in connection with the factory or the store ; but rich men can foster the means of culture to which all have access. In these days, when there is a strong tendency among the wealthy and their imitators to educate their own children in private schools, there are distinct signs of indifference or even hostility toward the free public schools. Yet these are precisely the institutions which must give character to our people, as they are the only means of education for wage-earners. Rich men can give time and thought to the management of the common schools.

Elevation of soul. Grandly did Channing, in his noble lecture "On the Elevation of the Laboring Classes," say : "I know but one elevation of a human being, and that is elevation of soul." The improvement in physical and economical conditions is nothing save a means to this end ; and employers have the power to contribute to this in varied ways. Sagacious and magnanimous men, as the Coopers, Drexels, Pratts, have set a worthy example. Some of the trunk line railroads have provided reading-rooms, baths, and even religious services of the Y. M. C. A. for the employees. The expenditures are justified on the ground of economy and humanity.

The capitalist, optimistic with success, tells the wage-earner that the only way to gain more is to earn more. This is partly true. But so far as it is true it shows how intelligence and riches, the gifts of the "higher classes," can improve the income of the poor, by providing instruction in those arts by which wealth is increased and finer goods are produced. *Increased earning power.*

Railroad companies and other corporations have encouraged their employees to buy stock and thus become, in a sense, partners in the enterprise. Aside from the insecurity of such stock and the extreme fluctuations in their value, the possession of shares gives little real power over the management. The method has a value, but only within narrow limits. It is not the ideal of the working people.

Students of social history have long since corrected the notion that a system of industry to which we are accustomed is a part of eternal order and is not subject to change. In other times the laborer was a slave, bound to render service to a particular person according to his will on penalty of death for refusal, and subject to sale like any chattel. The slave received his living because he was useless unless he was fed. But he could not, as a rule, accumulate wealth, and he was liable to be separated from his family. No very high development of character was possible. Under that system, which is called serfdom, the laborer belonged to the territory rather than to a person; and while he could not move about as he chose, and owed certain duties to his lord, he also found security, maintenance, and social consideration in his position. But slavery and serfdom *Profit-sharing.*

have passed away from civilized lands, and a third form of regulating labor, which also lived by the side of the others, has come to be very general in industrial communities.

The wage system.

This is called the capitalistic wage system. Its distinguishing characteristic is that it is based on a free contract which can be enforced at law, but may be terminated by consent. This system admits of a higher degree of personal freedom; it permits a man to go where he thinks he can do best for himself; it opens to the workman some hope of becoming a manager of business; and there is a general correspondence between effort and reward, since the more efficient workman usually receives higher pay than one who lacks capacity and skill. But there are disadvantages in this system, so serious that it is under a steady fire of criticism from many standpoints. As capital becomes more concentrated in large masses, and as division of labor is carried further, the workman is more separated from the employer; he no longer owns and controls the instruments used for production; he is exposed to the risks of business without having any voice in its management; he is under the power of the managers of capital to such a degree that freedom of contract

Its defects.

is frequently a mockery, since the places open to him are all under the sway of similar principles of government. The wage-earner has no direct and tangible interest in the product, save as it affects his rate of wages; and the interests of his employer frequently seem in antagonism to his own. The disputes relating to the rate of wages, the length of hours, the regulations of the shop, and the competition with outsiders have been so bitter as to endanger and sometimes destroy the social peace. The history of mankind shows that a change of some kind is to be expected, and that a method of employment which brings with it so many losses and perils cannot be regarded as absolutely final.

It is not strange that both philanthropists and business men should cast about for some mode of ameliorating the situation and promoting a more satisfactory arrangement. Among the proposed experiments is profit-sharing. This means, as here used, "An agreement spontaneously entered into by which the workman or employee receives a share of profits determined in advance." This method must be carefully distinguished from many schemes of bonus, piece wage, pensions, benefit funds, and other forms of remuneration and stimulus which sometimes go under this name. Strictly speaking, the word profit-sharing should be reserved for that form of industrial remuneration in which a fixed part of the profits shall be divided among the employees according to their wages. Certain advantages are claimed for this system: that it makes the workmen more industrious, careful of waste and wear, less likely to strike and thereby lessen their chances at a share of profits. It is claimed that workmen would not be so likely to disturb social peace if they had hope of a share in the profits of business. *Definition of profit-sharing.*

Objections have been urged from various points of view. Employers have objected that wage-earners would be quite willing to share gains but in bad years could not be reconciled to sharing losses. The answer to this objection has been made that the workmen in fact do share losses every year, since they lose income every day and hour they are not engaged. It is further urged in reply that the manager can create a fund in good years which will provide for the years of loss. Social- *Objections.*

ists are inclined to ridicule the scheme because it depends on the generosity of capitalists, a trait of character which they are not inclined to count a large factor. In reply to this objection it is urged that the capitalist employer who adopts this method would succeed so well that he would compel competitors to come to his way of doing, and that the success of the system does not rest entirely on philanthropy.

Conflicting opinions.

Economists are generally favorable to a trial of the scheme. Some business men are very enthusiastic over it, but comparatively few managers have attempted it, and more have abandoned it than have persisted. Where the cost of superintendence is high and the possibilities of waste of material and time are relatively great, with a superior type of men on both sides, a fair degree of success has been won.

Experiment must decide.

Perhaps the most serious theoretical objection is that the men may deserve a share and fulfill their part perfectly, and yet, owing to the incompetence or misfortune of the manager, they may fail to secure what they deserve. It is claimed that workmen should not be exposed to the danger of losing the results of their extra efforts on account of defects in that management in which they have no voice. Since wages are and must long remain the major part of income, and since a wage contract can be enforced at law while a gratuity cannot be so enforced, it does not seem likely that wage-earners will abandon their union when it comes to a real conflict of interests between the rate of wages and the fluctuating and uncertain share in profits. The verdict at present must wait on further experiment. There is enough to recommend it as worthy of trial in suitable conditions.

CHAPTER IX.

ORGANIZATIONS OF WAGE-EARNERS.

THE wage-earners, like all other men, should have a universal and supreme ideal. Character, in its widest and highest sense, is the ripe fruit of all social growths. The need of knowledge of God, man, and nature is common to all, not peculiar to a class. The enjoyment of vigorous and robust health is a good which most persons can appreciate. And while multitudes of people care little for æsthetic values, for beautiful sights and harmony, all have a latent faculty for art and are defective unless it is developed. But the condition of securing all the blessings of life in any high measure is the possession of income. Economic welfare is the condition of all other welfare. The primary "labor question" is a question of money. Wage-earners are not alone in this situation. All men are alike in depending upon the acquisition of at least a minimum of wealth for the attainment of spiritual satisfaction. The ladder which reaches heaven rests on the earth. This is not "materialism," it is common sense. Those who declare that money is not essential to noble life give the lie to their theory by their conduct. An all-wise Creator gives us bodies before there is any mind to speak of. Paul himself affirmed that the natural comes before the spiritual in the order of time, although it is not first in dignity. A minister seldom accepts a call until he has an agreement about salary.

While there is so much in common there are some

Common interests of humanity.

Natural before the spiritual.

important differences. Modern machine industry, with the accompanying concentration of capital, has, during this century, produced a wage class whose permanent interests are bound up with a particular form of income. Looking now at industrial communities we see that wage-earners are usually compelled to act together as wage-earners because of the method of industrial organization to which we all are subject. A relatively small minority can rise to be managers of industry, but the ratio seems to grow smaller every year.

<blockquote>Certain it is that the prospect of becoming capitalists does not act as so powerful a motive on the laborers to-day as on those of a generation ago. The opportunities to save are as great or greater ; but the amount which has to be saved before a man can hope to become his own employer has increased enormously. (Professor Hadley.)</blockquote>

Many wage-earners may be able to lay aside something in savings banks and can purchase stocks in manufacturing and transporting corporations. But ten hours a day, six days in the week, the large body of operatives are separated from the controlling and directing persons by distinct interests relating to the hours of labor, the intensity of labor, and the rate of payment. Naturally men desire to secure themselves against arbitrary and unreasonable regulations of their captains. One means of doing this is the trades union.

It is almost impossible to mention trades unions without exciting feelings of hostility on the part of those identified with the fortunes of rent, interest, and profit. But a calm and rational consideration of their history will temper this bitter hatred without committing us to unqualified admiration. The simple historical fact is that the development of the factory system has created a class of capitalists and a class of wage-earners ; that the capitalists are already the embodiments of concentrated power because of their control of machinery and their known power to wait without suffering, while wage-earners are urged by hunger and danger of starvation; and that wage-earners have constructed a semi-military organization to defend themselves, to meet the concentrated power of managers, and to secure more favorable wage contracts than they could secure as individuals.

From the standpoint of this discussion no very strong eulogy of trades unions is reasonable. This book is written in the interests of social peace, while trades unions and capitalistic organizations to meet them are on a kind of war basis. The best word we can say for the union is that it is relatively justifiable; that it is indispensable to progress, somewhat as the powder-cart is a vehicle of advance. We cannot give it high praise nor unqualified rebuke. It is an effective weapon in an apparently unavoidable strife. We may think of it just as of ancient slavery and armies, ugly but necessary means of climbing out of the barbarian pit. And yet trades unions are the work of the social spirit and manifestations of solidarity of interests; a primary school for a coming wider coöperation. Just as all affections must take deep root in the nursery of the home before they can bear transplanting and exposure in the wide world, so the semi-militant coöperation of the trades union is on the way to the parliament of man, the federation of the world. *Relative necessity.*

The guilds of former centuries were organizations of manufacturers and of merchants, or of persons who looked forward to becoming masters in the small industries of their times. The trades unions are of a different character and are constructed on a different principle. *The past of trades unions.*

They are composed of wage-earners who know that only an insignificant part of them, thought of as "deserters from their class," have the least chance of rising to the ranks of regulating agents. Since their home and company must be with operatives they are determined to make their permanent place as comfortable as possible. This class consciousness may seem very narrow and selfish, but is much better than dull, swinish apathy.

English history. At the beginning of this century in England and other countries of Europe it was a crime for laborers to combine for the purpose of resisting the demands of the masters. It was only after the most bitter and prolonged resistance that they fought their way to self-respect and conquered the respect of the employing classes by exciting their fears. Adam Smith had said, "Masters are always and everywhere in a sort of tacit, but constant and uniform, combination not to raise the wages of labor above their actual rate"; and for a long time the employers, as political rulers, were able to enforce their will by the help of force. But after the struggle which so much resembled war, the right of coalition has been recognized by all modern nations. At first prohibited, then tolerated, trades unions are now legalized, regulated, with definite rights and duties. "Capital is not absolute; and it is idle to compare the position of the capitalist nowadays with his position when his workmen were slaves and the law-makers were his creations." (Theodore Roosevelt.) The conquest of the laborers has been won by their unions.

Relation of unions to strikes. There is no necessary connection between these associations and strikes. Long before there were unions there were strikes of the most desperate and cruel kind. Even now among unorganized laborers there are strikes, lawless and bloody acts, and obedience to demagogues. On the other hand, some of the strongest unions do not strike, and all of them tend to become conservative as they gain wealth, funds, power, and reputation. Perhaps the very common prejudice against unions in this country is due to the fact that they are comparatively new, have had but brief experience, and are composed of a mixed multitude of city men who have come together from all nationalities. Perhaps a further reason for the excesses and irregularities of American unions in the past has been that our agricultural civilization had not provided us a legal ideal and rule, such as England has formed. A new country, where manufactures are just beginning to be a prominent factor, must work out suitable social regulations which will anticipate deeds of violence and bring associations under the direction as well as protection of law. As these temporary conditions are changed we may hope to find the use of strikes by unions less frequent and characteristic.

Trade unions new to us.

Indeed, the function of organization is to regulate action. Men who are accustomed to discuss their plans, to weigh, criticise, and resolve after debate and deliberation, are much less inclined to rash and precipitate conduct than the same men would be if they were without the means of comparison of views. The same aggravating conditions would arouse the same resentments and reactions of feelings as now, but without a society for deliberation the outbursts of indignation would be more frequent and more desperate. It is true that a strong union is more likely to be successful than one composed of raw recruits, but that is because it is more able to find out whether the employer is able to give better terms, and whether success is within reach. This knowledge and power

Aim.

make a strike less necessary just because it is known to be fairly certain of success.

One of the labor leaders has said that the object of their movement is to secure a larger share of the world's treasure, leisure, and pleasure. They, in common with all men, desire shorter hours of drudgery, higher income, wider opportunities, more respectful and considerate treatment.

Methods. The trades unions succeed by bringing the representatives of a trade into a society which can present a united front, formulate demands, sustain their members long enough to endure a siege while strength of both sides is put to the test, restrict the competition of other laborers, influence legislation on matters of interest to wage-earners, and provide funds for various exigencies of life. Illegitimate methods, as violence, intimidation, and insult, belong to the campaigns of the unions only in the sense that mutilating non-combatants and burning libraries belong to war.

Legal status of trades unions. Even war has its rules, and these tend to become more humane. International strifes are likely to be referred to judicial courts. And so modern nations, recognizing trades unions as necessary evils, or at most only relatively good, seek to restrict their militant operations as much as possible and to see that the contest is carried on in the spirit of fair play. Trades unions have always been legal in this country since the Revolution. Strikes are lawful. Men can continue to promote their own interests so long as they do not seek the injury of their fellowmen by threats, disturbances, riots, or insult. It is ordinarily lawful to do by union what is permitted the individual to do. Whether a strike is good policy is an economical question, an affair of bookkeeping. But the hoodlum cry of "scab," the bludgeon of the assassin, the incendiary torch, are to be judged on other grounds. In a country where any citizen can appeal to law and where manual workers are the majority of voters violence is inexcusable, and experience shows that it will not be tolerated.

Passing out of the warlike atmosphere of the trades unions, we feel more confident of ascribing the creation of the friendly societies to the social spirit which is our theme. To one who moves about among the poor of a great city there are few signs more beautiful and hopeful than the various associations of wage-earners formed to provide funds against times of exigency. On our cards of investigators for relief societies there is often printed the question: "Do you belong to any club, lodge, or friendly society?" The number of these societies is legion and their modes of work as varied as the colors in a kaleidoscope. Among the foreigners about our social settlements these associations constitute one of the foremost factors making for elevation and protection. They raise a lofty and strong barrier against pauperism, and bring men and women into relations of mutual helpfulness and friendship.

Pacific organizations for mutual benefit.

The older trades unions have generally tended to add these features to their more belligerent functions, and history seems to teach that this gives them increased power. May we not hope that when the labor insurrection is over, and labor has won proper recognition, that the benefit factor will be left as the element of permanent interest and value? We have already noticed that employers have sometimes taken the initiative in providing income for times of sickness, accident, and death. A weekly fee is not severely felt by a wage-earner, where fifty dollars would be a crushing burden. Sickness of the bread-winner is robbed of its worst terrors

The benefit factor in trades unions.

and made more amenable to remedy if there is a fund to provide for immediate wants. On the average a man will be out of employment from illness and accident so many days in a year, the average being different for various occupations. This average can be calculated and a sum can be made up by coöperation which will sustain the family until working capacity is restored.

Invention of insurance. The discovery of the principle of distributing individual risks by social action ranks with the invention of the steam-engine. The association for giving this principle effectiveness is at once cause and consequence of the disposition of sociability. Indeed, the cultivation of the friendly nature and the increase of knowledge and good breeding are among the most important elements. Those who are cut off from "society" find in these clubs and lodges a society which gives them pleasure and, in the long run, refinement of manners and a certain intellectual power. While the same financial benefits may sometimes be obtained at even less cost where employers manage the business, the highest results cannot thus be attained. Just as fast as wage-earners can learn to gather and manage their own funds, as they do in the friendly societies, the more rapidly will they acquire business tact, insight into the nature of our economic world, and those qualities of independence, self-reliance, and foresight which lift men in the scale of social rank.

Coöperation of others than wage-earners. Every sincere lover of working people must rejoice at every sign of independence. This does not mean isolation from the employing class. Any of us can join such associations if we pay our dues. It is a great deal better for the capitalist to knock at the door of a lodge and ask admission than it is for him to keep his employees in a state of minority and dependence by methods of patronage. As the wage-earners become more intelligent and self-respecting they will more and more conduct their own affairs. Even their losses of money will teach them wisdom, and the increase of mental and moral force will compensate for many disappointments. *Experience teaches.*

If young capitalists, with real gifts of financial wisdom, wish to be of the most benefit, they must give over their foolish and meaningless class pretensions and become members of some of the existing benefit societies. Politicians are doing this now "for what there is in it." It is an unworked field for genuine democrats who despise the narrowness of class arrogance, have a sincere desire to be useful, and are not itching for political preferment. But an unselfish and earnest political purpose would be promoted by membership in the clubs of workingmen. Merely personal ambition, however, is soon detected. Workingmen have been deceived so often that they are sensitive and suspicious, and nothing short of a serious and persistent devotion to their happiness can remove the moral barrier.

Life insurance is a much more difficult science than that which underlies the mutual benefit societies. The history of life insurance on some of the assessment plans is strewn with wrecks and marked with sorrows. There are certain fixed principles clearly ascertained by the experience of the century. Here as elsewhere the word "cheap" is likely to prove a deceiver. Life insurance costs, on the average, a certain sum. To be real and secure, a staff and not a reed, certain conditions must be observed. The modes of operation may vary but these conditions cannot be ignored with impunity. The terms of admission must be such as to exclude the feeble and the aged, or extra sums must be charged sufficient to cover the risk, or provide a fund from the young *Insurance fraternities.*

and strong ready to meet the certain loss. To omit medical examinations on grounds of "fraternity" without facing the inevitable loss in advance is to invite ruin. Then the premiums must be paid according to ages, or as the old men begin to die off rapidly the younger will find the burden unbearable and desert the sinking ship. There must be a reserve fund sufficient to meet the drafts made by deaths as they occur, since life insurance is simply a device for distributing a given sum over a number of years. Furthermore a society must cover a wide territory so as to be able to divide the losses of a particularly unfortunate locality over a large number of members.

Invariable laws.

The insurance department of Massachusetts has published opinions on these points. The English "Friendlies," described by Baernreither, have tried all sorts of experiments and won success after mistakes and failures. If a friendly society enters the insurance business it must submit to rational laws or disappoint the hopes of confiding members.

There is no device for extracting light from cucumbers or producing perpetual motion without a constant renewal of force. There is no magic in life insurance which will enable men to pay in fifty dollars and take out a thousand dollars. The average member must, in order to secure to his family the sum of one thousand dollars at death, pay each year a sum which, together with the interest compounded, will not only equal the amount desired at the calculated time of anticipated death, but also a sum for the expenses of the business. No philanthropy, sentiment, or brotherly goodness can circumvent mathematics.

Sentiment and mathematics.

It is highly desirable that these very useful societies should be placed on a sound basis. This can be done in several ways. The diffusion of scientific statements of the essential principles of safe life insurance is the first method. Only as wage-earners learn accurately the experience of the English societies and the results of statistical and actuarial study will they make the necessary sacrifices to secure sound insurance. The ordinary assessment plan is so enticing to beginners and looks so much cheaper on its face that many are led astray. Knowledge arms the worker against mathematical fallacies. Another method is state inspection and regulation. It cannot be hoped that all wage-earners can at once master the principles of insurance. These are complex and difficult. Just as the government protects citizens against short-weight coins and tainted meat, so it should protect citizens against societies built on deceit or even on unreliable plans.

Baernreither, historian and eulogist of the English societies, recognizes defects and shortcomings which are in general more common in America: *Limitations of friendly societies.*

These societies, as a whole, are imperfect in two respects. They do not reach equally all grades of the working classes, while for the more helpless and the poorer portion of them they provide only imperfect forms of insurance; and then, they are not yet sufficiently consolidated to prevent the insurance, purchased perhaps by the sacrifices of many years, from being frustrated by insolvency, an eventuality to which the poorer workingmen are necessarily more exposed than their brethren who can afford to join the sound societies.

What is here set down is the warning of a friend of mutual benefit societies. True friendship is not satisfied with flattery but seeks absolute clearness and safety.

One form of work of the social spirit has found little more than a beginning in America, although it has promise of future extension. In 1844 the Rochdale Pioneers of England started a humble store in Toad- *Coöperation on the Rochdale plan.*

lane with twenty-eight members and $140 capital. In 1892 there were reported to the Royal Commission of Labor in Great Britain 1,459 retail distributive coöperative societies, having 1,098,352 members, with £11,520,045 capital and £1,207,204 loans. The sales during 1891 amounted to £31,514,634, on which profits of £4,342,373 had been realized. Why does not this movement extend more rapidly in America? There are several reasons. Our economical conditions have been very different from those of the old country. Until within the last ten years every man had a chance of escaping from the wage status to ownership of cheap government land, if he chose to do so. The easy prospect of becoming a capitalist by taking a homestead tended to dissolve the bond which connected the members of the same occupation. A permanent residence in a city or manufacturing town was not thought of as necessary. Wages were higher than in any other country and the necessity of small economies was not seriously felt. It was more convenient to be served by retail dealers and pay for the luxury. Such were some of the reasons for the belated introduction and success of coöperation.

And even now the principle is not generally understood and appreciated in the United States. There is confusion of thought in respect to the objects, principles, and methods of real workingmen's coöperation. The idea has been made so popular by the English success that the title has been appropriated by various promoters of schemes for profit. More legitimate, yet still misleading, is the use of the term by all kinds of joint stock companies in which the members invest capital and draw dividends in proportion to capital invested. There is no objection to this method of investment. For a long time it will be one of the best ways for wage-earners to improve their conditions. But this is not coöperation in the proper sense.

In all these plans the gain goes to capital and the control is in few hands. This is a business method but not a workingman's ideal. The fact that there is a large number of partners and that they are manual workers, as is the case in so-called coöperative production, does not change the matter in its essential basis. It is still a company in which the profits are confined to the members, while the great public is excluded from the benefit. Probably for this reason the form of coöperative production under consideration has not been able to command sustained enthusiasm either in Great Britain or America. It appeals to too narrow a range of interests. It leaves control in the hands of a select set, to the exclusion of the community. A moderate degree of success has been attained under very favorable circumstances, as in the case of the coopers of Minneapolis who have a contract with millers to take their entire product of barrels, and who on this account are not exposed to the vicissitudes of competition. No doubt the management of business on such terms is a valuable education to the members of the association. Probably it is a financial advantage to them. But it leaves the great body of wage-earners about where they were before. The trades unions in time of strikes have repeatedly tried to establish business to compete with the employers and have almost uniformly failed. The instructed leaders say that failure is due to lack of education and business qualifications. But Beatrice Potter, in reviewing the English movement, said that all such efforts ought to fail because they are too selfish and undemocratic.

<small>Limited success of societies for profit.</small>

<small>Democratic ideals must rule.</small>

Democratic principle of coöperation.

There is an element of spiritual and prophetic ambition in the English movement which is thus expressed by Thomas Hughes, who did so much to advance the work in England: "Human society is a body consisting of many members, not a collection of warring atoms. True workmen must be fellow workmen, and not rivals. A principle of justice, not of selfishness, must govern exchanges." The dominant aim is the welfare of the community, not merely the interest of the trader and manufacturer. The joint stock company divides profits according to capital and gives power according to investment. Coöperators divide profits according to purchases, and management is based on the principle "one man, one vote." The one plan is limited and feudalistic; the other is frankly and thoroughly democratic; its aim being "to place all men on the same level in respect to control over management, eligibility for office, and equally divided profits."

Economic advantages.

The immediate advantages of coöperation are seen in the superior quality of goods, in protection from short weights and adulteration, in assurance of moderate prices. Since the management is in the hands of consumers and not of capitalists, there is no interest in adulteration nor excessive prices, but the interest is all the other way. Since a market is assured by the membership there is small expense for costly advertising. As the payments are for cash there is no loss for bad debts to be charged up to the prompt customers as a punishment for being good citizens, as is the rule in capitalistic establishments. Wage-earners in Great Britain have become owners of millions of dollars of capital by an insensible process. Every pound of coffee, meat, or flour purchased at market prices represented a minute investment. The coöperators have grown rich literally by buying.

Coöperators have something of that education which managers of business enjoy. They must discuss and decide questions akin to those which tax the powers and train the intelligence of merchants and bankers. They must learn to compromise with their fellows, to cultivate tact, courtesy, patience in debate, and submission to the majority after vote is taken. It is manifest that such training tends to fit wage-earners for that true democracy which comes nearer each generation. Coöperators have been leaders in the movements to secure fair and humane treatment of employees; as in granting shorter hours, half-holidays, and the best wages; and in mitigating the evils of sweating, child labor, and unsanitary physical conditions. Many societies own libraries and halls for discussion, provide lecturers and entertainments, and set apart a per cent of the profits for these educational purposes. *Moral advantages.*

There must be one price plainly marked, and that must be about the market price; cash payment must be insisted on without exception, since credit is ruin; dividends are assigned to purchasers according to the amounts of registered purchases; the members buy shares, but each member has only one vote; the investment pays a certain rate of interest like any other capital; the employees of the association are paid fixed salaries, but have no more control in the management than other members, although they may be permitted to vote as shareholders; there must be efficient and honest management, since defective administration will wreck the finest scheme, and salaries must be high enough to secure competent persons and remove temptations to steal. In order to diffuse the benefits of the association *Conditions of success.*

The coöperative spirit.

as widely as possible the coöperative stores are open to the public. "The coöperative spirit" is one of the essential factors, as one of the publications defines it:

A true coöperator has three qualities, good sense, good temper, and good-will—good sense to dispose him to make the most of his means; good temper to enable him to associate with others; and good-will to incline him to serve them and be at trouble to serve them and go on serving them, whether they are grateful or not in return, caring only that he does good, and finding it a sufficient reward to see that others are benefited through his unthanked exertions.

The financial success of the movement indicates that these qualities are not altogether lacking, although no one would claim that they are universally present.

The movement in the United States.

In the appendix will be found recent statistics gathered by Dr. E. W. Bemis. Outside of New England the conditions are not yet very favorable for the Rochdale plan of coöperation. The returns for 1886 showed a business of about $1,000,000, while the partial report for 1895 yields only about $900,000. The years of depression have told heavily on this form of business as well as on others.

In New England, with a more concentrated population of industrials, there has been greater success. Dr. Bemis says that "while six of the stores that had a trade of $134,000 in 1886 are now closed, the trade of the remaining thirteen of those in existence in the former period has grown from $479,000 to $978,951.48, and nine new stores report a trade of $251,409.49. The total coöperative trade in New England, almost entirely on the Rochdale plan, is thus twice as great as ten years ago."

He adds: "A few coöperative societies secure discounts elsewhere, not only on boots and shoes, dry goods, coal and wood, hardware, oil, meat, bread, clothing, and furniture, but on bicycles, jewelry, watches, milk, musical instruments, laundry, photographs, athletic goods, and the services of the tailor, dentist, and physician."

The next stage of development, corresponding to that of the English associations, is the federation of all the societies of the Rochdale type. *The Bulletin of Labor*, No. 6, gives an account of the beginnings of this movement. Federation.

It is well known that managers of business are members of the debtor class, the heaviest borrowers in the nation. When they pay six per cent interest they have reason to hope they can make the money bring ten per cent or more when it has been mixed with their powers of direction. Credit is itself capital to one who can use it. And this is as true of poor men as of rich men. The story told for Continental Europe in Wolff's "People's Banks" is more interesting than a novel. It points out the path to a gold mine. It shows how the wage-earners can redeem themselves from the clutch of the usurer and win for themselves property. Throughout the civilized world the workingmen are coming to be aware of this instrument of elevation. Their necessities bring them into coöperation, which is itself civilizing. Popular credit.

There are societies known in this country by various names, as Building and Loan Associations, Coöperative Banks, Coöperative Savings and Loan Associations. They are to be carefully distinguished from the joint stock companies of private capitalists and investors who have appropriated the name. The "national" building and loan associations have no particular interest to us here, although they are not under criticism. All the associations here mentioned are combinations of persons Coöperative banking.

154   *The Social Spirit in America.*

of limited means, largely mechanics and clerks, to win a possession by means of small regular payments. The first of these societies was formed at Frankford, Pennsylvania, in 1831. In the Ninth Annual Report of the Commissioner of Labor there were reported from forty-eight states and territories 5,598 "local" associations, with 710,156 male shareholders and 263,388 female shareholders, of whom 29.83 per cent were borrowers. The total dues paid in on installment shares in force plus the profits amounted to $413,647,228. If we add the figures for the 240 "national" societies the amount would be $450,667,594. Mr. C. D. Wright pays this tribute:

<small>Statistics of business.</small>

> A business represented by this great sum, conducted quietly, with little or no advertising, and without the experienced banker in charge, shows that the common people, in their own ways, are quite competent to take care of their savings, especially when it is known that but thirty-five of the associations now in existence showed a net loss at the end of their last fiscal year and that this loss amounted to only $23,332.20.

<small>Method.</small>

The plan of organization and operation is not complicated. The capital is collected by the letting of shares of $200, more or less. These shares are paid for by monthly installments of one dollar. If a member has already paid for a lot and wishes to build a home without ready money he can borrow on this security enough for his purpose and pay it back with interest as he is able, meantime enjoying the use of his house. It is true that he must often pay a premium to secure the loan, and the interest is often somewhat higher than he would have to pay private parties. But the arrangement to pay in small sums is an encouragement to undertake and carry through a plan which involves foresight and self-denial. There is a danger that the saving may be made at the expense of health and culture, in which case it comes too dear.

It may be asked whether there is any field for credit among wage-earners in cities and manufacturing towns. It may be thought that credit is the bane of persons so situated, even if it might be a blessing to small landholders like renters and peasants. While pondering this point the following advertisement fell under the writer's eye: *Occasion for other forms of credit.*

> We advance money to honest employees holding good positions with first-class firms or corporations, without security of any kind, at bankable rates. Positively confidential. Your employer will not know anything about it. Established 17 years.

It is evident from such notices that mechanics and clerks have frequent occasion for making small loans, that honesty and occupation can be coined into capital, and that capitalists find profit in lending to such persons. Whether the advertisements are in good faith, and whether they keep their word, is not to be here discussed, since the question is whether such a social expedient is superfluous or not. Why not organize for mutual benefit rather than for the benefit of capitalists? The Raiffeisen method seem applicable to this country as well as to the continent of Europe. Here also we have honest and capable mechanics and clerks who, in a pinch, rather than ask alms or favors, are compelled to borrow at usurious and ruinous rates from private parties. This is especially true after a long period of depression in business. There are also many cases in which a man could secure a bit of valuable property at a bargain if he had a little more money to add to his limited hoard. In other instances the head of the family might be assisted by the mother or mature daughter *Demand for small loans.*

if they could command a little capital to set up a store. In the suburbs of towns, near schoolhouses in cities, near depots of railroads, and in other situations there is, in spite of the colossal department stores, an opportunity of carrying on a small business which will be a convenience to the neighbors. In the suburbs the older children might cultivate a garden, or keep a cow and sell milk, or raise chickens, or keep flowers for the markets, if they had a little capital. These illustrations indicate a permanent field of no mean significance.

Renters need capital. One thinks also of the colored people of the South, struggling to escape the grasp of the money-lender, yet compelled to employ some form of credit, buying everything at exorbitant rates and paying a crushing interest on his loans. And what is true of the negro is true of multitudes of white men, North and South. Of what use is it to advise men to leave the crowded cities and till the soil when they have no tools, no food, no wagons, plows, and cattle? Nature in the most fertile regions has no pity on a man who has nothing but his bare hands. There are beginnings of associated efforts to furnish mutual help which might be promoted by applying the principle of the Raiffeisen banks so successful in Germany.

Raiffeisen. F. W. Raiffeisen was born in 1818. As a young man, being incapacitated for a military position by physical infirmity, he obtained a position in the civil service as burgomaster in Westerwald. It was a bleak and impoverished land, with barren soil, shut off from large markets, the people ill-fed, oppressed by usurers who lent them cattle and money on terms which pulled them down into slavery. Raiffeisen raised a small sum of money to carry out his social invention and pushed his plan through to success past many forms of opposition.

The plan as developed includes the following elements: the capital is obtained from any source, and is frequently advanced by rich men, savings banks, and trust societies. Interest is paid of about three and one half per cent. The borrowers pay about five per cent. There are no salaries except for the accountants. The expenses are kept at the lowest possible point because the management is contributed by the rich and experienced business leaders of the community. There are no dividends, because all profits go to a reserve fund or to the poor, on the ground that the least taint of selfish motive would spoil the enterprise. The district of operations is so small that the borrowers are acquainted with each other, and this is an essential factor in success. The members are personally liable without limit for the payment of the loans, and this makes them very careful about accepting new debtors. The only security is character. No mortgages or pledges are taken. The note of hand is signed by the borrower and perhaps one or two friends as sureties. Of course there is the most careful inquiry as to the habits, honesty, industry, and outlook of the borrower. A lazy, inefficient fellow might get credit from distant strangers, but never from his neighbors.

<small>Raiffeisen's plan.</small>

Germany has a system of relief for paupers, and these associates are independent peasants, proud of' independence and rejoicing in freedom from usurers. The moral influence of such a system is so great that rural pastors have fostered it on this ground, and many have declared that its effects are surprising. Drunkenness, idleness, wastefulness are diminished ; thrift, economy, industry are promoted. There is higher ambition and less discontent. The system is a new and powerful social bond and deepens the sense of local attachments

<small>Moral effects.</small>

and solidarity. There is little danger from vicious radicalism where the people are connected by a bond of mutual helpfulness. The borrower must show that he can make good use of the capital intrusted to him. In forty-three years no member or creditor has lost a cent. Various other forms of coöperation have grown out of this movement. The People's Banks are known, under modified forms, in Switzerland, Italy, Belgium, and France.

Unselfishness a factor in business.

It would seem from this survey that the coöperative schemes in all countries have failed of the highest success just so far as they were narrow and selfish; and that the most frankly democratic have taken deepest root and borne most abundant fruit. It may be several generations before the largest enterprises can be conducted on a democratic plan; but a beginning has been made of no mean proportions and with splendid promise.

The ethical and religious idea involved in this chapter has been thus expressed :

> Man thinks of the few, God of the many; and the many will be found at length to have within their reach the most effectual means of progress. . . . I have expressed a strong interest in the laboring portion of the community; but I have no partiality to them considered as laborers. My mind is attracted to them because they constitute the majority of the human race. My great interest is in human nature, and in the working classes as its most numerous representatives (W. E. Channing, " On the Elevation of the Laboring Classes ").

CHAPTER X.

ECONOMIC COÖPERATION OF THE COMMUNITY.

WE have in the chapters immediately preceding considered the working of the social spirit as expressed in the helpful acts of employers and of organized wage-workers. It has been very clear that there are some achievements beyond the power of isolated individuals, and even beyond the power of vast private associations. Every great community has under its control other organs of regulation and enterprise—public opinion, custom, law, and government. The "struggle for existence" is no longer mere brute conflict for the means of animal satisfaction. The struggle of civilized and Christianized men is for beauty, amiable character, dignity, inward worth. In the family the violence of antagonism has always been tempered by the instinctive affections of parents. In all higher societies sympathy, regard for the welfare of neighbors, patriotism, and at last humanity as cosmopolitan sentiment, have transformed the motives which enter into the contest. There are still trials of strength, ever necessary to determine the fitness of each man for his place, but the trial is no longer a scrimmage but a game played according to rule.

<small>Agencies of public opinion.</small>

Slowly but surely public sentiment is crystallizing into a conviction that the disputes between employers and employees shall be decided by rational means rather than by brute force. There is a community interest closely connected with quiet and order. There is a sen-

<small>Reconciliation and arbitration.</small>

sitive area which is wounded where hunger and gunpowder are asked to decide between capitalist and laborer. This sentiment is shared by the wage-workers and the employers as members of society and participants in the spirit of the age. It finds expression in various arrangements and institutions.

America has already shown numerous examples of conciliatory conferences. If the great world only knew what was going on in factories and shops they would be surprised to learn how few occasions of dispute ever become public. Incipient riots at the bench are daily quenched by good sense, and soft answers on both sides turn away wrath. As the social spirit takes the place of a mere egoism and animal instincts the settlement of differences will be more frequently a direct and friendly act. Both in England and this country various methods have been devised for anticipating trouble by agreement or by a principle of settlement. The sliding scale, common in the iron and coal industries, is an example of this type. Under this arrangement the wages go up and down, automatically, according to the market price of the product. It is by no means an unobjectionable method, but it is preferable to war. It has been accepted as a rough standard of justice, until a more equitable scheme can be devised. In scores of instances, on the eve of strikes, trouble has been avoided by an informal, friendly conference of managers and representatives of the workingmen.

Since 1806 France has had its *Conseils des Prud' Hommes*, a tribunal for decision of disputes between employers and employees. These courts take cognizance only of past agreements and do not consider future rates of wages. Their first step is to secure an adjustment by conference and they usually succeed.

Afterward the matter may come to trial and be concluded without litigation, and enforced as in the ordinary cases. Germany and other countries have adopted the principle. Massachusetts, generally most advanced in labor legislation, as in so many other things, has for several years worked upon this line. The conscience of the nation will not long tolerate a strike or a lockout without previous resort to some method of conciliation and arbitration. Whether a just law can be framed to make the verdict of arbitration final and compulsory, is doubted on both sides, and cannot be regarded as a settled question. In respect to the enforcement of contracts and specific agreements there is no great difficulty. But neither employers nor employees are willing to submit the future rate of wages to a tribunal. *Arbitration in Massachusetts.*

It would be impossible to enumerate the services already rendered by our national and local governments for the economic welfare of the people. Every dollar that we earn has greater purchasing power because we enjoy, in a high degree, the help and defense of the state. It would allay discontent and subdue distrust if all the children of our schools could be shown what they and their parents owe to the government. Life, liberty, property, good name are under the great shield of the nation. The fire department of the metropolis hurries its engines to quench the flames which are consuming the two-room cottage. The health department is busy fighting diseases to which the poor are especially exposed. The police department upholds those laws which are made for the universal welfare. The officer of the law is proud to escort the ragged girl across the street, as well as to warn back the drivers for the lady clad in rustling silk. Many and dark are the *Protective legislation.*

iniquities of the police, and cruel and shameful deeds are done by courts and sheriffs ; but these are done in the dark, they are inconsistent with the genius of our constitution, and they are in express violation of oaths of office.

Doubtless we should urge more efficient execution of these sacred trusts. The adulterations of food by grocers, the short weights and measures from which all suffer, the concealed traps set by unscrupulous plumbers or careless builders, require vigilant notice and unsparing criticism. Reformers have yet more enemies to conquer.

Factory laws.

The necessity of placing workshops under government control has long been felt in older countries. Farmers little realize what this means because they work alone, have all the air they can breathe, are not obliged to conform to the motions of machinery or of fellow-workers, and can control their hours and methods of labor. Most of our legislatures are composed of men who, generally speaking, have formed their ideas according to rural conditions. They cannot easily appreciate the necessity for special legislation regulating the life of operatives in city shops and stores. A conscientious farmer elected to the legislature owes it to himself and to his country to visit the factories, and the city legislator should visit the farmers, and both should exchange opinions in relation to the various demands of a complex and growing community.

Protection of working children.

There are men who declare that legislation should not be invoked to protect adults from the neglect, greed, and cruelty of employers. But few intelligent and humane persons will object to laws on behalf of helpless children. Experience has shown in all modern countries that not even parental affection can be trusted when deep poverty presses and blind ignorance is set to watch. In the ranks of the noble medical profession unworthy charlatans can be found who, for a petty bribe, will sign a certificate of health for a feeble child. Employers may be found who accept the perjured affidavit of parents that their children are of age, or take from them a release in case of injury in the shop. Nothing but the most rigid law, carefully enforced by state inspectors and physicians, and supported by enlightened public opinion, can defend child life from heartless, pitiless greed.

Young persons are more easily affected by unwholesome trades than adults. Saturated with the nicotine vapors of tobacco works their growth is stunted, their heart action is impaired, their powers of digestion are enfeebled. Set to work in stockyards and butcher-shops the sensibilities are blunted and the moral nature perverted. Glass-works are so hot that children working in them go blind, become rheumatic, or develop tuberculous tendencies. Boys are permitted to grind steel cutlery at emery wheels, and are murdered by the dust. At an alarm of fire a throng of girls crowded in a box or candy factory trample each other in panic on the stairs. Young people do not appreciate the value of guards for dangerous machinery; the young are less ready to use safety devices than are the old. The figures show that the girls under sixteen have thirty-three times the probability of being hurt of those over sixteen, and that practically all accidents to female factory operatives befall the young and inexperienced. The figures also show that a boy in a Minnesota factory has a probability of accident about twice that of an adult; and that his chance of fatal accident is over seven times as great as that of a grown man. (Minnesota Labor Report.)

Perils of the young.

Boys and girls at greatest risk.

When it is thus made clear that accidents are certain to occur in undue ratio among children the necessity of state intervention ought to be clear. It is amazing how the pressure of poverty blinds parents and avarice blinds employers to the significance of these facts. The place for the child is not in the factory but in school. A reasonable amount of work in the garden along with kind parents may not injure a young person, but work in a close factory, a steamy laundry, amidst the vapors of chemical works, is murderous. For the sake of the coming race all children should be given a chance to start in the race of life with the elements of education and without the handicap of acquired disease. Very pitiful is the condition of many children who work at errands or as cash carriers in great stores. Years after factory children are protected these weary little ones are overlooked. Ladies who buy their goods so cheaply in these magazines should not forget that the child employees are paying a part of the price. If extreme poverty has compelled parents to send young children to labor then the community must assist. The result would be that when the children are taken out of public occupation adults, the natural breadwinners, would find employment. As it is the little ones, because their labor is cheap, drive out their own parents from wage-earning employments, and reduce whole families to beggary. There is no apology or excuse in any American community for permitting children under fourteen to be out of school and chained up to serve pitiless machinery.

Regulation by law has been found necessary in case of the public work of women. It is idle to say they are able to take care of themselves; they cannot. They are practically shut out from employing the methods of trades unions just where those are most needed. All

Compulsory education.

Women workers.

modern states have been compelled to prevent women from working in mines, in dark places, and at all-night occupations. And while legal restrictions must not be made to hinder women from earning an honest living under suitable conditions there is one principle which may be applied as a test of suitability in all situations: the proved tendency of the occupation under given conditions to destroy health and unfit women for their duties as wives and mothers. The character and health of women workers are not a mere private concern; the very existence of society is involved. Therefore society is not violating individual rights when it adopts wholesome measures of control.

It is said that the fatal accidents in the mines of Great Britain and Ireland show a decrease during the last forty years of more than double per 1,000 tons of coal produced, and a decrease from 3.9 to 1.6 per thousand persons employed. This is due in part to the increased efficiency and perfection of machinery, but still more to the legislation which excluded women and children from the perilous mines, which required the use of safety lamps and other devices, and which made employers liable in costs for injuries for which the management was responsible. What can the reader of these lines do to help our miners? He can ask a labor leader to tell him the present requirements in his own state and write a letter to the representative in the legislature asking him to give it attention. He can study the reports of the factory inspectors and assist in urging their recommendations. The persons best informed as to the dangers and injuries to which wage-workers are exposed are the leaders of trades unions. Ministers of the gospel and all other defenders of human rights, health, and happiness, should learn from the representatives of the

Efficiency of factory inspection.

Appeal to the legislature.

workingmen and give voice to their reasonable demands.

Mr. Henry White, general secretary of the United Garment Workers of America, thus defines the sweating system: "A condition of labor in which a maximum amount of work in a given time is performed for a minimum wage, and in which the ordinary rules of health and comfort are disregarded. It is inseparably associated with contract work, and it is intensified by sub-contracting in shops conducted in homes." The most serious evils grow out of the crowding of strangers into the homes set apart for the family. Foreign immigrants without skill, but thrifty and industrious, unacquainted with the laws of health and with a low standard of living, are the victims and causes of this evil. The crowding of cities, the excessive cost of rents, and the method of contracting-out work are favoring conditions. The community, once awake to the misery and degradation of this system, can coöperate to reduce its danger by refusing to buy goods without the guarantee of a union label that they are not made in insanitary rooms and at starvation wages. Community action is also necessary in order to secure and sustain laws which prohibit the manufacture of clothing in rooms occupied by families; or in infected, filthy, and dark places; or by little children. Public opinion should also demand an adequate number of efficient inspectors and give them moral support in enforcing the statutes. The ministers ought to discover, by faithful parish work, the existence of these wrongs and should direct the moral opposition of religious people against the iniquity. Philanthropy and patriotism must join with religion in invoking the ordinance of government on behalf of the oppressed slave of the tenement as well as on behalf of public health and purity.

All the mutual benefit societies, the incorporated companies, the lodges, the fraternal insurance associations require the recognition of public authority. They cannot live as legal persons, sue and be sued, and carry on enterprises, without legislation. They cannot defend themselves from fraud and unscrupulous competition without legal help. So that some social coöperation and oversight are essential in the promotion of self-help. The building and loan association needs to be protected against dishonest competitors and managers; and the public requires safeguards against wily schemers or incompetent organizers of companies.   *Enabling legislation.*

Some of the states are providing agencies for the registration of men seeking employment. Much time and money are lost by traveling blindly and aimlessly from place to place in search of occupation. Business men do not know where to look on the instant for workmen. To bring the two parties together is the function of the employment bureau. The private bureaus are not always reliable, and are often distrusted. The charitable agencies are shunned by independent and skilled workmen. The state bureau meets the need.   *Free employment bureaus.*

The great industry which began with the century has grown to colossal height. The progress of combination of capital has been resistless and magical. What has the social spirit to say and do in presence of this phenomenal product of the age of steam-driven machinery? Can the ordinary patriotic citizen do nothing but fold his hands in despair, or cry to a pitiless and relentless fate? There is not a citizen so humble but can help himself and his country. The vaster the corporation the more it attracts public attention. Child labor was a hidden and incurable evil until it was massed in a huge bulk before the public eye in factories, and there it   *Trusts and combinations.*

began to be corrected by law. Corporations are very powerful but the state which gives them a charter can take it away, modify it, or make better terms. The matter is not nearly so difficult or dangerous as it is sometimes represented by excited alarmists. Let us see first what the social spirit has for its work.

First of all, if criminal acts have been done, there is the machinery of the courts to discover, to prove, to punish by civic or criminal process. We have learned in the case of the most powerful robbers that detection is possible and punishment can be inflicted. Before a jury a corporation is already at a disadvantage. The fewer the rich criminals the greater interest has the public in suppressing them.

Criminal acts.

In the second place, if the corporation is acting contrary to public policy and contrary to its charter, we have courts and legislatures through which to revoke charters. Again, charters are given for a limited period, and when they are about to expire the public can make better terms.

Some of the worst injuries have been done by city and state legislatures elected by the people. Franchises have been given away because the people chose representatives who were either dishonest or weak. A town or state will have as good government as it deserves. If the honest men refuse to take aggressive part in carrying on their own government they must not whine if venal and treacherous men sell out the public interest for private pelf.

Politics and franchises.

A community is not shut up to one single method of reducing a monopoly to serve instead of dominate. For example : a city council disposed to be honest can either let out contracts for street-car service on the best terms to the highest bidders ; or it can tax the franchises when

they expire ; or it can build its own lines if it thinks that
the most economical method. In the same way rail- *Control of corporations.*
roads, refineries, coal oil corporations, and all other
large combinations of capital can be brought under control. It is simply a question of whether a democracy
can command the services of honest and capable legislators and legal advisers. There is absolutely nothing in
the nature of the case to fear. The great corporations
have developed a machinery for production which has
marvelous efficiency and economy. The consumers
have shown their appreciation by buying the product
where it was produced most cheaply. It remains for the
public not to destroy this elaborate and magnificent
industrial and commercial machinery, but to put a yoke
on it, and compel it to work in the way most friendly to
the common weal. Niagara Falls have been harnessed
and compelled to serve the public. Great trusts can be
brought to terms by the invention and use of suitable
political machinery, managed by capable and honest
legislators and administrators.

In Mr. Spahr's "The Present Distribution of Wealth
in the United States" we are told : "Less than half the *Danger from great estates.*
families in America are property-less ; nevertheless,
seven eighths of the families hold but one eighth of the
national wealth, while one per cent of the families hold
more than the remaining ninety-nine." The method by
which this astounding result was reached is not beyond
criticism. But the accumulation of portentous fortunes
is unquestioned. It leaps to the eye. When this accumulation is the result of a service to the public worth far
more than its cost, and while the wealth is employed in
legitimate and useful industries, we have nothing but
praise for owners and managers. If a great capitalist *Function of the millionaire.*
becomes a millionaire or a billionaire by taking a moder-

ate commission on a commercial invention or achievement which enriches the nation, no reasonable person can complain. He remains still a mere trustee through whose hands the stream of public capital flows.

But so far as such fortunes are accumulated by perjured assessment lists; by bribing the assessors to return property at a rate far below that returned by poorer men; by bribery of legislators and courts; or by any other inequitable and atrocious process—that is matter for a new criminal law adapted to the new temptations of recent commercial life.

Taxing power. And if the evil presses until it becomes intolerable a way will be found, perhaps with a new Supreme Court, to lay an income tax. Already the principle of the inheritance tax has been grafted upon the legislation of some states and it is always a means of turning the attention of heirs to the wisdom of cultivating habits of industry in their youth. The truth is that the democracy has absolute control. It is a sleeping giant not yet fully conscious of its strength. The chief danger always is that when it wakes up it may at first, drunk with a sense of power, become unjust and foolish. The remedy for that is the schoolhouse and the church, knowledge and justice, the social spirit.

Positive ministries of government. Examples of the helpfulness of state agencies in relation to economic welfare may be given to show not only what has been done but what remains to achieve. At this writing the United States government is behind most of the great nations in respect to postal savings banks, and it is to our reproach. Here are the offices of the postal service ready at hand, in every city, town, and village throughout our great country. There is a corps of trained officials who could, with little additional clerical assistance, handle the small savings of the people, as is done in Europe. What would be the advantage of such a system? The very poor would be encouraged to save a little from hard-won earnings and set it aside for the days of need. Timid people, who are frightened by the rare cases of failure of private banks, would trust the government. Inhabitants of suburbs and of remote villages would find it convenient to make deposits if there was an office near them to keep their treasures securely. Regular banks would not be disturbed by the new agency, because large deposits would still go as they do now to commercial houses. People would thus be able to accumulate a moderate capital for favorable investment, and they would become still more deeply attached—German, Irish, Bohemians, Russians, Italians —to the government which takes care of their slender but precious hoard. *(margin: Postal savings banks.)*

The public schools should not only teach thrift but should give discipline in the habit of saving by collecting the pennies by means of a stamped card, and so assisting the growth of a social custom which is more valuable than a gold mine or a diamond field.

What can you do, reader? Sit down at once and write a letter to your congressman and another to your senator at Washington, and ask them what they are going to do about the postal savings bank? By the way, do you know the names of these gentlemen?

Those who oppose such uses of municipal and state government as is here urged are fond of calling it "paternal," and of representing that self-respecting workingmen do not want to be "patronized" by the government. But what is the government? Is it, as it once was, a royal person who grants favors to subjects in answer to a beggar's plea? Is not our government, under a democracy, simply our own tool to use for the *(margin: "Paternalism.")*

common welfare? If we choose to employ our own institution in this way are we receiving a patron's favor, or are we helping ourselves? Paupers are not in the habit of combining to extend the functions of government: it is the most sagacious citizens and manual workers who are engaged in this movement.

<small>Municipal pawnshops.</small>

The tyranny of the usurer in some American cities is unchecked by practical legislation. The ordinary usury laws simply make the very poor pay a heavier rate for risk and add a crushing weight to their burdens. The poor are compelled to pay the highest rates for all they consume and also for money borrowed. The pawnbroker is not always cruel and unscrupulous, but his business tends to make him so and to drive out all self-respecting persons into other callings. Yet it is often necessary for the honest poor to borrow on the security of their chattels. Chattel mortgage-lenders and private pawnbrokers squeeze from unfortunate borrowers, by illegal methods, interest at the rate of twenty to one hundred per cent, and this means ruin. Such shops are often receivers of stolen goods and tend to increase crime. The police supervision of these places is a costly item in a city budget. European cities have taught us a way to avoid these evils, in great measure, by the institution of municipal pawnshops which secure capital at low rates (about three and one half per cent) and lend to the poor in their extremity at six to nine per cent.

<small>Municipal markets and slaughter houses.</small>

The governments of American cities, following European examples, have undertaken to protect consumers from the excessive charges of private dealers, and from their neglect of the conditions of health in the preparation and distribution of foods. With the growth of cities it seems certain that the local governments will be compelled to regulate and, perhaps, monopolize the establishments where perishable forms of food are prepared and marketed. In other connections we have touched upon various contributions of the governments to the common welfare : as parks, bath and wash houses, public toilet booths, libraries, museums, poor relief. The examples here given may serve to illustrate a principle and a tendency toward providing for the public welfare by public means. The provision for free education, especially manual training and technical schools, is closely related to the economic progress of the people.

This would be the chapter where, in the course of logic, should fall a discussion of socialism. The advocates of socialism have already contributed, along with serious error, many just criticisms and practicable suggestions of reform. But since the most popular of the collectivists in this country dates his vision in the year 2000, and life and chapters are so short, we must pause on the border of that land which yields so large a crop of promises. We shall have our hands full of work during the remaining years of this century. Perhaps when practical reforms are carried socialism will not be desired.

Socialism.

CHAPTER XI.

POLITICAL REFORMS.

<small>More power, more responsibility.</small>

WE have been considering the wisdom and methods of extending the functions of our various governments. But these governmants are only so good as our political morality and skill can make them. Unless we can improve our city councils and secure better officials it will be dangerous to intrust to them more responsibility. There is not a business man in the country who would, in the present condition of things, confide to a city council the management of his bank or his railroad. Good citizenship must now resolutely set itself to the task of securing honest, efficient, trained administrators of public business.

<small>Political duty.</small>

The first political duty of a patriotic person is to master in thought the framework and activity of our national, state, city, county, and township governments ; to fix clearly in his mind what are the actual duties of each official in the executive, legislative, and judicial branches of government. How can we criticise the conduct of our public employees until we know what they ought to do? The constitution of the United States is not a long document and it tells the essential things in relation to national officials. The constitution of every state describes the work laid out for governor, judges, courts, legislators, and county officers. The charter of a city prescribes the task of municipal agents. There are books, written by able men, which explain constitutions and laws, and recite their history. Even young persons are capable of learning the fundamental elements of our government. No one can read the daily newspaper intelligently who has not first studied the general outline and history of all these governments. But with a map of the whole field in his mind the reader knows how to find the right pigeon-hole for every fragment of information which is supplied by the periodical press. Without this systematic study of government the daily newspaper is confusing, and the reading of it induces partisanship. Only when the mind is prepared by a theoretical and historical study can the journal do its best service for the mind and for conduct. *[Preparation for newspaper reading.]*

There are some kinds of work which a government must perform as a condition of social existence and order, and these may be called necessary functions. For example : the nation must provide an army and navy to protect it against foreign invasions and injuries, and to maintain peace at home. A nation or a state must determine who shall be citizens and who shall have a share in political control as voters and officers. Laws must be made to decide disputes among citizens about the rights of property, the ownership of land, the inheritance of estates, the obligations of parents and children, of husband and wife. Evil-doers must be restrained and convicted, and measures must be taken to prevent crime. No society can maintain its existence, much less its peace, without such general regulations from an authority which the people recognize. Legislatures must make laws; courts must tell what they mean ; governors, presidents, and mayors must administer. *[The essential work of the state.]*

We have already seen that a government may go beyond the merely protective work of maintaining order and may be made an agency of progress. A vigorous,

Government agencies of progress and convenience.

ambitious, humane people will not merely employ their legal machinery to maintain the being of the nation; they will also employ it to promote well-being. They will not permit a dry theory, a mere arbitrary assumption as to the right use of government, to cripple its usefulness. If they believe a national post-office can serve the public need of communication they will suppress all private competition in that field by a national monopoly. If they come to believe that the telegraph, as in Europe, should be owned by the public rather than by private companies, they will erect their government telegraph lines and go into the business. If the people of a city come to think that gas, electricity, water, or street-cars can be furnished more cheaply by local government, they will find a way of adding this department. A government is simply an organ of public convenience; it is the means by which the people in a given territory get what they want. That is the definition given, not by theorists, but by the actual life and conduct of all modern countries. If a community find it has made a mistake and can secure commodities or services better through contracts with private parties it is always able to lease out its streets, watercourses, roads, or other common property on favorable terms.

Party politics.

In our age and country the citizen must generally act through a party. Edmund Burke defined a party as "a body of men united for promoting by their joint endeavors the national interest upon some particular principle in which they are agreed." And he urges that a citizen ought to seek to make his convictions felt by coöperation with his fellow-citizens. "I find it impossible to conceive that any one believes in his own politics, or thinks them to be of any weight, who refuses to adopt the means of having them reduced to practice."

Lieber declares: "It is impossible for civil liberty to exist without parties. . . . A sound party, which the conscientious citizen may join, ought to have the following characteristics: Its principle ought to be an enlarged and great one, a noble principle worthy of moving masses ; its members ought to be, if possible, large ; its consistency and mutual adherence ought to be chiefly a moral or mental one, and it should have its strength in physical organization ; its members ought to feel, and act as if they felt, that before all they are citizens of their country." *Party principle.*

Selfishness, narrowness of interest, unpatriotic use of party machinery for sectional and personal ends are the bane and curse of parties, the diseases of political organization. A healthy, worthy party is a voluntary association of citizens for promoting the welfare of the whole nation. The existence and maintenance of political parties at great cost are proofs of the high estimate placed by the people on their institutions. Of course corrupt and designing men contribute to party funds and work for party success for unworthy ends, and even criminal use is often made of the "machine." And yet political machinery is just as necessary as educational, commercial, or ecclesiastical machinery. It is not a sign of healthy morality when people sneer at parties and talk loftily of the mean tricks of politicians, while they stand aloof from the conflict in order to keep their cuffs clean. It is sheer cowardice and poltroonery, not ethical and religious superiority, which regards political wire-pulling with contempt. Jesus did not pray that his disciples should be taken out of the world, but that they might be delivered from the evil ; that they might maintain their integrity in the caucus, the committee, the club, the mass-meeting, the lobby. *National aims.*

False independence.

When party spirit is no longer identified with the national interest, with all the elements of welfare for the entire people, and becomes a mere breath and voice of class, or set, or sect, or trade, or profession, then it is evil. Lieber names several classes of citizens according to their relations to parties: "apathists, neutrals or independents, party-members, partisans or zealots, factionists, and trimmers." Too many fastidious and conceited citizens who pretend to be independent deserve his definition and stigma: "an independent man is a man you can never depend upon." To defend the policy of neglect, to retire into the desert or the closet of prayer, on the pretext that politics are wicked and worldly, is a base denial of religion, and of the fundamental law of Christ that his followers should be leaven, salt, and light for the world. It is a good man's duty first to learn, second to talk, and third to work for his country. It is better to vote in error than not to care what becomes of the nation, because interest will lead to intelligence, while mere sulky fault-finding leads to nothing.

Independent action.

There are times, especially in connection with local and state questions, when the independent voter finds it his duty to part company with his party, to oppose the nominations, to organize effective resistance to tricky, unfit, and unscrupulous leaders. This simply means another form of party, not isolated and impractical action.

The questions affecting national parties have little or nothing to do with municipal or town problems. The tariff question, currency, foreign policies, may properly divide the nation into parties, but they have no bearing on such matters as street-cleaning, supply of water and light, local franchises and public schools.

For the election of city officials men should unite in entire disregard of party affiliations in order to secure the most perfect administration possible. As there is little hope of reaching this ideal at present, leagues of honest voters must be formed to fight the professional politicians and franchise "boodlers" at every point by independent nominations.

The patriotic citizen ought to be alert, vigilant, and energetic at every stage of a campaign : in the discussion of issues ; in the local committees and clubs ; in caucuses, primaries, and circles where "slates" are made up ; in town, county, state, and national conventions. If his party refuses to select measures and men according to his conviction about the general good, the independent voter has several ways open. He can assist in the formation of a new party ; or he may persist in efforts within his party to influence conduct ; or he may join others in securing a balance of power between parties and in casting a strong vote with the best candidates available. Circumstances must determine which is, on the whole, the wisest course. "Going to the polls" or even "going to the primary" is not the whole duty of a good citizen. Even the primary, if the party machine controls its nominations, is not primary but secondary—a mere agency for giving popular approval and endorsement to the schemes of men who plot to debauch and rob the public.

Vigilance all along the line.

Some social movements must be carried on by a part of the people : civil service reform is a vital concern of all the people. The administration of national, state, and city affairs has been corrupted and perverted by the "spoils system," and the people have been robbed and misgoverned because we have not had a reasonable, fair, and sensible method of appointing public officers.

Civil service reform.

The men who live by concocting schemes to steal from the city or state dread nothing more than the civil service reform. Therefore they misrepresent it, ridicule it, hate it, try to cripple it.

Principles of this reform. The principles of the civil service reform are simply those of all successful private business. The offices of all governments should be filled by persons who have proved their fitness for the particular work, and no other basis of choice should be considered. All citizens, without regard to party or sect, should be eligible, and none should be excluded. The principle of merit carries with it the law of tenure and promotion. No civil officer—as postal clerk, policeman, school-teacher, superintendents and attendants in charity institutions and prisons—should be discharged save for incompetency, failure, dishonesty, or neglect. While the duties are well discharged the office should be secure. Refusal to contribute to party funds or to take part in a canvass should not affect tenure of office.

Promotions to vacancies should be according to merit and preparation. So far as possible there should be an ascending order of promotion for faithful service, so that every official should feel at the beginning that there was hope of advance if he gave himself unreservedly to his work.

An appeal signed by Mr. Carl Schurz sets forth the common interest in this reform.

The poor man's interest. A poor man has a personal interest in the abolition of the spoils system, because he is not incompetent in consequence of being poor, and he has a right to a chance for appointment if he wishes it; because if not competent himself, his son or daughter, educated in the public school, may readily become so; because the spoils system wastes the public money, and the poor man pays his full share of taxes, in house rent, and food, and clothing, and everything that he uses; because it is the interest of every citizen that the business of the government shall be honestly managed; because the politician who is trying to feather his own nest is always the worst enemy of the citizen, while pretending to be his friend, and the abolition of the spoils system means the destruction of the boss, whose power rests on the distribution of offices as spoils; because no other reform is safe or can ever be successfully prosecuted until the abolition of the spoils system has been secured.

This reform is necessary in order to enable the executive officers, presidents, governors, mayors, to give time and strength to their duties. The mayor of a certain city was compelled to lock himself in his office during business hours in order to keep off the swarm of office-beggars who besieged his door. Public business is impeded or paralyzed by this pressure. It should be no part of the work of an incoming executive to satisfy the "claims" of low ward politicians who did mean work in saloons to help elect him. If every applicant must pass an examination and then take his place according to his capacity, the crowd of office-seekers would be smaller and of a better quality. *The necessity for civil service reform.*

Corruption of political life comes largely from the power of executives to appoint civil servants. Under our present system the executive is almost compelled to pay his political debts with appointments to office; and the ground of his selection must frequently be private interest and not public welfare. Hence we have militia officers who never learned the manual of arms, and heads of insane asylums who get mad from drink; and teachers in public schools who have diplomas from ignorant aldermen, but none from the normal school; and park commissioners who never heard of landscape gardening; and overseers of the poor who have not imagined there ever was a treatise on scientific charity. This state of things disgraces our nation in the eyes of *Misplaced power of appointment.*

the civilized world ; it introduces rascality, wastefulness, and inefficiency into our municipal administration ; it makes further extension of useful state and municipal activity seem impossible. The civil service reform is honored and recommended by the character of the enemies it has made. All scoundrels, "ward-heelers," mean drudges of unprincipled leaders hate it. Their hatred is a high and deserved compliment and an excellent argument for all good Christians to fight for it.

<small>How to help.</small>
Individuals, churches, associations can assist the National League by small contributions of money; by purchase and distribution of their literature; by offering prizes to students in schools and colleges for able discussions of the subject; by holding conferences; by investigation of the appointments made by mayors, governors, and congressmen. Gradually the principles of civil service reform have made the way in nation, states, and cities, and in many public institutions. This progress is the fruit of the social spirit; of self-denying, high-minded, intelligent, and courageous agitation and hard work. Advance has been gained in spite of the combined opposition of mercenary office-seekers in both parties, and it is a moral triumph which should encourage every good citizen who is engaged in difficult social work.

<small>Municipal reform.</small>
The management of our American cities is thought to be the weakest point in our government. A few years ago we had few great cities. We had less experience in municipal administration than older countries where cities have grown quite as rapidly as with us. An agricultural people suddenly confronted the difficult problems of building large towns and learning to live in them. Perhaps the worst factor was a general feeling that one man knew as much as another about streets,

schools, taxes, finance, sanitation, and the thousand intricate questions of a great municipal business. Democracy has not yet become enlightened enough to respect the specialist and the expert. The simple affairs of a village or a rural neighborhood may easily and frequently change hands without serious results. But the complicated affairs of a huge manufacturing, railroad, and commercial town demand the study and experience of many years.

The whole difficulty lies in one point : how to get the right man in the right place and keep him there so long as he does the work well and responds to public needs. The following suggestions were made by Mr. Franklin Mac Veagh, and may serve as a basis for discussion. The mayor of a city should be independent, with full power to appoint executive officers without the interference of the council. The heads of departments should not be boards but single, responsible men, who should answer to the mayor directly, as in a great business house, without the possibility of sharing the responsibility with a crowd. The powers of the council should be limited by the charter to legislation within legal bounds. The members should be paid reasonable salaries "and should not be expected to steal them." They should have no power to appoint subordinate officers. The merit system should control the selection of all employees except the chiefs of departments and their private secretaries. *Right men in the right places.*

The city should have power to govern itself—under a charter granted by a general incorporation law of the state. The limits of taxation should be fixed by the state constitution and laws so that councils could not ruin and bankrupt the municipalities with debts. There should be a constitutional prohibition of special legisla- *Limitation of councils.*

tion. The state authorities should have no power to impose officials on a city. Reforms in election methods must accompany and supplement these measures. Ultimately all reforms depend upon the intelligence, the vigilance, the devotion of the citizens, and therefore popular education is essential to good local government.

It may be questioned whether the recent tendency to strip city councils of power is altogether wise. The representatives of the people must be trusted. To load the mayor with responsibility can never relieve us from the necessity of electing honest and capable aldermen. It is here that the chief difficulties lie.

Electoral reform.

The object of an election is to secure an expression of the real wish of the people. Under present conditions it is notorious that a clique of politicians, ruled by a boss, fortified by the hope of office, takes possession of the political machinery and registers their will in the name of all the people. So powerful, insidious, and unscrupulous have these gangs of politicians become that it is very difficult to break them up and defeat them. All parties come into their hands, and even honest statesmen are often subjected to a humiliating and compromising alliance with degraded and corrupt villains. A brief statement will be made of the current social movements to circumvent these nefarious schemes and make elections the genuine expression of the popular will. It is assumed that no improvement in elections can be of great value unless the popular choice is itself wise, instructed, and honest.

The Corrupt Practices Acts.

American patriotism is willing to learn of our English cousins, and they, being older, have some things to teach us. We need to learn how to secure and maintain a pure and free ballot, and patriotism in a land of universal suffrage has no holier task. The social spirit is moving toward this reform, and is calling all good citizens in all the states to assist. The temptations to bribe voters are constant and pressing, and the forms of bribery are numerous and subtle. Civil service reform would remove some of the prizes, the so-called "plums," which reward political success, but there would still remain powerful incentives to purchase votes, which means to set a price on the splendid and invaluable right of an American citizen. The possession of an office brings social consideration, honor, and sometimes a chance to plunder the dear public. It frequently enables a man to control the actions of inferior officials. Success of a party in some campaigns brings with it financial advantage in connection with tariff legislation. Hence employers are tempted to bring pressure to bear on their employees to vote with them; often with the sincere belief that their interests are common. Men of highest character are sometimes led to purchase votes, or wink at the act in others, when they see that a large body of ignorant and venal voters can be secured for the right side in no other way. The dangers from the southern negro and from the raw immigrant of the North are akin.

Bribery.

Plausible as are the apologies for buying votes, all clear-minded men must see that it is shameful, humiliating, and degrading. No body of people can long engage in such practices without deep moral stain. England has succeeded better than any other country in reducing bribery to a minimum. Professor J. W. Jenks reported that he found "still a very little bribery; a little persecution; more, but still not very much treating; some coercion by employers, some by priests; a good deal of trickery and misrepresentation that is mean but very natural," and some indirect cor-

English success.

ruption ; but on the whole he found the elections pure.

When the candidates are compelled to make out a sworn and itemized list of election expenses ; when the law punishes with disfranchisement, imprisonment, and heavy costs all acceptance or offers of bribes ; and liquor is kept at a distance ; and public opinion sustains the law, bribery can be reduced to a very inconsiderable amount. Several states have already passed such laws, and the task now is to extend them to all the states and enforce them with vigor.

The Australian ballot.
The new ballot-system has for its purpose the suppression of intimidation and bribery at elections. "The ballots are printed by the state, and contain the names of all the candidates of all the parties. Against the name of each candidate the party to which he belongs is designated, and against each name there is a small vacant space to be filled with a cross. At the polling-place the ballots are kept in an inclosure behind a railing, and no ballot can be brought outside under penalty of fine or imprisonment" (J. Fiske). The voting is absolutely secret and the voter is free from all pressure upon his independent judgment. It is beautiful to note how the impertinent and corrupt crowd which once haunted the voters has melted away under the action of this law.

Referendum.
It may fairly be claimed that the movement to refer all essential issues to a direct vote is growing popular in the United States. A democracy is frequently thwarted in its purposes by combinations among its own elected representatives. Laws carried by a small majority in the legislature have often been contrary to the actual will of the majority. The referendum is a means of giving direct expression to the will of the voters. State constitutions are thus amended. Critical and vexed

questions about taxation, control of the liquor traffic, important increase of debts for improvement are finally determined by submission to a popular vote. Measures thus decided are less likely to be causes of disturbance. The issue is disentangled from all foreign matter and discussed in a large way, free from personal and partisan considerations. As Mr. Lecky says, "Democracy has been crowned king. The voice of the multitude is the ultimate court of appeal." If the people err in judgment they must learn better by bitter experience, and the earlier they can put their theory to the test the sooner they will learn their lesson.

The referendum enables the people to check the legislature after it has acted. But Switzerland has constructed political machinery by which any large constituency can bring a measure to the attention of the legislature and so to decision. The democratic principle here finds its most distinct expression. That which is accomplished indirectly by newspaper discussion, popular agitation, resolutions by societies, congresses, and party platforms is, by the initiative, made the immediate issue before the community of voters, in a concise and legal form demanding attention. *Initiative.*

Majorities are often despotic and merciless. Sometimes they are ignorant and unjust. Victory means trampling the unsuccessful minority under foot, and the minority has rights and may have superior wisdom and worth. Republican government ought not to mean a new kind of tyranny. There is nothing in a majority worthy of worship. The ideal of a just government is the welfare of man, woman, and child, whether their votes count or not. The aim of "proportional representation" is to secure in legislative halls a hearing for the minority, and for every considerable body of citizens *Proportional representation.*

who have common convictions and interests. Indeed majority rule often means merely the rule of the "ring" which leads the majority by the nose.

Evils illustrated. Professor Commons illustrates the injustice of the present system. In 1894 "the total vote cast for congressmen was 11,288,135. Of this number the Republicans cast 5,461,202; the Democrats, 4,295,748; the Populists, 1,323,644; the Prohibitionists, 182,679; and 24,862 scattering. The result was the election of 245 Republican, 104 Democrat, and 7 Populist congressmen." The Prohibitionists, though they constituted a large part of the population, had not a single representative to voice their convictions in legislative halls, and the Populists with 11.7 per cent of the votes secured only 2 per cent of the congressmen. In some elections the other party has had the extreme advantage, but in no election is there a fair representation of the various interests of the nation. In 1892 Tammany Hall, with 59 per cent of the votes, elected every one of the thirty aldermen. The corrupt machine, under such conditions, can control the election undisturbed by the helpless independent votes. Sometimes the great corporations get possession of the bosses on both sides, and then the whole state legislature is in their grasp.

Advantages. Proportional representation carries with it the right and power of any respectable number or class of citizens, even if a majority is against them, to send legislators to the law-making bodies of the commonwealth or city to present their views, to urge their rights, and to check the arbitrary and tyrannical action of those who chance to be in power. If this plan was employed in electing city councils on general tickets, instead of ward tickets, it would enable reform parties to consolidate their strength, secure more competent representatives, and resist the corrupt organizations which now rule our cities. It would compel the party leaders to offer a higher class of men as candidates. It would induce honest men of ability, business men, wage-earners, and professional men to stand for election, since they would not be compelled to secure office by the degrading methods now so common.

A radical reform would still further encourage busy citizens to go to the primaries and the best men to accept office—the abolition of the caucus and convention and the substitution of a legalized primary. There should be in every state legal provision for the nomination of any candidate on the petition of a respectable number of voters in a party. Under the present order it is usually a waste of time to go to the primary unless one is an expert politician, and the consciousness of disappointment it is which prevents honest citizens from going to the place of nomination. Give them a fair chance to be on equal terms with tricksters and they will be glad to perform their duty. Give the independents power to place their own candidates on the ballot in as favorable a place as those of the professional ring and all dark and selfish schemes will come to naught.   *Legalized primary.*

Well does Mr. Fiske say:

Popular government makes many mistakes, and sometimes it is slow in finding them out; but when once it has discovered them it has a way of correcting them. It is the best kind of government in the world, the most wisely conservative, the most steadily progressive, and the most likely to endure.   *Optimism.*

> But our earnest must not slacken
> Into play;
> Men of thought and men of action,
> Clear the way.

Justice not automatic. Fortunately for national life no governmental machinery can be invented which will, once wound up, run automatically without intelligent supervision, devoted interest, self-sacrificing patriotism. The corrupt ward politician performs a useful function, though in a discreditable way, when he irritates the business community into paying some attention to the working of this divine institution of democratic self-government.

CHAPTER XII.

THE SOCIAL SPIRIT IN THE STATE SCHOOL SYSTEM.

It is a work of charity, and charity is the work of heaven—nay, it is the highest and noblest charity, for he that teacheth another gives alms to his soul; he clothes the nakedness of his understanding, and relieves the wants of his impoverished reason. He indeed who governs well, leads the blind; but he that teaches, gives him eyes. . . . Doctrine is that which must prepare men for discipline; and men never go so cheerfully as when they see where they go.—*R. South, Sermons.* The teacher's work.

OUR purpose in these pages is to show the good citizen how he can best work for the commonwealth. There are social services which all are bound to perform and which do not demand professional training. Treatises on pedagogy must be consulted by the teacher for direction in the technical processes of his calling. But in a democratic country, whether we like it or not, the quality of the schools will depend very greatly on the coöperation of the people. Let us in this chapter give attention to some of the ways in which intelligent citizens are assisting the school authorities, and to the measures which require very general interest and devotion. Many parents would be glad to take part in the movement for better schools if they realized how much they were needed, and if they saw any practical method of effort.

"You will hear every day," said Emerson, "the maxims of low prudence. You will hear that the first duty is to get land and money, place and name. 'What is this truth you seek? What is this beauty?' Schools and social ideals.

men will ask with derision. If, nevertheless, God have called any of you to explore truth and beauty, be bold, be firm, be true. When you shall say, 'As others do, so will I. I renounce, I am sorry for it, my early visions; I must eat the good of the land, and let learning and romantic expectations go until a more convenient season'; then dies the man in you; then once more perish the bonds of art and poetry and science, as they died already in a thousand thousand men." Thus does our great ethical inspirer and prophet call the leaders of a nation to unite firmly to promote the higher elements of popular welfare.

Function of the school.

The school system is that social institution by which the entire people consciously and of set purpose seeks to transmit its knowledge and its higher ideals to the next generation. The people of the United States, without murmuring or protest, have rapidly set apart a larger and larger portion of their growing wealth to these exalted ends.

Democracy and schools.

Amiel, a delicate and timid spirit, feared that all fine things would disappear with the leveling processes of a commonplace democracy. And many refined souls share his anxieties. We who believe in the future of democracy may do well to listen to these forebodings of gloomy prophets in order to prevent the fulfillment of the dark anticipations. "The age of great men is going; the epoch of the ant-hills, of life in multiplicity, is beginning. The century of individualism, of abstract equality triumphs, runs a great risk of seeing no more true individuals. By continual leveling and division of labor, society will become everything and man nothing.

"As the floor of valleys is raised by the denudation and washing down of the mountains, what is average will rise at the expense of what is great. The exceptional will disappear. . . . The statistician will register a growing progress, and the moralist a gradual decline : on the one hand, a progress in things ; on the other, a decline of souls. The useful will take the place of the beautiful, industry of art, political economy of religion, and arithmetic of poetry." But this delightful writer does not regard this tendency as final, and he thinks a craving for spiritual good will appear after the animal hunger is satisfied. There will "arise a new kingdom of mind, a church of refuge, a republic of souls, in which, far beyond the region of mere right and sordid activity, beauty, devotion, holiness, heroism, enthusiasm, the extraordinary, the infinite, shall have a worship and an abiding city." But this can never be unless the people provide liberally for the means of culture.

Fears for popular rule.

In the Report on Secondary Education, presented by the Royal Commission of England by Assistant Commissioner J. J. Findlay, we find the following testimony :

The sentiment which makes sacrifices.

> The contrast between ourselves in England as a people and the English race in America across the ocean lies mainly here, that in the most progressive states of America *the people believe in education*, and are willing to make sacrifices for the sake of their creed. Outside of the scheme of public education, we have presented in the United States an almost prodigal liberality in the establishment and support of private educational enterprises. On every hand colleges and universities and technical institutes are bountifully supplied with the gifts of rich men, and it is evident that this stream of wealth is the result of a national sentiment in favor of education. We have no parallel to this generosity either in England or in any other country.

President Garfield voices the best convictions of true Americans in his words :

> There is no horizontal stratification of society in this country

like the rocks in the earth, that hold one class down below forevermore, and let another come to the surface and stay there forever. Our stratification is like the ocean, where every individual drop is free to move, and where from the sternest depths of the mighty deep any drop may come up to glitter on the highest wave that rolls. . . . We confront the dangers of suffrage by the blessings of universal education.

The school unknown to citizens.

The schoolhouse to the average citizen seems almost as impenetrable as the French Bastile. He knows it is entirely harmless and that there is no legal obstacle to his entrance. But he fears to disturb the classes and teachers ; he is busy about his own occupation ; and he is afraid to expose his ignorance of many forgotten elements by asking questions. Therefore the average citizen passes the schoolhouse without much thought, unless the principal sends for him or punishes his pet bad boy. Still we are all proud of our free public schools, and are seldom disturbed in our placid dream of complacent contentment by stories of schools in the lands of Pestalozzi and Froebel. Indeed, we have imported and naturalized so many German ideas and living teachers, and even teach the language of Germany to such an extent, that we are acquiring a fine fruit from a Teutonic graft on a rude but healthy American stock. We are very sensitive to any attack on this institution,

Pride in our system.

to open criticism, covert insinuation, or distant suggestion of dividing school funds among the sects. An assault on the school system, with the stars and stripes floating over its buildings, is with us high treason.

Most of us know all too little of what is going on inside those walls where our children spend so many bright days of youth. It seems the affair of boards, normal schools, principals, and teachers. Our people feel incompetent to deal with the theory and practice of instruction and discipline ; and only occasionally does

The Social Spirit in the State School System. 195

one ascend the chair of the infallible and dogmatic anonymous correspondent. Very much of popular discussion is of these two irrational, extreme types, confident abuse or timid questioning.

It must be apparent that there is a close connection between the home and the school which demands a clear and friendly understanding. The primary teacher is merely the mother's assistant. The family is the real primary school and, for weal or woe, the mother is the first teacher. And then the school is educating children to live in society; imparting to them the knowledge which they will need to fit them to move in the great world's life; training them in the habits of regularity, punctuality, neatness, order, courtesy, honesty, obedience, coöperation which will fit them to be valuable and happy citizens. *Home and school.*

Divorce or any serious isolation of school from general society is, therefore, injurious and dangerous. And it becomes a serious question by what means and to what extent the non-professional public can, without annoyance and disturbance, be helpful to the school. Remember that the representatives of democracy hold the purse; that elected councilmen, boards of education, and legislators control school policies; that they reflect the convictions of their constituents; that expert educators cannot go faster than they are permitted to go by public opinion; and it will be seen that all citizens must either help or hinder the system of education. *Danger of divorce.*

Dr. Broadus's homely story brings home to us the necessity in a republic of giving moral discipline to our political masters: "I'll bet you five dollars on the gray horse," said a man, "and Squire Thornton shall hold the stakes." "And who will hold Squire Thornton?" said the other. It is the old query, "Who shall watch the guardians?" Our journalists, statesmen, legislators, financiers are our masters, and our schools form them. We must educate our masters.

From the report of Hon. W. T. Harris, commissioner of education, 1894–5, we learn the vast interest of the nation in common schools, as measured by property, income, teachers, and pupils. The entire population was estimated to be 68,748,950. The persons of school age (five to eighteen years) was 20,328,147, the number enrolled as pupils 14,201,752, to whom may be added all who were in private and parochial schools. The total number of pupils and students of all grades in both public and private schools is estimated at 15,688,622. The entire population is receiving an average of 4¾ years of 200 days each. Massachusetts gives 8.04 years per inhabitant. The people of the German Empire receive 7.2 years of 200 days each. The average for the United States is steadily rising. The South is advancing in a most encouraging way. The average amount of schooling given in the South Atlantic Division in 1870 was 1.20 years, while in 1895 it had risen to 2.85 years. The whole number of public school-teachers is 396,327, of whom 32.4 per cent are male. The average monthly wages are $46.82 for male teachers and $39.41 for female teachers. There are 237,416 schoolhouses, and school property is worth $439,071,690. The income is $177,597,691, of which 85.7 per cent is from state and local taxes. The average expenditure per capita of population is $2.59, in addition to all that is expended upon private schools of all grades. The financial aspect of the system is important enough to command the attention of every taxpayer. The expenditures are already immense and they are certain to increase.

In our cities there is a marked tendency among rich people to send their children to private and "select" schools. They claim that the teaching in the public schools is inferior; that the rooms are crowded; that the manners of the pupils are rude. Let us grant that there is a measure of truth in these charges. Let us give no undue emphasis to the counter-charge that there is among us the beginnings of a class spirit, an aristocracy, and that "select" schools are patronized by those who wish to keep their children afar from the common herd, and form them to become the imitators and lackeys of the rich.

Duty of wealthy people to public schools.

Mr. Robert Grant, in his "Art of Living," brings out a phase of the problem too often overlooked.

Moral influences.

> Excellent as many of our private schools are, it is doubtful if either the morals are better, or the liability to disease is less, among the children who attend them than at a public school of the best class. To begin with, the private schools in our cities are eagerly patronized by that not inconsiderable class of parents who hope or imagine that the social position of their children is to be established by association with the children of influential people. Falsehood, meanness, and unworthy ambitions are quite as dangerous to character when the little man who suggests them has no patches on his breeches as when he has, and unfortunately there are no outward signs on the moral nature, like holes in trousers, to serve as danger signals to our darlings.

Let us not question the legal and moral right of a parent to give his child the best opportunities he can afford, and the kind of an education which he believes most suitable. Surely the father is under no obligation to sacrifice his own child to an institution, even if it be a national institution. The nation has no right to require such a sacrifice.

But if those who are rich can afford to give their

children costly opportunities the people generally cannot do so. The foundation of national education cannot be laid in private and parochial schools. If our common schools are really so inferior the duty of all is to bring them to a higher grade, to provide them with the best facilities.

Danger from private schools.

The danger from private schools is that their patrons will be alienated from the common schools and come to regard the school tax as an injustice. "Why should we be taxed to educate the children of other men?" This is the question so ominous of danger. It comes from the egoistic, atomistic, individualistic theory of society. The children of the poor are our children. They also are members of the same community. Their labors help to create wealth in which all share. Their character is the character of society. Their votes will ultimately decide all political fortunes.

The Earl of Shaftesbury warned against those great English schools which some of the wealthy people of America are patronizing or seeking to copy. He said that they made admirable gentlemen and finished scholars, but did not prepare men for the life of our age. "We must have nobler, deeper, and sterner stuff; less of refinement and more of truth; . . . a contempt for ridicule, not a dread of it." The great philanthropist may have spoken too bitterly against Eton and similar institutions, for certainly they have sent out many noble servants of humanity. But such schools ought not to be built up at the expense of the free high schools of the democracy. And there is always a real danger at this point.

Resources of influence.

Citizens have it in their power to assist the public schools and their administrators by sympathetic study of education, by listening intelligently to the expert leaders of schools, by generous financial support, by activity in promoting improvements. It is possible to build up a consensus of opinion in the country which will represent a high average of conservative judgment and which will make progress certain and constant.

Public opinion should require that the buildings which represent the public taste, and are the homes of fourteen millions of pupils and four hundred thousand teachers, two hundred days in the year, should be so constructed as to favor the health, the refinement, and the intelligence of the coming generation. Of school hygiene we have already spoken. Its importance cannot be overestimated. *The schoolhouse.*

If the people are to be redeemed from coarse, rude ways and are to rise to the appreciation, enjoyment, and creation of beautiful things, then the forms of art must be set before them when they are young. Miss Starr, of Hull House, who is doing so much to bring fine things into schoolrooms, thus illustrates the necessity for bringing beautiful objects into a child's life: *Art in the schoolroom.*

> Two small girls who were going to one of our Hull House picnics were crossing the bridge over the Chicago River. "I hate rivers; don't you?" one of them said, and the other answered, "Yes, they smell so awful bad." Now that is what the absence of beautiful sights and sounds did for those children. You could never make them see a river as anything better than bad smell, because purling brooks and pebbly bottoms and green banks meant nothing to their minds.

Many teachers are trying with limited means to adorn the assembly halls and places of recitation. One will frequently see a home-like curtain at the window, a pot of flowers on the sill, some colored chalk drawings on the board.

Societies are formed in some cities for the purpose of

beautifying the walls of schoolrooms. Photographs of famous pictures, plaster casts of classic sculpture, supplied at moderate cost but excellent of their kind, are placed before the eyes of youth and left to plead the cause of an æsthetic perfection. The color and decorations of the walls and ceiling are made to conform to the canons of good taste, and children carry back into their homes standards of beauty. There is a general movement to make the grounds about the buildings beautiful with sward, flowers, and suitable play-grounds.

Art in the course of study.

From appreciation we pass to creation. To many minds the introduction of drawing into the schools seems a piece of foolish extravagance. And yet its value ought to be obvious. Every one can learn to draw well enough to add a new power of expression to the written or spoken word, while the practice of drawing fits one for the finer processes of mechanical arts, gives a power of criticism and pleasure in the presence of pictures, and awakens and discovers the latent genius of genuine artists who are scattered throughout the country. European countries have introduced art studies partly in order to hold the markets for manufactured goods. The Educational Committee of the Women's Industrial Council of London discovered that French artificial flower-makers were better paid than the English and had a surer market even in England.

Art in industry.

The cause was sought and found in the École Professionelle of Paris, in which pupils are thoroughly trained in drawing and design, and become competent to make entire flowers. In the manufacture of furniture, metal work, textile fabrics, upholstery, stone-work, mere crude handwork is displaced by machinery. But if artistic skill and taste are added the product earns for the workmen a superior reward.

The final cause of education is not mere industrial efficiency, but that for which mechanical skill is itself a means, namely, the production of a complete and happy life. Dr. James MacAlister's words express the higher truth : "While we are extending our system of education on the utilitarian side, we must not forget that the right enjoyment of life—that is, the exercise of the higher faculties—is as much a function of living as earning one's daily bread ; and for our education to be useful in the true sense of the term, we cannot ignore the training of the æsthetic faculties as much for moral as for practical ends." It is because the public in America is so slow to realize the larger meaning of education, and has had so imperfect a training in art, that it is so difficult to introduce and foster this branch of culture. But there are numerous signs of a better day.

Educational end of art.

If we are to provoke a revulsion against untidy streets, hideous alleys, tumble-down houses, ugly and weedy spaces, repulsive garbage-heaps, offensive advertisements of black and yellow on barns, dead walls, and mountain sides, and other sins against human perfection, we must make our schoolrooms teachers of beauty.

And far above these gross abuses the finer natures among us have entertained visions of a complete life, full of noble sentiment, instructed in the laws of the universe, reverent toward the infinite goodness and holiness. Such a life perfected is an æsthetic product on which all rightly constituted minds can gaze with complacency. To that perfected and beautiful life the common schools may offer a most essential contribution.

In a former place we have insisted on the fact that the family is itself the first and most important of all schools. Dr. Dike's report for 1896 emphasizes this point with fresh illustrations.

School and home.

Early influences.

The rapidly-increasing interest in child study and the incorporation of the kindergarten into the public-school system can hardly fail to accelerate this movement back to the home; for the demand for the kindergarten rests largely on the recognized educational importance of the years immediately preceding the former school age. But child study is now pushing us still farther back. The years before the kindergarten age are seen to be immensely potent in education. The prenatal life of the child, its ancestral inheritance, and all the supplementary life of the home and the hours of play outside school, are coming into view as being full of educational meaning.

This is profoundly true. And the inference is natural: the trained professional teachers must be pioneers in the social function of preparing parents for their educational duties. There is no other body of persons fitted for this service. Rarely do we see it hinted that a young woman should go to a normal school in order to fit herself to be the teacher of her own children. Yet this doctrine is a logical inference from that of the educational value of the family. Some socialists are also logical when they say that mothers are not fit to educate their offspring and therefore the children

Parental training.

should be brought up in communal establishments conducted by trained and competent nurses and instructors. The only entirely satisfactory reply to the socialistic theory is that we must teach the mothers to perform duties which cannot be delegated without fearful increase in mortality and without violation of the holiest instincts of our nature.

Fortunately there is a movement already widely extended to bring school and home into relations of reciprocal helpfulness. In some places the initiative is taken by teachers, in others by parents.

The leaders of kindergartens and their training

schools are calling conferences of mothers which have already proved very important. Principals of public schools have long been in the habit of having exhibitions and festivals in which the community was invited to enjoy the entertainment given by the pupils. Courses of University Extension lectures on the principles and methods of teaching might be offered in schoolrooms and attract for their audiences teachers, parents, and Sunday-school workers. The familiar discussion in mixed classes would reveal to those persons the essential unity of their labors, and fit them for more effective coöperation in the social task. *Conferences of teachers with parents.*

What institution of society can so well give the necessary knowledge of the difficult art of household life as the common school? Elementary instruction in regard to the chemistry of foods, the functions and dangers of bacteria, the reasons for cleanliness, the selection and care of furniture, bedding, and clothing, ventilation, heating, plumbing and drainage, and household accounts is entirely possible. Primary text-books are already provided. Interesting experiments are easily made. The educational value of the study could be kept up by making it contribute to language and mathematical work. With some care the scientific facts and principles could be presented in beautiful literary form, as has been shown in many charming juvenile books on nature studies. The health and happiness of multitudes depend on the universal diffusion of existing knowledge on these subjects; and there is no educational institution save the common school which can reach all members of the nation. *Domestic science in the school.*

We leave the seriously defective and perverted to be studied at a later stage. They do not belong to the public schools, but to special institutions. There are *"Nature's step-children."*

many children, however, who must be dealt with in the common schools and who require peculiar treatment. Miss Alice J. Mott, in a suggestive paper, has called them "Nature's step-children." They are not imbecile nor criminal, but slow. They cannot keep up with ordinary classes in all studies and the effort to push them produces bewilderment, discouragement, despair. If they are sweet-tempered constant failure in the presence of superiors breaks their hearts and subdues their spirit. If they are impetuous the school discipline turns them into rebels, criminals. Most school-teachers and many parents are acquainted with children of both types.

The duty. Society must provide for the suitable training of these children or have to fight them as lawless adults or support them as parasitic paupers. The methods appropriate for normal children tend to repress and stupefy the slow pupils.

Invent methods. What should be done? Let the school boards discover from the teachers the number of such children and provide the necessary facilities for their development. Here is a boy who turns truant and barn-burner because he cannot learn language; but in a machine shop he discovers his talents and works out a good heritage of character. Here is a girl to whom history is one long torment; yet in a sewing-school and kitchen she can be made a model housekeeper. Colleges are offering elective courses; why should the rigid curriculum be reserved for the younger students? Why should boys and girls be driven along in a way ever associated with disgrace, humiliation, and unintelligible lessons? The lady just cited tells of one who confessed: "I never had a happy or even comfortable moment in all my school life, excepting three times: once when the schoolhouse chimney burned out; once when the plastering fell on our heads, and once when one of my schoolmates had an epileptic fit."

Some one has related that Dr. Arnold, of Rugby, though usually patient, once spoke sharply to a dull pupil, who replied: "Why do you speak angrily, sir? Indeed, I am doing the best I can." Dr. Arnold said he never so felt a rebuke in his life. And surprises sometimes await the impatient teacher who measures all scholars by one rule. An Edinburgh professor once cried out to a dull boy in his class: "Dunce you are, and dunce you will always remain." That student was afterward known by the name of Sir Walter Scott. Angels even in modern schoolrooms are sometimes entertained unawares. One of the greatest orators in America was as a schoolboy more famous for throwing paper wads than for mathematics. The stupidity ascribed to a pupil may really belong to the teachers who lack insight and carefulness of observation. *Patience required.*

Principal Parker, of the Chicago Normal School, illustrated the injustice from which slow or defective children suffer. *Example of injustice.*

> He spoke of a boy who had been brought to him by his mother. Her story was that the boy was fifteen years old, that he had attended school regularly from the age of seven, and he had reached only the third grade; he was years behind boys of his own age. He was lovable, kind, had no bad habits—just stupid. Colonel Parker spoke to the boy, and discovered from the way in which he held his head that he was deaf. The mother protested that it could not be. Colonel Parker insisted that he was right. The boy was put in charge of a careful, observing teacher, who, at the end of a session, announced that the boy was near-sighted—so near-sighted that he could not distinguish letters or figures on the blackboard.

In all cases of unusually slow children careful tests of their physical condition should be made by physicians and teachers, and special methods of patient instruction should be adopted in order to unfold their powers.

Improved rural schools. To stem the tide of migration to cities; to give the best advantages of education to the sturdy and healthy inhabitants of farms; to equalize the privileges of civilization; to prepare all for the duties of citizenship, better rural schools are required.

Obstacles. The difficulties in the way of raising the quality of schools in the country are very serious. In many districts there has been a steady decline of population, due to the flow toward towns. The average number of children in families is much smaller than in former times. When the population is scant and poor the financial burdens are very heavy.

As a result of these causes many schools have fewer than ten pupils. With so small a number it is impossible to secure the services of a competent and energetic teacher. In the absence of competition and emulation the best energies of students cannot be called forth. There is an atmosphere of discouragement and depression. In a small school where youth of all ages, from six to eighteen, come for instruction, even a brilliant teacher would find it impossible to meet their wants. There can be no adequate grading of classes; no specialization of instruction. The teacher is distracted, fretted, confused by the multiplicity of subjects, and falls into the mechanical habit of hearing by rote recitations out of text-books. In a poor district the schoolhouse must be scantily furnished with maps, charts, globes, and other indispensable apparatus.

Remedy. It has long been evident that the townships should pursue a policy of consolidation. The inefficient small schools should be closed up; the children massed in the villages and centers of population; fewer and better teachers set over larger and more inspiring classes; higher salaries paid so as to command better ability. Since the towns keep their schools open a longer term the number of days of schooling would be materially increased.

One of the chief objections to consolidation came from the parents who lived at a long distance from the village. They complained that their children could not walk so far. This difficulty has been overcome in Massachusetts by providing carriages for the conveyance of children to school in case the distance is too great for them to go on foot. By a law approved April 1, 1869, towns of that commonwealth were permitted to use school funds for the conveyance of pupils to and from the public schools. After a trial in that state the experiment has extended to New Hampshire, Vermont, Connecticut, Rhode Island, Ohio, and is urged for adoption by educational authorities in New York, Wisconsin, and elsewhere.

Conveyance of children to school.

The pupils are aroused to their best effort by the enthusiasm of numbers; they are arranged in grades and classes more nearly according to their requirements; they are trained to habits of promptness and punctuality; their conduct on the way to school is under the supervision of a mature and trustworthy person, and the moral dangers can be reduced; they do not come to the day's work in wet garments, chilled by winter's cold; in the schools they come under a higher quality of teaching ability; and the supervision of directors and superintendents can be made more thorough. The movement seems to have passed the stage of experiment and to deserve careful attention and imitation where the conditions call for it.

Advantages.

The rural schools, it is complained, are making young

Adaptation of rural teaching to rural life.

people discontented with farm life and sending them to the wicked and crowded cities to beg positions and to sleep in garrets. Then let the rural schools show how to turn the farm into a laboratory of science; let useful learning illustrate the infinite forces and everlasting laws of soil and vegetation and atmosphere; and the intellectual attraction of the craft of husbandry will act powerfully to retain the inquiring spirits upon the land. The work of the real teacher must point to the future calling of the farmer and not away from it.

While class work must remain the chief element in the high schools there is the beginning of a movement to bring this institution into closer relations with the home, the shop, the store, and the common interests of the adult population. Thousands of people are compelled to leave school just at the time when the wider outlook of the high school was opening to them a land of promise. There is a deep and bitter feeling of antagonism to this essential part of our system which may be mitigated if not removed. No reason exists for the exclusion from these advanced privileges of any citizen. Those who have gone into business or trades can continue their studies all through life.

High School Extension.

A quotation from a report by Principal F. A. Manny, formerly of Moline, Illinois, will illustrate one method of approach. "A college day program by Moline College students, an address on eastern college life, a program illustrative of high school work, lectures on travel, current events, clubs, receptions for pupils and parents —all these have helped to make the high school building mean more to students and at the same time have brought many hundreds of parents and friends to the school. The purchase of a stereopticon makes the possibilities of this department vastly greater than ever."

The teachers and students have maintained night classes in the town for persons who must work in the daytime. A slight additional expense for teachers and care of rooms would multiply the usefulness of the institution and endear it to multitudes. Such a high school promises to become the college for the people.

In April, 1895, the legislature of New York made an annual appropriation of $25,000 for four years of free lectures. During the first year the report of Dr. Bickmore shows that the lectures were enjoyed by fully a million people of the state, in country and city. Essential factors in this attempt to popularize instruction in art, science, history, travel, and literature are the magic lantern, music, and, for some subjects, dramatic representation. Those who are not pursuing exhausting avocations and have some powers of attention can do better work in classes. Various methods, adapted to local conditions, must be employed, and the field for invention is practically boundless. *Lecture courses.*

The scholars of a community ought to take to heart the boast of one quaint English classic :

> I make not my head a grave but a treasury of knowledge. I intend no monopoly but a community in learning. I study not for my own sake only, but for theirs who study not for themselves. ("Religio Medici.")

Social history points to a very important change in industrial life. In a former age there was an apprenticeship system; the boys lived with a master and learned his trade. That time has gone by, never to return. The millionaire manager will have no apprentice lads under his heels, and his diamond-decked wife will not have the care of a hundred awkward youth who work in her husband's iron-mill. Simply to suggest the picture is to make thought of a renewal of the old sys- *Trade schools.*

tem ridiculous. And then the machine has driven out the apprentice. A machine costs money, goes by steam, and cannot stop to wait even while a boy picks up the finger which he has just cut off with a buzz-saw. The foreman cannot wait to teach a lad. Enough if the stout laborer is instructed to manage a single machine "so strong that no fool can break it, so simple that any fool can run it." There are no trades, only processes.

Vicissitudes of the trades.

Looking over forty years of industrial history we see the death of the trades, one by one : type-setting is gone, killed by the linotype; house-building is composed of many arts, and these are passing into sash, door, and blind factories ; the electric motorman is displacing the locomotive engineer ; the machine-cutter is expelling the tailors. The shoemaker is a factory hand.

This swift transformation makes it at once impossible and useless to have a full trade. And yet some special arts can be taught and there is a limited demand for technical schools. Mr. Auchmuty's building schools in New York, business colleges, classes in type-writing, telegraphy, and various technical institutes show what may be done. Gradually the public system is being extended to give instruction in any art which will fit people for their place in life. If the state teaches physicians, lawyers, dentists, and pharmacists, why not smiths, weavers, decorators, and machinists? These are questions democracy is sure to ask until it gets answer.

Manual training.

A discussion of manual training methods addressed to teachers would be out of place in this book. But the success of this new branch of education depends so much on public sympathy that the grounds of appeal for support should be frequently restated. In some cities the manual training department has been established by private enterprise and conducted at the cost of far-seeing and liberal men until the community could appreciate its value and consent to the necessary tax for support. But private enterprise can never supply the wants of the entire school population.

The modern fact just noted, that there are no full trades, and that all mechanical arts are ever in process of dissolution and transformation, implies the necessity of training youth in versatility and adaptability. If a course of instruction could be devised which should give young people the key, the alphabet of all possible trades, the principles common to all the arts, the persons so educated would be able to pass over from one trade to another. *Lost arts.*

Now there is just such a method of education. This method goes by various names. In its best form it is "kindergarten" for children of the ages of three to six. At a later stage it is called "sloyd" and "manual training." Educational experiments are now being tried which promise to show that this constructive, creative method should run through the whole school life. A few tools are the elements of all complex machines. A few principles govern the development of all industrial processes. Therefore what we want is an education of all youth which will enable them to change from one process to another without undue loss of time and energy.

The best years for this kind of preparation are those from twelve to sixteen. Up to the twelfth year a boy cannot be trusted with many sharp tools or swift machines, nor can he carry on the mental processes which make part of the manual training school method. Professor C. M. Woodward's tables show that the average age of withdrawal from schools in St. Louis is 13.3 years; in Chicago, 14.5 years; and in Boston, 15.9 *Lengthen school life.*

years. In many communities this age is lower. Boys leave school earlier than girls, but without equipment for the life of our industrial system, and, because many of them are not prepared to be self-supporting, they drift into idleness, vice, and crime. School boards should be authorized and required to provide a course of study fitted for these years; the age of compulsory attendance should be made as high as the industrial conditions will permit; and factory laws, enforced by inspection, should prevent the employment of youth not duly prepared for specialized industry.

Neglect of crime causes.

In these ways we should avoid the necessity of guarding lads by a costly system of police, of punishing them by an expensive series of courts and prisons, and of supporting them as vagrants in poorhouses or by dole charities and woodyards. Is it not a sorry tribute to national shrewdness and insight that we first deny our boys all chance to learn an art in its principles, import skilled men to displace our own sons, and then, all too late, give our boys in reformatories just that manual and technical training the lack of which sent them to those penal institutions?

Imported competitors.

It has actually come to this deplorable result that the only way in which a boy can learn a useful mechanical calling is by committing some crime which will take him to a manual training or trade school. As the "social spirit" becomes more enlightened it will reverse this order; it will build additions to the schoolhouses for tool work and it will diminish the reformatories. A list of cities which have already introduced these improvements and which carry the honorable banner of pioneers of progress would be an argument of hope and good cheer. Teachers' institutes and conventions are eagerly discussing methods of fitting youth for life in this actual world which encompasses us all. Education is not merely preparation for life, it is life. To make manual work honorable we must give it rank and place along with literature, history, art, and classics, and thus associate the useful occupations inseparably with ideal pursuits.

Why should we tax the entire community to support schools and then permit the children to pass school age without using them? Children have a right to a fair opportunity of unfolding and discovering their native abilities. The word "compulsory" education is a misnomer. With the right sort of instruction, and with good home influence there is seldom need to compel attendance and work. Shakespeare's

Required attendance.

> whining schoolboy, with his satchel
> And shining morning face, creeping like snail
> Unwillingly to school

lived before the days of tool practice, drawing, clay modeling, sand maps, and illustrated histories. And yet even he, with all his whimpering, learned to read, and afterward wrote laws and books and found his way around the world.

If the avarice of parents robs their offspring of school such parents must be prevented from carrying out their base intention. If extreme destitution is the obstacle, then charity must remove it.

In some parts of the United States there is a general demand for religious services and very little opposition. But in large towns and cities with a heterogeneous population sectarian differences and secular antagonism have banished Bible reading, religious teaching, and public prayer from the tax-supported schools. It is impossible to foretell the issue of this unhappy controversy, but some consequences are already becoming clear. If

Religious teaching.

the state must refuse to teach religion then this duty is all the more to be felt by the family and the church. Probably it will be found in the event that the instruction will be more vital, sincere, and potent than if it were imparted in a perfunctory way by teachers who are not always in sympathy with the exercises. The mode of imparting knowledge may be less systematic and accurate, but even this may be improved.

We can also see a tendency to recognize the Bible as an indispensable factor in history, literature, and ethics. Suitable selections can be made from it which will not give offense to any reasonable person nor come into collision with our fundamental law which separates church from state and forbids the use of public funds for sectarian uses.

Ethical teaching.

There is a general and growing demand for the teaching of human duties and virtues on the general basis of social obligations. All well-ordered schools are, without formal and set lessons, agencies for moral discipline, for the formation of habits of respect, honesty, punctuality, sympathy, and order. The best lesson in morality is the life of the teacher and the daily conduct of the student community. But in addition to these provisions for forming character it is coming to be generally believed that a graded, comprehensive, and systematic method of instruction and discipline should be adopted for forming, by conscious effort, the social impulses and habits of the pupils.

Higher education by the state.

There is no logical stopping-place in the development of our public schools. Mr. Huxley's ideal of free education for all citizens "from the gutter to the university" is realized in the United States. It is too late in the day to resist this tendency. Our governments throw no obstacles in the way of privately endowed colleges and universities. There is no danger of an all-powerful state monopoly of higher education with a fixed and fossil type, secure from competition. The nation will keep faith with the endowed institutions of learning to which it has granted sacred charters. But the whole people will not depend upon the capricious working of private benevolence to make sure the opportunity of the highest culture to all its youth who are competent and ambitious. There is room for all and a generous rivalry will not exclude a patriotic coöperation of all for the nation's honor and progress.

The members of the teaching profession are obliged to instruct their directors. It is a delicate and difficult work, and the pupils are not always docile and humble. A great manufacturer or even a successful saloon-keeper, once elected to a school board, suddenly feels inspired with unlimited confidence in his own ability as an educator. Fortunately, most of our directors are capable of learning enough of the principles of education, after some experience, to select good superintendents and support them. When we can keep the "spoils system" down, the boards can be turned into normal institutes and fit their members for the business. It must be confessed, however, that there is room, wide as the continent, for improvement. The electors should require proof of all candidates for these honorable offices that they have themselves had a good education and have studied the literature of pedagogy. *Boards of education.*

The library should be regarded as an essential part of the school system. If the teacher's labors have been successful the pupils will have a hunger for knowledge and a taste for reading. The town or village which has no public library and reading-room is resting under a cloud of disgrace. Here is an appropriate object for *Free public libraries.*

the gifts of wealthy citizens whose real estate has risen in value because of the growth of population and of the industries of the locality. Here is a new profession, the office of librarian, which ranks in dignity and usefulness with that of teacher and preacher.

Traveling libraries.

The New York method of sending small libraries to villages, to rural communities, and to groups of responsible persons should be rapidly extended to all our agricultural states. These libraries are sent on the application of twenty-five resident taxpayers or other trustworthy persons who must agree to seek the establishment of a local free library as soon as public interest will warrant the venture. This method has already been adopted in several western states and promises to be popular and beneficent.

Reforms before us.

We have given generous praise to our public school system because it deserves praise. We should seek to improve the quality of teaching ; and this demands more normal schools and students for them ; greater permanence in the office, to secure the fruits of experience ; a higher grade of examinations for certificates ; freedom from partisan, personal, and sectarian influence on appointments ; better salaries ; smaller classes in the cities where teachers are overwhelmed in the crowd of children ; more thorough and sympathetic supervision.

The corrupt methods of agents of text-books are a serious hindrance in our schools. There seems no escape from this evil save by providing free text-books at public expense. But all reforms in one of our dearest institutions must come with civic interest, higher estimates of culture, purification of political administration, and the general diffusion of knowledge relating to the development of human faculty and the real values of human life.

CHAPTER XIII.

VOLUNTARY ORGANIZATION OF EDUCATION.

THE institutions of culture did not come down to us from the clouds, carried by bodiless angels who can work without salaries. They were not the free gift of foreign rulers nor even the product of a system of taxation. The fact that education is a growth of the free social spirit, native to our soil, is evidenced by the creation, maintenance, and endowment of many schools and associations which owe nothing to the government save charters, protection, and exemption from taxation. *Spontaneity.*

Some of the data for this opinion may here be set down. The ambition to secure an education, the intense craving for knowledge, the altruistic impulse to diffuse the blessings of truth and beauty, the longing of parents to give children a larger opportunity than they themselves enjoyed, the patriotic pride in our own institutions have been among the motives which produced our free school system and many other educational agencies. Throughout many parts of the United States the private school preceded the public school. It was a common custom for the wealthier men in a community to employ a teacher and then invite the neighbors to share the expense according to their ability. It was this spontaneous and philanthropic effort which prepared the soil and sowed the seed for our present universal system of state instruction. *Societies.*

The experiments in educational methods are usually tried at the cost of progressive and enterprising men in

Experiments.

private station. Free libraries have been furnished in many localities by individual benefactors or by voluntary associations, until the appetite for reading became so general and keen that a tax could be ordered for extending the institution. In the same way at present the kindergartens and manual training schools are being brought before the public for consideration. Associations of charitable and energetic citizens who believe in the efficacy of new methods are content to give proof of their faith by investment in schools unlike any heretofore familiar. It cannot be expected that large masses of men will move so promptly as small companies of superior persons. When the value of a method has been demonstrated on a small scale it can be pressed upon the attention of municipal boards. For this reason

Freedom.

it would be injurious, perhaps fatal, to progress, if the state had a monopoly of education and should drive private associations from the field. There would be danger of stagnation, routine, formalism, death.

Happily the American people care little for mere theoretical assumptions. They desire a satisfaction or a means of culture and go about procuring it by the most direct way. If they can induce the public to pay for it, well. If the public is reluctant to risk capital in a change, then some one will be found wise and rich enough, or fanatical enough, to try it. Thus by a gradual process of experiment and agitation kindergartens, drawing, tool-practice, manual training, sloyd, and

Pioneers.

many other novel features have come to form part of the free school system. The pioneers, mocked, abused at first, compelled to try their inventions at cost of their own funds, are finally rewarded in honor for their wisdom and their courage. If the scheme fails the promoters are mercifully forgotten.

The statistics not only of denominational institutions but even of state and city schools and colleges show how large a factor in higher education philanthropy has become. In the most recent report of Dr. Harris, 1894–5, the following significant figures are given in relation to colleges and universities in the United States. The whole number reporting was 481, with 11,582 instructors and 149,939 students. The total increase reported was $16,789,638, of which 37.8 per cent was derived from students' fees, 31.7 per cent from endowments, 17.6 per cent from municipal, state, and national appropriations, and 12.9 per cent from miscellaneous sources. The entire amount of benefactions reported for the year was $5,350,963, but the year before it was nearly four million dollars greater. The value of all property belonging to these institutions is $232,195,461, of which amount $102,574,808 are reported as permanent endowment funds. Benefactions amounting in 1895 to $495,760 were shared by 140 secondary schools.

Statistics.

The Roman Catholics report 3,361 parishes with schools, and about 800,000 pupils. The Evangelical Lutherans report 3,079 parochial schools and a little more than 200,000 pupils. The German Evangelical Synod of North America reports 410 schools and 17,911 pupils. The Protestant Episcopal Church reports 336 teachers and 6,860 pupils. The Holland Christian Reformed reports 17 schools and 2,229 pupils. There are a few others of minor importance.[1]

Parochial schools.

The total number of pupils taught in parochial schools in the United States is given as 1,028,843. These schools, with few exceptions, are supported by voluntary gifts without taxation. But it must be remembered that many of these children go to parochial

[1] Report of Commissioner of Education, 1894-5, pages 1662-3.

schools only for a time previous to confirmation and attend the public schools at other times.

The Chautauqua idea. The writer of these lines has had the honor and joy of knowing the work of Chautauqua; first as a somewhat skeptical observer and critical visitor, then as lecturer and teacher. He was first drawn to study the institution by way of observation of local work in a western city and by impressing the benign effects of its inspiration on many individual lives. The central impulse of the movement is belief in God. It is a religious work, founded and conducted by men to whom love, hope, faith are the supreme realities of existence.

Breadth. Religion with these founders was not a rite, a mere literary deposit, a concern of Sabbaths, priests, castes, or special occasions. It was the atmosphere and vital element of all life. In its definition were comprehended the faithfulness of the mother in kitchen and nursery, the courage of the soldier, the sturdy manliness and industry of the village blacksmith, the vigorous and confident march and toil of the pioneer, the devotion of the philanthropist, the sacrifice of hospital nurses, the wise services of statesmen, the iconoclastic zeal of reformers, the patience of the scholar's research, the enthusiasm of the poet or preacher, the sensuous and spiritual ecstasies of the musician, the craving curiosity of the student. All days are Sabbaths. All labors are sacred.

All life sacred. We should study the works, the ways, and the word of God, and that for the good of all, not for ourselves alone. Education is never finished. The spirit never grows old. They who think, learn, serve, hope, and trust have immortal youth. We have seen a woman of eighty years receive her certificate after a course of reading with the blushing pride of a girl of sixteen.

President Hegeman, of the Metropolitan Life, gave to high school pupils counsel which reveals the law of personal perfection and the condition of highest usefulness. It declares a principle on which Lincoln acted in preparation for his career, and the advice has the authority of a successful business man.

Economy of time a duty.

Be careful about the odds and ends of your time. If you are tired and need rest, take it, that's as much your duty as to be occupied. But look out and guard against the habit of loafing, of murdering time, of wasting hours that once gone never can be reclaimed.

In your later lives especially, watch the fifteen minutes this morning and the half-hour at noon and the hour at night—those intervals that make up a day in the course of a week and that might be given to some good deed. After a large stained-glass window had been erected in a noble edifice across the water, an artist picked up the discarded fragments of glass and made one of the most beautiful cathedral windows in all Europe. So one boy will pick up a splendid education out of the odds and ends of the time which he carefully saves, as against another who carelessly throws them away.

The beautiful window.

Two mechanics in a near-by city had each his hour at noon. When lunch was finished one busied himself in studying some improvements in the machinery he was using. He pegged away patiently, at last succeeded, had his invention patented, exchanged his overalls for broadcloth, and became a rich and useful man. The other spent his time in teaching a dog to stand on his head and do tricks, and at last accounts was traveling with a circus at ten dollars a week, matinées thrown in.

We have free common schools, but most of our youth leave them before the years of maturity and with scant knowledge of the vast world in which they must live, whose conflicts they must face, whose problems they must solve. Evidently the common school can do no more than start the intellect on its voyage of endless discovery. Then we have the college and the university.

The field.

But these are for the elect few; and many a college graduate, caught in the whirl of business, forgets his classics and his science, and permits his better faculties to become a garden of weeds and briars. College graduates must have impetus to learn, motive to continue systematic mental activity, incentive to assist less favored neighbors. Then we have the public library, at least in favored towns and cities, and it is a boon of inestimable value. But the average reader is lost in the labyrinths of literature. Aimless, purposeless, planless, the reader is often more injured than benefited by contact with the literary treasures of dead or absent teachers. The principle of selection is wanting. The clue to the maze must be put in the reader's hand. What is true of public libraries is even more true of newspapers. For here the laws of choice must be observed in order to avoid not only the dyspepsia of surfeit but even the poison of vice, the insanity of fragmentary presentation of detached paragraphs. The broken bits must be placed in the general scheme of color and outline which compose a picture; the thread of history must string the isolated beads; the groundwork of philosophy must give unity and comprehensiveness to the jumble of impressions, images, stories, statistics.

The casual visitor at the Assembly grounds by the beautiful lake in New York may pass weeks in simple, wholesome recreation, if such is his sole purpose. There are boats on the lake, and long drives and walks, a bracing climate far above sea level, charming woods, gymnasium, races, plenty of incitements to out-door life. In the vast amphitheater the multitude can listen to excellent music, to witty lectures, to delightful readers, or, in the evening, with the help of the stereopticon, take a journey in the world. There is much entertainment and never an objectionable word or gesture. It has been demonstrated that the fund of pure humor and of exciting entertainment is so great that it is a sign of incompetence in one who must use degrading means in order to sustain interest and give pleasure.

Entertainment itself easily shades into instruction. Indeed, the recreations are designed to have some higher, wider view of life and duty. Noble sentiments are rendered attractive by the arts of the orator, the photographer, and the elocutionist. Those who are hungry for knowledge can attend the more serious "public lectures" in the Hall of Philosophy. Naturally the audiences here are not so large as in the Amphitheater. The tax on attention is greater, and a great many people who go to Chautauqua are already under sufficient mental strain. For those who at home have been distracted with cares, too busy to give much connected thought to great themes of philosophy, theology, economics, politics, sociology, and natural science, these lectures serve a valuable purpose. Attendance is voluntary, and there are no examinations. If one is weary or bored he can walk away. *Informal instruction.*

The conferences, formal and informal, which are held at the Assembly are of considerable educational value. Here may be found meetings for the discussion of temperance reform, kindergartens, secondary education, training of defectives, microscopy, labor movements, social settlements, and a hundred others. The informal conversations on the piazza of the Hotel Athenæum, or in walks about the grounds, or at the cottages are frequently most delightful and informing. *Conventions.*

More serious and systematic is the college work. Instructors from many colleges and universities go to Chautauqua to visit each other and to give instruction *The college.*

by lectures. Examinations are offered for those who desire to test their progress or to gain credits toward degrees. Its work is conducted throughout the year by the correspondence method.

The C. L. S. C. and Home Reading.

Perhaps it is through the C. L. S. C. (Chautauqua Literary and Scientific Circle) that the movement has been most widely felt. From its central office in Buffalo, New York, this agency acts all the year around. First of all a course of connected reading is mapped out by a competent committee, and it requires four years to complete the required work, although the course for each year is a unity and a satisfactory whole. The time is laid out by the week and month. A monthly magazine is published which carries the reader out in different directions beyond the books. Papers for reviews and testing examinations are prepared for those who wish to use them. In order to do the work of a year it is necessary, in the average, to devote one hour daily for nine months. A certificate is given to those who complete a course, and to this certificate seals are attached as evidence of advanced and collateral reading. Brief courses are provided for those whose time is very limited, and many special courses are laid out for the large number who desire to advance in particular directions.

Relation to college work.

The circulars distinctly assert that "the circle is not in any sense a college, either in its course of study or its methods of work." There is no sham, no false pretense about the department. And yet it is true that many young people have been inspired by the circle to enter college and pursue their studies in regular classes; that tens of thousands who could not attend college have gained accurate and liberal knowledge concerning the sciences, the literatures, the great race ideas which command the attention of college students.

Throughout North America, in church parlors, in homes, in schoolhouses, in rooms of the Young Men's Christian Association, or Young Woman's Christian Association, may be found little groups of the readers of the C. L. S. C. books and magazines. Many persons read alone, report to the secretary, and receive their certificates and seals. But better work can usually be done when the members assemble in local companies, discuss the topics, ask and answer questions, enjoy sociable evenings, promote lectures, provide musical entertainment and in all ways keep faculties alive. By combination museums are established, magic lanterns and slides can be owned or rented, maps and pictures may be purchased, and many appliances used which individuals could not command. The circles are encouraged to promote local improvements in sanitation, parks and roads, education, and in all that helps general well-being. *Local circles.*

Mr. John Fiske said: "I am convinced it has not been equaled by any other system of popular education." Dr. J. G. Fitch, English inspector of training colleges, said: "It seems to me you have hit upon one of the most admirable and fruitful devices ever yet adopted when, by means of reading circles and correspondence helps, the solitary student has opened to him what he shall read and what use he shall make of his reading when he has it." President Garfield's words seem especially significant when we remember the efforts which it cost him to secure an education. "It has been the struggle of the world to get more leisure, but it has been left for Chautauqua to show how to use it." And Dr. E. E. Hale: "After the general system of public *Opinions of the value of Chautauqua.*

school instruction, the Chautauqua system is the most important organized system of education at work in the nation."

In the Report of the Commissioner of Education, 1894–5, page 1488, may be found a "check list" of 319 summer schools, with address, length of term, time of sessions, character of course, and other information.

Outgrowth.

The Chautauqua movement has been fertile. The Jews and the Roman Catholics, encouraged and inspired by the example, have established similar systems. Summer schools are formed all over the country, North and South, East and West. Clubs and circles quite independent of Chautauqua have taken up its ideas and methods. England has felt the influence of the home reading method. The students of the circle are found in all parts of the civilized world.

Women's clubs.

No survey of voluntary educational efforts in America, however brief, can omit the women's clubs. The actual functions of these important agencies of culture are briefly indicated in reports collected by Mrs. Henrotin. Four hundred and ninety-five clubs were united in the General Federation in 1896. Of these fifty were pursuing purely literary subjects. In the department clubs 371 have a department of literature, which includes art, science, and philosophy; 232 have a department of education, including practical work in kindergartens and public schools; 174 have a department of philanthropy, which implies sociology as applied to philanthropy, theoretical and practical; 165 are pursuing household economics; 163 have social economics as applied to the history and practical application of municipal and legislative work, with village improvement associations, etc. These organizations would justify their existence and cost if they limited their activity to the higher education of their own members; for women have a right to the best life for their own sake. But women with larger knowledge see the social needs of the age and therefore give attention to charity, to schools, to reforms, to all that affects home, children, happiness, and character.

There is a movement to establish in all cities institutions for the training of housekeepers and domestic assistants (called "servants" in the feudalistic phraseology which marks defective democracy). Many intelligent women desire to lift household work to its true dignity by making it the expression of a scientific and disciplined culture. The National Household Economic Association is fostering this tendency, and many of the women's clubs have departments especially devoted to this backward art and industry. Something more is required than a merely mechanical and routine drill in dish-washing and pie-making according to fixed recipes. Fundamental studies in chemistry, bacteriology, physiology, sanitary science, must prepare wives, mothers, and their assistants for the intricate business of making and keeping healthy and beautiful homes. And this same accurate and comprehensive knowledge will fit women to be inspectors and directors of schools, councillors of cities, reformers of customs and morals. *Household economic associations.*

The agricultural population in many portions of the United States are greatly in advance of those in all other countries in accessibility to new ideas. They use more machinery and of a better kind. They are inventive and progressive. From their ranks have come many of the first men in our national history. The great organizations of farmers have promoted the interchange of ideas and have quickened their intellectual life. *Farmers' reading circles.*

And yet there are many difficulties in the way of

literary and scientific study. The farmers are isolated from each other. A visit or a party becomes a serious and difficult matter when the winds are keen and frosty, or the roads miry. In the summer labor is too exhausting to leave vitality for an evening class or discussion. Work in the open air induces sleepiness after the hearty evening meal. There is not that constant social irritation and impetus which keeps the city dweller in a state of mental ferment.

And yet the farmers should not rob themselves of all participation in the heritage of science and the humanities. The introduction of machinery has somewhat lightened the burdens of exhausting toil. The sulky plow, the horse rake, and the steam thresher have transferred to senseless matter part of the strain which once wore out the muscles and nerves of country folk. With better roads, postal service, schools, cheap books and papers, and free libraries the obstacles to culture are gradually melting down.

Machinery lightens toil.

The farmer of the next generation must know more than his ancestors or go to the wall. No tariff can help him against the competition of the wheat plains of India, Siberia, and South America. Knowledge is power, but only to him who knows. Uncle Sam has no more farms to give away. The trusts are making a profit out of what ignorance once cast aside. Mining experts are working over rejected ores with new scientific method. Agriculture must become scientific. The clumsy, wasteful methods which were suitable and economical when free land was abundant must be succeeded by precise calculations of the values of fertilizers, plant foods, drains, and machines. The farmers have come to see this. The agricultural colleges and experiment stations, bulletins, professional papers, and the general press have

Higher attainments necessary.

had influence. Associations for discussion, institutes, granges, county fairs have become important media for the interchange of technical information.

A distinguished director of agriculture has said: "The great nations of Europe strain every effort to make science the handmaid of war. Let it be the glory of the great American people to make science the handmaid of agriculture" (Hon. Jerry Rusk).

The farmer governor of Indiana, Mr. J. A. Mount, voices the true aspiration of an awakened rural population:

> I have never favored, nor do I now favor, the exclusive study of literature pertaining to the farm. Let the reading circle be a diversion from farm topics and the routine of farm life. . . . The gathering of farmers' families, alternately in their farmhouses, and spending an evening, rendered enjoyable by social good cheer, made instructive by literary exercises, and enlivened by good music, cannot fail of good results. . . . Our rural homes must be surrounded with elevating influences, and afford the means for the development of cultured men and women. Let these homes possess the wealth of books, the charm of music, and the fragrance of flowers, and the boys will not spend their evenings at the village store in the fume of tobacco smoke and the atmosphere of stale jokes.

Higher elements of culture.

More's Utopia anticipated University Extension. In that happy land, far, far away:

> It is a solempne custome there to have lectures daylye in the morning, where to be presente they onely be constrained that be namely chosen and appoynted to learninge. Howbeit a greate multitude of every sort of people, both men and women, go to heare lectures, some one and some another, as everye mans nature is inclined.

University Extension in Utopia.

Mr. George Picot has given articulate expression to the social incentives of the scholar:

> Every person ought to apportion his life in two fields; and

while one of these is consecrated to the duties of his special profession or even to the affairs more agreeable to his taste, the other should be dedicated to those collective enterprises without which a nation would be a collection of egoistic beings without common bonds.

Every teacher or special student, in the course of his particular studies, comes into possession of certain general ideas, great race truths, which can be made clear to all intelligent citizens and which are essential to the common welfare.

It is true that a chemist or geologist cannot put in popular form any part of his processes which involve close mathematical reasoning or highly intricate methods. But all sciences of nature, language, history, politics, economics, and sociology issue in certain well-established principles which can be stated in plain English and illustrated from familiar experiences and phenomena.

The duty of scholars to the people. The University Extension movement has grown out of these two considerations, that scholars are in possession of truths which the wide world needs to guide its conduct and enlarge its vision, and that scholars owe a part of their life to the people whose labors sustain them and whose institutions protect them.

It is not implied that University Extension is the only method of popularizing knowledge, for there are many methods. It is not asserted that all college professors are under obligation to give public lectures, because not all have the gift of exposition, and many are so engaged in specialized research that they have no time or strength for this method of teaching. But it is claimed that institutions of higher culture, as soon as they can command the means, should train a special body of instructors and keep them in the field for this particular educational task. Even busy professors can often find time for occasional courses of lectures to the people. In discussions of social problems the teacher will often receive as much as he gives, and return to his study with fresh materials for elaboration. Here again philanthropy frequently pays ten per cent on investment.

The *Hospital* illustrates the social necessity of popularizing knowledge :

> Science, more especially physiological and medical science, suffers enormously from lack of able exposition. The inventor, the man who has a "good thing" for sale, often fails to realize a fortune because he has not the means or does not know the best methods of "placing his goods upon the market." In like manner discoveries have been made in science from time to time, improvements are made in the art of healing, which remain a dead letter to the world, sometimes for years, because there has been no man of adequate expository faculty to place them in clear, intelligent, interesting, and convincing terms before all those who have actual or potential interest in them. Sir James Simpson had not the merit of discovering chloroform, nor even of making the first experiments with it. He had the merit of so convincing the medical mind that its general use became a necessity with hardly a day's undue delay. But the real discoverer was a medical student whose name is unknown to most of the medical men of our own time. Science which is not adequately expounded is lost to the world.

Social necessity of popularizing science.

Now, while it is true that we have a multitude of periodicals and newspapers which have wide circulation, and these printed forms are useful and necessary agencies of exposition, it is also true that the personal assistance of a living teacher remains the most impressive, economical, and expeditious method of helping people to get at the essential elements of a scientific or literary subject.

Living teachers.

When the old Universities of Cambridge and Oxford

Origin.

began to awaken from their selfishness and cloistered indifference to the world's needs, their apostolic fervor, kindled and fanned by such men as Dr. Arnold of Rugby, took many forms of expression. Missions were manned by heroes. Popular traditions of error were bravely fought down. The desire seized such spirits as Denison and Toynbee to let poor men share with them the high thoughts of the ancient seats of learning. Thus University Extension came to be. It is a movement marked by many failures and errors, but also by many triumphs.

Methods.

Three general methods are pursued. The "lecture-study method" provides a lecture, popular in mode of presentation, but given by a specialist in his own department. In order to fix attention, to save time from note-taking, and to preserve a permanent outline of the lesson, a syllabus of the lecture is distributed in the audience. In connection with the lecture an opportunity is given for an informal discussion and conference. A list of books is printed with a syllabus, and a traveling library containing the volumes is kept in the town during the weeks in which the lecturer is making his visits.

The "correspondence method" is designed to assist isolated students who cannot reside at college and who wish to be under the direction of a living teacher. In this case the instructor prepares an outline of topics, with directions for reading and study, and the student after careful use of the instructions returns papers and answers for criticism. Excellent results have been obtained in this way when the student has time and books, and is capable of sustained effort without the spur of class work.

The "class-study method" does not differ from

ordinary college work. It is designed for persons who must recite in the evening and can give only a part of their time to the subject.

In all these methods the student comes into direct relations with a living teacher, and the personal element is found to be very valuable.

Voluntary agencies have their opportunity in connection with the splendid movement to supply reading for the people. In some cities rich men have furnished the building and a fund, or have given the first "plant" to the community upon a contract that the institution should afterward be maintained at public cost. The "traveling libraries" have often been furnished by wealthy people and they have been eagerly and gratefully used by persons who lived far from the towns. *Libraries.*

A beautiful work is that of the home library associations. The members of these societies purchase a few carefully-selected books, attractively bound and neatly arranged in a portable case. This miniature public library is placed in care of a family in a quarter of the city where the incentives to culture are as meager as the opportunities. The managers of the library become personal friends of the children of the neighborhood; read to them delightful stories; show them pictures; talk with them about the subjects of the books; and when the set of works has performed its mission it is exchanged for a fresh set, which may have been busy elsewhere. This plan requires a very small capital; it offers a very natural occasion for introducing a visitor to the poor; and it has produced the most delightful fruits of gracious social relations and eagerness for good reading. By such means vile and trashy publications can be driven out and a taste for better things so established as to make them positively offensive. It is very well to *Home libraries.*

burn pernicious printed stuff—it cannot be called "literature"—but still better is it to cultivate a taste which revolts at the unclean and demands healthier intellectual food.

Social settlements.

Social settlements and University Extension had their origin in the same time, place, and inspiration. The settlement has found a home and a native development in American cities. The "subjective necessity," to use Miss Addams's phrase, is what we call the "social spirit." "It is more blessed to give than to receive." A true culture is communicative. A right education increases sociability and sharpens conscience. A wholesome education makes the mind creative. A mother is never hired to make sacrifices for her child; it is natural to her. If the ideas of Pestalozzi really take possession of family, school, and college instruction and discipline, the philanthropists will come forth burning with social zeal. If the ethical philosophy of T. H. Green, the life-giving sayings of Carlyle, the humanitarian periods of Mazzini, the poetic creations of Lowell, the divine messages of Channing and Phillips Brooks ever enter the red blood of a scholar, then a new spiritual birth occurs. And if the contemporary and indwelling Christ comes to his throne in the heart there is ready, if need be, the martyr, the hero, or heroine. To be sure, the real martyr is never conscious of doing any extraordinary thing. It is all so natural for a large soul to do a generous deed and not know it to be such. "When saw we Thee a hungered and gave Thee meat?"

Objective necessity.

Then Miss Addams tells us there is an "objective necessity" for social settlements. The form taken by philanthropy is fixed by the mold of circumstances. Within a few decades the great industry has come to dominate our life. It masses people in cities. It divides rich from poor. It separates the population geographically and socially, and sets them down in camps of indifferent or even hostile citizens. People live in the same town, work under the same roof, and yet never touch each other in school, or church, or hall. The non-conducting class spirit breaks the electric current of social sympathy.

But it is this same colossal and imperious great industry which increases the democratic feeling and the class consciousness of wage-earners. Wage-earners are not the "poor" of Charles Booth's analysis. The "workingmen" hate charity. To offer it to them either offends or crushes them. They want justice and they unite to get rights. They feel the slights of the rich and the well-dressed. By living with persons of the same occupations they form a class feeling which is not a national feeling, and make a public opinion of their own. Even the public school in great cities does not unite the classes, because the well-to-do and the wealthy live in their own part of town or send their children to private schools. *Democratic feeling.*

This moral alienation is fraught with dangers to the commonwealth. It makes city government more difficult and corrupt. It enfeebles the influence of religion and art on common life.

The settlement is primarily a person, not a system or a contrivance. The very essence of it is the gift of one's self to a certain locality. One who has nothing superior to impart, or who has no talent for fellowship, or who thinks of self-display as a patron or Lady Bountiful, cannot make a true settlement—not if there were a legacy of a half million of dollars to support the scheme. Working people are clairvoyant. They discover shams, sometimes where they do not exist. They *Personal factor.*

are sensitive—and who can blame them? Hence, one must be a real democrat to be of any value. The least skepticism as to the capacity of the plain people for all that is really noble and valuable in art, in religion, in the essentials of high living, is fatal to the leader or resident. No one should attempt the life without a period of probation.

Methods.

Stereotyped plans are of no value. The resident becomes a citizen. He discovers certain needs—better sewers, sanitation, lights, houses, libraries, schools, police, poor relief, political customs. In order to remedy the evils and promote the health, happiness, and progress of the neighborhood he acts as he would anywhere. He discovers the best people, the salt, the "saving remnant" in the street or ward. There are conferences and discussions. There is division of labor. One set believe the sun of life rises and sets in entertainments, and they start out to supplant the low variety theater. There are people who enjoy music, and they organize to expel bad spirits, as David did, with harp and psaltery and—dance! There are others who have not bowed the knee to the ward "boss," who have discovered that he is vulnerable, and they know his tricks dark and vain. These people with a genius for political war join hands to put a decent shoemaker in place of a boodle saloon-keeper in the city council. Still others wish to promote a finer worship, a more real and human religion ; and so there comes to be a pleasant Sunday afternoon, or some additional help to the neighboring churches. Thus life in its fullness is defended and assisted ; and this is a social settlement. For a list of clubs and classes of all colors and kinds, for baseball, football, German, embroidery, dancing, Bible classes, foreign travel, flower missions, coal purchase,

Variety of gifts.

book-keeping, cooking, painting, dressmaking, kindergartens, crêches, and all the rest one can consult the bulletins of the settlements. But such printed exhibits can tell little to one who has not by visits or work or residence entered into the sacred intimacies of the life itself.

Among the most remarkable manifestations of the confidence of Americans in education are the gifts of individuals and churches for schools among the Indians and negroes, the "wards of the nation." Various denominational societies have raised and expended vast sums for these institutions. *Missionary education.*

We give an illustration of the spirit and method of this educational philanthropy. In 1882 Mr. John F. Slater, of Connecticut, gave $1,000,000 for the uplifting of the colored population of the South. The income of this fund was to be devoted to education, and it was stipulated that instruction should be on a broad but positive Christian basis. All schools assisted must provide manual training to fit the youth for industry. The annual appropriations are nearly $36,000, and at the end of the year 1894 the trustees had distributed $439,981. In the year 1896 $5,000 was given to "employ pious and intelligent women to travel in the rural districts of Virginia and Alabama to start mothers' meetings, where the average ignorant woman, who cannot now hope to receive an education, may at least be taught the way to keep a decent home, and to elevate the moral standard of her humble life."

Out of many splendid examples of the union of all social motives we may select the school of which Booker T. Washington, a negro of fine ability, is principal. This remarkable man won his way through poverty to an education at the Hampton School. In 1881, with *The Tuskegee, Alabama, Normal and Industrial School.*

$8,000 furnished by General Marshall, of Boston, Mr. Washington started a school with one teacher and thirty pupils. The last report shows sixty-six teachers and 959 pupils, 2,000 acres of land and forty buildings. The state appropriated $2,000 a year to aid the enterprise. This history is typical of the spirit and method of educational progress even under the most unfavorable circumstances.

Peabody fund. In 1866 Mr. George Peabody gave $2,500,000 for the promotion of popular education in the South. Afterward he added another million dollars. A sum equal to the original gift has been distributed and the principal remains for further beneficence.

The first appropriations were made to selected schools and towns and cities, to educational journals and agents, for the purpose of creating a sentiment in favor of free education supported by public taxation. When this sentiment was well developed special efforts were made to induce the states to organize public-school systems and make them a part of the organic life of the commonwealths; and when this end had been attained there was a gradual withdrawal of grants for local schools, and a concentration of the income upon schools and institutes for training teachers. (*The Independent*, December 17, 1896.)

Vacation schools. Enlightened philanthropy has before it a serious and hopeful field in the care of poor children during the summer when regular work of the public schools is suspended. Then the little ones are turned wild upon the streets, or shut up in small rooms to torment weary and overtaxed mothers. The year's work of teachers is undone. Habits of order are broken up. Temptations assail the idle on every hand.

School colonies or vacation schools for the poor children were first tried in Zurich, Switzerland, in 1876, and have passed into other European countries. They are supported by benevolent societies in conjunction with the public authorities. The plan includes the opening of the schoolrooms for informal work and entertainment under the direction of a competent teacher; picnic excursions to parks, lakes, rivers, and the country; and, best of all, a sojourn of several days upon farms. The schools of several cities, aided by enterprising philanthropists, have already made a promising beginning of this beautiful work. For example, in New York City six schools were opened in the neighborhoods crowded with poor families. The number of children who enjoyed these privileges was, in 1894, 2,100; in 1895, 5,225; and in 1896, 6,762. As the numbers increased the per capita cost decreased. The expense each day for each child was, in 1894, 11.7 cents; in 1895, 5.6 cents; in 1896 it was only 4.9 cents. The expense for each teacher was $75 for the season. In other cities the most encouraging results have been obtained. The young people whose parents are able to send them out to green fields and mountains, to seaside resorts and foreign travel, should not forget those who are shut up within the furnace-hot walls of city tenements and streets.

Example.

CHAPTER XIV.

SOCIALIZED BEAUTY AND RECREATION.

The most trivial question acquires dignity when it touches the well-being or rouses the passions of many millions.—J. R. Lowell.

Play and art.

THERE is a deep organic relation between the play instincts and art. The men of the Reformation and of English puritanism failed to appreciate this factor in life at its full value. They thought of duty and of work, and they became industrious, rich, powerful, morally and religiously the leaders of the world. On the other hand, the men of the Renaissance discovered another side of life, its joy, its charm, its passion, its human worth. It is coming time to wed the Reformation and the Renaissance, the glory of integrity and the grace of art, for both come from the one divine source, and their separation is perilous to all social interests. Some men and women have already united them in a very high degree, as the classical Milton sought to do when puritanism was fighting its way to recognition.

Teaching of physiology.

There is a physiological need for play and for beauty. The joints stiffen and the muscles remain undeveloped if youth is passed in the mere mechanical processes of "useful" labor. Free play, whose end is in itself, which is undisturbed by the care for something beyond, is a necessary condition of a sound body, a long life, an even temper, and a cheerful and wholesome disposition. The most difficult tasks become light if done in sport. Mark Twain's story of the way in which Tom

Sawyer made his comrades do a disagreeable and tedious piece of whitewashing is an illustration taken from life. That father who induced his boy to clear the field of mullein and other weeds by calling them hostile Indians to be exterminated with a sword made out of an old scythe-blade understood human nature.

Beauty is not for something else, it is a good in itself. A tree which bears no fruit, if it is symmetrical and casts a grateful shade, does yet bear fruit in an inward satisfaction of the soul. In the inspired vision of that lost paradise for which we human wanderers are still seeking through the centuries, it is said, "The Lord God made to grow every tree that is pleasant to the sight, and good for food." There is a clear distinction between the mere animal satisfaction and the æsthetic pleasure. In the revelation of the City of God all jewels and precious metals become symbols of the glory and beauty of streets and walls. The huckster and auctioneer see the dollar mark on the frame of a picture and cry its worth in terms of currency; but the amateur or the artist gazes upon the Sistine Madonna or upon sunset colors with a wonder and worship which it would be cruel to disturb with low talk about prices and markets. Beauty is a good apart from money values and lower uses. It is a pearl of great price for which coarse wealth may be lavished. The end of a tedious and costly journey is reached when one stands in rapture in Lincoln Cathedral or before Angelo's Moses.

Beauty is a good.

These assertions of the ultimate value of music, poetry, pictures, dramas, operas, can no more be "proved" than religion can be demonstrated to the unsusceptible. If the man is color blind an army of witnesses could not make him see the difference between green and violet. Fortunately most human

The want innate.

beings, of the higher races, in their normal condition, can be awakened to interest in beautiful objects by the sight or hearing of them.

Song of nature.

>   Whence and why
> Man's tender pain, man's inward cry,
> When he doth gaze on earth and sky?
> I am not overbold:
>   I hold
> Full powers from Nature manifold.
> I speak for each no-tongued tree
> That, spring by spring, doth nobler be,
> And dumbly and most wistfully
> His mighty prayerful arms outspreads
> Above men's oft-unheeding heads,
> And his big blessing downward sheds.
> I speak for all-shaped blooms and leaves,
> Lichens on stones and moss on eaves,
> Grasses and grains in ranks and sheaves;
> Broad fronded ferns and keen-leaved canes,
> And briery mazes bounding lanes,
> And marsh-plants, thirsty-cupped for rains,
> And milky stems and sugary veins.
>   . . . .
> Yea, all fair forms, and sounds, and lights,
> And warmths, and mysteries, and mights,
> Of Nature's utmost depths and heights.
>   . . . .
> So, Nature calls through all her system wide,
> Give me thy love, O man, so long denied.
>   . . . .

Closed doors.

> But oh, the poor! the poor! the poor!
> That stand by the inward-opening door
> Trade's hand doth tighten ever more,
> And sigh their monstrous foul-air sigh
> For the outside hills of liberty,
> Where Nature spreads her wild blue sky
> For Art to make into melody!
> Thou Trade! thou king of modern days!
>   Change thy ways,

> Change thy ways;
> Let the sweaty laborers file
>   A little while,
>   A little while,
> Where Art and Nature sing and smile.
> —*Sidney Lanier, "The Symphony."*

There are many excellent folks who can see the use of art when they can be persuaded that it will prevent pauperism, vice, and crime. There are some very useful citizens who never get beyond that conception of "reform." They seldom reflect upon the notion that the bad people might attain that level of virtue which is just above the jail and the almshouse and yet not be very attractive members of society. Few of us would think we had achieved any remarkable or praiseworthy success if our highest claim to respect was that we had never been arrested for drunkenness. Apparently there are very zealous reformers who would find this a terribly dull world if there were no idols to smash, no idiots to feed, no lepers to cleanse, no drunkards to sign total abstinence pledges. If we permit ourselves to reflect a moment we can see that where "reforms" come to an end the real humanity begins to appear. Beauty and play are valuable reformatory agents. *(Reformatory power of beauty.)*

Dr. E. Chadwick notices the effects of closing up the walks and open grounds in Scotland. The only remaining places of entertainment being the public houses, the people went there for social intercourse, and drunkenness greatly increased. At the time of which he writes the Sabbath was observed with Judaic strictness, but drunkenness and other vices were worse than in England or Ireland.[1] The Sabbath has no reforming power if its hours are left empty and ugly. Probably it would be better for many people to work on Sunday than spend *(The Sabbath in Scotland.)*

---
[1] "Health of Nations," Vol. I., Chaps. XII. and XIII.

the time as they do in debauch. Saint Monday wears a sad face among the laborers whose pleasures are purely animal. The guilt of neglect is enhanced now that we know by experiment the moral influence of pictures, music, and green parks made charming with flowers. Permanent reforms are carried by substitution.

Expert valuations of play. Mr. G. E. Johnson has written a special paper on education by plays and games, and gives an estimate of the value of 440 recreations. He has gathered testimonies of masters of the art of teaching which it is worth while to consider. "Play is the first poetry of the human being. It is the working off at once of the overflow of both mental and physical powers" (Richter). "Man is wholly man only when he plays" (Schiller). "Education should begin with the right direction of children's sport." "The plays of children should be along the line of their future occupation." "Do not use compulsion, but let education be a sort of amusement" (Plato). "Instruction should be amusing to the child" (Quintilian). "Children should have entertaining employment" (Aristotle). "Plays are efficacious in education" (Fenelon). "Studies should be made amusing and interesting" (Rabelais). "Play is the purest, most spiritual activity of men at this stage, and at the same time typical of human life as a whole, of inner hidden natural life in men and in all things. It holds the sources of all that is good. The plays of children are the germinal leaves of all later life."

Testimony of Jevons. A serious economist like Jevons says, with careful emphasis: "Among the means toward a higher civilization, I unhesitatingly assert that the deliberate cultivation of public amusement is a principal one." Among the agencies he mentions as having already had a civilizing influence on English workingmen are expositions, theaters, science lectures. But he sets music in the highest place because it can be enjoyed sitting down, in a posture of restful repose ; it is absolutely pure and remote from trivial ideas ; and it is, more than any other power of excitement, devoid of reaction and of injurious effects of any kind. Musical gifts are widely diffused and the art is socializing. Every town and village can easily have its bands and chorus.

<small>Advantages of music.</small>

But play and art have, even on this lower level of social ministry, a considerable and demonstrable value. Music has charms to soothe the savage breast. Pictures redeem a garret from extreme vulgarity. Lowell, in his essay on the American Tract Society, written before emancipation, laid bare with just severity the helpless, futile, and irrational mode of dealing with degraded men by merely negative means. When the negro required education, liberty, opportunity, and help, it was not enough to publish tracts. "They would hold their peace about the body of Cuffee dancing to the music of the cart-whip, provided only they could save the soul of Sambo alive by presenting him a pamphlet, which he could not read, on the depravity of the double shuffle."

The wants of civilized and progressive people multiply in number and rise in rank. Savages have few and simple wants, but those are fiery and devouring passions. The influence of the highest religion does not issue in monasticism or asceticism, but in abundant life. Meat will not gratify the desire for music ; a symphony will not quench thirst ; a prayer is not a substitute for out-door exercise. There is a time for everything. Piety does not remove the demand for recreation, or for pictures, or for song. Healthy religion flows into all the interests of existence and sanctifies them.

<small>Many patterns of men.</small>

The drama. The heirs of the Reformation and of puritanism have never quite forgiven Shakespeare, the greatest soul who has lived since the prophets, for being an actor. We see the vice of the theater. We dread the stage and the greenroom. But we have not worked our way to clear thought and just discriminations on the subject. Our church rules and our social standards are in a state of confusion, full of contradictions and weakness. We have nothing consistent to say to youth. Our appeals are hopelessly uncritical and without authority. Meantime our young people go without principles, without guidance and insight. Every one knows that church discipline has broken down absolutely in cities, so far as dramatic entertainments are concerned. Some churches have attempted to meet the deep and universal craving for impersonations of character and life by giving shows of their own—frequently awkward, cheap, miserable failures. Denunciations without discrimination shoot over the mark. Mere harangues about "worldliness" react upon the speaker and rob him of moral influence, and give ground for accusing him of injustice.

Principles of discrimination. We have reached something like a sane and defensible method of dealing with books and papers, with fiction and poetry. We have worked out principles of discrimination. No longer do we indulge in declamation against all novels without critical measurement, but we select the wholesome, grade the volumes according to ages, and use the mighty art of story-telling as a vehicle of noble sentiment. Polluting printed matter we hunt down and consign to the flames, and have the conscience of the people with us, as we have definite laws in favor of these summary methods.

There is no reason why we should not arrive at just as

clear and definite standards in relation to the dramatic art. Give to criticism of the stage the same quantity and quality of study as has been given to fiction and dramatic writings, and the church could build up an intelligible and defensible standard which would command the respect of moral men and women and finally influence legislation and administration. The reform of the regular theater is, it is admitted, one of the most difficult tasks before us; but it must be resolutely attacked and patiently pursued if we are to rescue it from the powers of evil and compel it to minister to the education of society in all that is noble and worthy. It is difficult to reform municipal politics and many other ancient evils, but the good citizen does not despair. *Standards needed.*

Americans have yet to develop a defensible criticism of other forms of art. What could be more confusing than much of the current declamation against "the nude," as if garments could even conceal the most pernicious suggestions of baseness. As we gradually produce a native school of sculptors and painters we may be able to evolve a code of criticism which will leave us all that is beautiful and which will destroy all that can really harm the soul and corrupt morals. But so long as the people are deprived of great works of art they will be unable to see in pictures or statues any æsthetic value, and will think of them with the eye of lust or avarice. But the nobler day has already dawned. We have at work teachers of good taste and high purpose who are interpreting for us the meaning of line, form, color, expression in the aspects of nature and in the human body. *Pictures and statues.*

There are two forms of æsthetic enjoyment, passive appreciation and active creation. The audience at a concert or play, the spectators of a ball game or a running match, have a very keen pleasure in receiving impressions on eye and ear. But creative energy yields a higher delight. From this point of view it seems desirable not only to employ professional artists to entertain us and set before us the most perfect standards of professional training, but also to bring out all local gifts of every variety — song, instrumental music, bands, readers, elocutionists, interpreters of science and literature, and talents for modeling, carving, drawing, painting. Our social settlements have shown very clearly that the poorest people can appreciate the best music and pictures, and that they and their children have unsuspected resources of entertainment within themselves.

Develop native talent.

Many a sluggish intelligence has been awakened by the old-fashioned spelling-match, by amateur theatricals, by a whistling chorus, or by a debate on some matter of current interest. And every time a man comes into the conscious enjoyment of a new activity he is armed with a new weapon against vile lusts and irregular appetites.

There is one great art which every family in the nation can help to cultivate and which all local governments and associations can assist — the art of making the face of nature beautiful.

Art helps nature.

Miss Mary C. Robins, in an interesting series of articles in the *Atlantic Monthly*, suggests the central principle of the social movement for making the landscape attractive and pleasing:

It is in dealing with nature that we can best find an opportunity to gratify our need for a great art, an art the people want, an art they can love, one that will give them true joy, that will appeal to the humblest and the wisest alike ; for we crave something popular to please the masses, something large to gratify the race instinct for the colossal, something bold and far-reaching to strike an answering chord in every American heart. Ours must be an art that men are ready to pay for.

Where shall we begin? Perhaps with a window garden overlooking an alley in a crowded city. At least one spot shall have color. A pot of earth and a few seeds may give hints of Eden. Or if the home is a cottage, with space between wall and walk for a few plants, that narrow plot shall tell the passer-by a story of contentment, peace, and aspiration, and make him wish as pretty a picture for the eyes of his own wife and children. The rude laborer may be redeemed from his cups and his degrading pleasures by the garden and the flowers. *Beginnings.*

Or it may be we think of a grave, marked now by sunken ground, overgrown with grass and weeds, these in the cemetery outside the town. All the graves around it are neglected. Why not invite the neighbors to help rebuild the fence, to mow the grass, to plant some flowers, to secure an intelligent gardener to trim the walks and adorn the unoccupied spaces? An appeal to love's memory will generally meet with a response, and affection will necessarily and instinctively express itself in beauty. *God's acre.*

The village churches may not be large and costly, but they may be made attractive. About each one should be a protected space, every inch of it telling a story of order, neatness, propriety, grace. Missionary societies should employ the best architects in the country to furnish plans for the houses of worship. The schoolhouse and its play-ground, in country, village, and city, should enlist the service of local patriotism. The style of building should be determined by a state commission of consulting architects, and not by the village carpenter.

Parks.

All towns need parks for public meetings, for holiday festivals, and for display of natural beauty. It is happily becoming fashionable for rich men to give tracts of land for public uses. But it is not necessary to wait for a shower of manna. Towns can buy or condemn land for this noble use, and they should not wait until it becomes costly.

In cities "every group of houses should as a matter of course have its play-grounds for children, five per cent of all building land being compulsorily set apart by law for recreative purposes" (Jevons). It is not enough to have vast areas at a long distance from the people. In the center of every block must be a play-ground, a fountain, a bit of green, room for color.

Failure of egoism.

Egoism, "private enterprise," is an æsthetic failure as it is morally vicious. Mere individualism makes ugly towns. Selfishness compels us to find a half-dozen planes of motion in a single square, since the free American citizen chooses the level of his sidewalk to suit himself. Here is a shanty next door to a house of six stories; a coal yard opposite a ribbon shop; a vacant lot full of thistles next a neat and charming garden; a sharp gable contrasting with a flat cornice.

Sociality, neighborliness, mutual respect will some day put this bold, rude, ungentlemanly ruffianism to shame. The inhabitants of a street will form an association to bring the entire street up to the level of the finest taste anywhere displayed. The poor widow will have her house painted since she cannot afford to do it herself; but the selfish rich man who defies public opinion will be rebuked and whipped into line.

The ugliness of our towns usually arises from the fact that they are like original chaos, without form or plan. Each man builds his own house as he pleases or can. The result is a wilderness of chimneys and roofs and irregular lines. The mind is distracted by the view.

Some suburban towns have been laid out according to plans. Intelligent landowners have set down "building restrictions" in contracts of sale, preventing the erection of unsightly residences or shops. But the poor are seldom thus protected against themselves. Nothing short of municipal regulation can bring order and beauty into the deformed streets where so many are compelled to dwell and rear their children. Every city should have an architect who should draw plans and assist in the arrangement of new houses. {Hopeful examples.}

Who that has ever enjoyed the Italian cities can rest in peace when he returns to America? The vision of Florence and Milan haunts him. Patriotism is flattered by our rapid growth and delights in the prospect of still greater cities. But refined patriotism desires to see the next generation born in the presence of buildings and parks which will insure health and culture.

Not only foreign travelers in America, but visitors from the picturesque regions of New England and the mountains of the South report a feeling of depression after a long journey across the plains of the West. They readily acknowledge the wonderful fertility of the soil, the energy of the inhabitants, the amazing achievements of the pioneers. They can see that this central plain must come to support a vast population whose numerical preponderance will give it the political leadership of the republic. But men accustomed to hills, valleys, cascades, and charming parks cannot conceal their discontent, perhaps their disgust, at the dull level monot- {Monotony of prairie scenery.}

ony of the country. Many of the prairie towns, with their streets in spring mere lanes of sticky mud, with their shabby and unpainted board houses, their ill-kept yards, their half-dozen ugly churches, their long rows of unwashed country wagons ranged along the principal thoroughfare, horses standing in filth, irregular wooden sidewalks, and general air of neglect and disorder, leave in the memory of the visitor forbidding and disagreeable impressions of the æsthetic and moral character of the people.

Examples of better things. But each country has its own peculiar attractions and possibilities. Holland is a very flat region, and much of its soil was originally a sand in which no plant could grow. But The Hague, Leyden, and many less famous places have been made attractive for artists. Having only too much water, they have lakelets and canals. By liberal use of fertilizers they have redeemed the soil, planted trees, cultivated flowers, and covered the naked, sterile earth with living forms of beauty. Along the sluggish canals are trees and windmills and interesting quaint houses. The western towns and villages may be transformed under the magic touch of refined taste. Flower gardens, hedges, artistic houses, watercourses lined with all varieties of shrubs, lakes which mirror the sky, arched bridges, roads become avenues of noble trees, windmills as useful as those now at work but more attractive to the eye, these are among the possibilities of the future. Mr. Pullman has demonstrated what can be done on level ground, and discovered to the western world the economic value of beauty. Here and there a farmer has surrounded himself and his family with a landscape which suggests a paradise. There are villages, first settled by New England people, where a charming refinement is manifest in houses and public buildings.

But only too often it will require a long struggle with stupid apathy, with coarse and vulgar indifference before the rude pioneer constructions and arrangements yield to the demands of art and the villages and rural neighborhoods become ministrant to a rich and splendid human life.

Apathy.

Missionaries of beauty, with a zeal for the education of æsthetic faculties dormant in the people, will be required for the crusade. We need men like Jonathan Chapman, nicknamed "Johnny Appleseed," who was born in Boston in 1775, and who carried apple seeds into Ohio, planted them in open spaces, sold or gave away his infant orchards, and left behind him living and grateful mementos of a worthy and devoted life.

We need city commissions who will call in a real landscape gardener to plan their parks and decorate open spaces and cemeteries. For example, the visitor of Detroit can see at Belle Isle what a genuine artist can make of a perfectly flat and swampy piece of ground; how he can transform it into a "vision, a delight, and a desire," by comparatively simple means.

There is a close connection between the movement to preserve and improve our natural scenery and the movement to promote good roads. Senator Chandler, in an address before the National League for Good Roads, touches this point:

Good roads again.

> The question of good roads in New Hampshire has connected itself with that of forestry, because, in order to keep New Hampshire prominent among the summer resorts of the United States, it is necessary for us not only to have good highways and good roads, giving easy access to our natural scenery, but we must preserve our forests and our watercourses.

The public highway, now too often a dreary and

saddening stretch of monotony, gives opportunity for rows of trees, clambering vines, fountains, resting places, artistic wayside inns for bicycle riders and pedestrians.

Village improvement societies.

In union there is strength. The enthusiasts will be obliged to organize their friends, to excite discussion, to induce lawyers, merchants, pastors, teachers to commit themselves in essays and speeches to a large and worthy policy of improvement. Agitation itself will educate. In order to prepare for discussions there must be reading and thinking. On Arbor Day, when trees are planted, the children will be told their uses and the modes of caring for them. At the annual festival those who have made unusual sacrifices will be praised and honored. When men walk under the grateful shade on hot summer days they will think of doing for posterity what others have done for them. Village will vie with village for the honor of first place in attractiveness.

How to form them.

It is not difficult to form a village improvement society. A dozen earnest people can engage all the professional talkers and writers to set the air vibrating with eloquence. The poets will proffer their rhymes appropriate to the season and the subject. A president can be induced to accept the honors and dignities of the chief office. Various committees may be appointed to collect funds, plan enterprises, persuade the slow, ridicule the patrons of ugliness, and to do particular pieces of betterment. It is not difficult to form such a society, but it may prove a very weighty burden to carry it afterward for several years.

Perhaps in the present state of public opinion we must generally look to the women's clubs for leadership and persistent agitation. The county fairs are institutions which may be seized upon for autumn conventions, while the farmers' societies may be enlisted with great social advantage.

Miss Margaret J. Evans, president of the Minnesota State Federation of Women, reports that

> The state work embraces: first, fostering town and country clubs in order to provide women from the country rest rooms when in town, to give the stimulus of social intercourse, and a monthly literary program; second, fostering public and private libraries; and, third, city and village improvement associations. Parks and streets have been made orderly and beautiful in several towns in Minnesota, the children in the schools have been interested and instructed by placards to lend their help, country school boards and teachers have been entreated to make country districts attractive, and much use made of the public press in educating public sentiment.

Agency of women's clubs.

And what is true in Minnesota promises to be contagious in all parts of the union. Fashions soon travel from Paris to Oshkosh.

Village improvement societies and similar associations in cities will confront the problem of expense. Of course the niggardly old fossils who never did care for anything but money, and whose noblest craving is land-hunger, will ridicule private effort and resist the levy of taxes. But we are learning the value of franchises. We have come near the end of giving away the use of streets and roads to make rich capitalists still more rich. We are growing weary of yielding the streets to be deformed by unsightly poles and wires without compensation. We are coming to the decision that a part of every fare we pay shall go to some public use. Now that electric roads are running out in all directions it is time for the country people to look after their interest and exact compensation for the use of roads. Here is a source of revenue for improvements. Many a company

Cost.

will be glad to keep the highway in order for their privileges, if the county town authorities are honest and awake early in the morning of the day when the franchise is to be let.

Social luxury. We may return to the subject of luxury in connection with the topic of recreations and art for the people. Professor Giddings has classed under the head of "culpable luxury" expenditures for objects which are æsthetically bad; which do not increase the sum of beauty, of refinement, and of general cultivation in the community. There are so many improvements to be made; so many ways of investing wealth which might add to the rational happiness of hundreds of thousands of people, that selfish and reckless outlays on momentary pleasures seem doubly immoral.

As the social spirit pervades and masters all minds, and as rich men come to see that the path to honor lies in the direction of public service, they will make their grounds and their picture galleries minister to the elevation of all their neighbors. Exclusive and insolent walls will not obstruct the vision. There are already many who have set the example of generous stewardship and who bring their treasures of art before the eyes of the entire community.

Let us hear the verdict of one of the principal economists of this century:

Luxurious expenditures of selfishness. That useful function, therefore, which some profound writers fancy they discover in the abundant expenditure of the idle rich, turns out to be a sheer illusion. Political economy furnishes no such palliation of unmitigated selfishness. Not that I would breathe a word against the sacredness of contracts. But I think it is important, on moral no less than on economic grounds, to insist upon this, that no public benefit of any kind arises from the existence of an idle rich class. The wealth accumulated by their ancestors or others on their behalf, where it is employed as capital, no doubt helps to sustain industry ; but what they consume in luxury and idleness is not capital, and helps to sustain nothing but their own unprofitable lives. By all means they must have their rents and interest, as it is written in the bond ; but let them take their proper place as drones in the hive, gorging at a feast to which they have contributed nothing. (J. E. Cairnes, " Political Economy.")

Let us heed the voice of a historian, commenting on the service of the father of political economy :

Again, no rich man need fear that he will learn from political economy the moral sophism that luxury may be laudably indulged in because it is good for trade. On the contrary, he will learn to distinguish between productive and unproductive consumption, and the results of each to the community ; and he will have it brought home to his mind more effectually, perhaps, than by any rhetoric, that if he does live in luxury and indolence, he is a burden to the earth. The words, "I give alms best by spending largely," have indeed been uttered, and they came from a hard, gross heart. But it was the heart not of a political economist, but of a most Christian king. Those words were the answer of Louis XIV. to Madame de Maintenon when she asked him for alms to relieve the misery of the people. (Goldwin Smith, " Lectures on the Study of History.") *Witness of economists.*

Mr. Lecky, whose study of modern life has been profound and extensive, declares :

The evils that spring from plutocracy are great, and increasing. One of the most evident is the enormous growth of luxurious living. The evil does not, in my opinion, lie in the multiplication of pleasures. Amusement, no doubt, occupies a very disproportionate place in our lives, and many men grossly mismanage their pleasures, and the amount of amusement expected by all classes and ages has within the last generation greatly increased. But those who have realized the infinite pathos of human life and the variety of human tastes, characters, and temptations will hesitate much to abridge the sum of human enjoyment, and will look with indulgent eye on many pleasures which are far from cultivated, elevating, and refined, provided they are not positively vicious and do not bring with *A historian.*

them grave and manifest evils. What is really to be deplored is the inordinate and ever-increasing expenditure on things which add nothing, or almost nothing, to human enjoyment. It is the race of luxury, the mere ostentation of wealth, which values all things by their cost.

This feeling is wholly distinct from the love of art. To minds infected with it beauty itself is nothing if it is common. The rose and the violet make way for the stephanotis and the orchid. Common fruits and vegetables are produced at great expense in an unnatural season. The play is estimated by the splendor of its scenery. Innumerable attendants, gorgeous upholstery, masses of dazzling jewelry, rare dishes from distant countries, ingenious and unexpected refinements of costly luxury, are the chief marks of their entertainments, and the hand of the millionaire is always seen. Nor is the evil restricted to the small circle of the very rich. From rank to rank the standard of social requirement is raised, making society more cumbrous, extravagant, and ostentatious, driving from it by the costliness of its accessories many who are eminently fitted to adorn it, and ruining many others by the competition of idle, joyless, useless display. It is a tendency which vulgarizes and materializes vast fields of English life, and is preparing great catastrophes for the future. ("Democracy and Liberty.")

Luxurious expenditures "give work" to and distribute money among wage-earners—cooks, milliners, coachmen, florists, decorators, cosmetic venders. That is true. A certain amount of this expense is justifiable. But $200,000 in a single evening! Is there no limit? The voluptuary not only apologizes for this extravagance but demands praise for a service to the poor. "Have I not given employment to scores of people with this $200,000 spent upon my ball?" Yes. And in a few hours nothing remains but wrecks and waste. Who has not heard of the cruel tyrant who commanded a sculptor to make him a statue of ice? The genius which might have left an imperishable work in marble was whipped by fear to serve a moment's caprice. There is something akin to this in the cruel wastefulness of the plutocrat for whom the Jenkinses of society apologize and whom they praise. Charles Kingsley suggested, in "Alton Locke," that the same money spent on houses would also give far more employment to wage-workers and leave behind the permanent means of comfort. Wealth spent on private and transitory pleasures if distributed on public parks, museums, galleries, music halls, decoration of our ugly schoolrooms and mission chapels, would give paying occupation to many more people and diffuse satisfactions among hundreds of thousands instead of a few hundreds, and for centuries instead of seconds. To the student of history and economics the insulting excuses and praises of extravagance and barbarian ostentation are as exasperating as the spectacle itself is revolting when placed in contrast with the misery which is near it.

A better way.

The chant of the English socialist leader and artist paints a vision worth cherishing in every democratic land :

And what wealth, then, shall be left us, when none shall gather
    gold
To buy his friend in the market, and pinch and pine the sold?
Yea, what but the lovely city, and the little house on the hill,
And the wastes and the woodland beauty, and the happy fields
    we till,
And the homes of ancient story, the tombs of the mighty dead,
And the wise man seeking out marvels, and the poet's teeming
    head,
And the painter's head of wonder, and the marvelous fiddle-
    bow,
And the banded choirs of music, all them that do and know.

Chant of a socialist.

CHAPTER XV.

CHARITY AND CORRECTION.

Thus we have two distinct types of mind—the egoistic, which may be called the statical, and the altruistic, which may be called the dynamic. The egoistic, or statical, type of mind looks at things as they are, and has no thought of improving them. . . . Strong sympathies may, indeed, coexist in such minds, but they are impulsive only, and extend no further than the concrete case which may happen to appeal to them at the moment. The dynamic type of mind, on the other hand, sees in everything a potential superiority to its present condition. It demands the elevation of the low, not by almsgiving, but by education and enfranchisement, until no distinctions shall exist except those of actual native capacity to do and to be, and in many ways it agitates moral reforms for the future and the many when no direct gain to self is to follow.—*L. F. Ward.*

THE works of the social spirit in America are chiefly those of the healthy, vigorous, progressive members of society. When Commander Booth-Tucker, of the Salvation Army, speaks of our country he no longer writes of the "submerged tenth" but of the "submerged twentieth." We have not yet a very great permanent pauper and criminal class. The best energies of our people are not to be expended on the defective and delinquent. We are finding a way to deal mercifully with the miserable, and yet not permit revenues and energies to be absorbed in caring for those of whom least can be made. There are, indeed, selfish persons who should be made ashamed of their hard hearts and unmerciful apathy. Some part of every strong life

Social pathology a small section of sociology.

should be given to the weak. But those persons who represent "charity" as the chief business of mankind are in error. Almsgiving and rescue missions ought to occupy a relatively small place in the sum of social labor. It is ridiculous to identify sociology with that corner of it which considers human depravity. The arts of navigation and marine commerce deal only incidentally with hulks and wrecks, with rocks and roaring straits. The science of health might be absolutely complete without a section devoted to cancers and fevers. Social pathology is but one aspect of the science of society and the arts of social control and amelioration.

It is true that contrary opinion is current, and that some people feel guilty because the whole city is not treated as a hospital. But the general instinct is sound and wise. The jail and the almshouse have nearly as much room as they require and more than would be necessary if the laws of general moral and physical health were better understood and universally obeyed. *Poverty is not pauperism.*

There will always be differences in ability and in wealth. We shall always have with us some who are poorer than others. Poverty is a relative matter and it is in imagination as really as in the purse. But pauperism is not necessary, any more than yellow fever. Both are diseases. The people of the Middle Ages cultivated pauperism as a gardener grows mushrooms. Any community can have all the beggars it is willing to pay for to adorn its church porches and furnish Lady Bountiful with a background for her "charity." But the nation which does not extinguish its pauperism and its defective stock, or at least reduce them to a manageable quantity, is itself to blame. *Cultivation of pauperism.*

There will ever be occasion for neighborly kindness;

for family care of helpless infancy and decaying age; for the organization of mutual assistance and insurance against the unforeseen risks of life. Altruism will have occasion enough for display and development without keeping a degraded multitude of undeveloped or perverted human beings on hand for practice of the supernatural virtues.

Abolition of pauperism.

The best relief agencies are those which tend to make themselves unnecessary, not those which report the largest disbursements of money, coal, and old clothes. The best prison or correctional system is that which shows the fewest prisoners in proportion to the population.

The ideal of charity is to rid the world of the picturesque vagrant, the professional burglar, the begging child, the gypsy mother, the drunken sot. No method of relief was ever devised which did not tend to make human beings in some measure parasitic, weak, helpless, and base. All rational charity tends to sincere fraternity, to development of self-reliance and self-support.

The cannibal method impossible.

It is important that this ideal of charity should be held fast through evil report and good report, just because it is impossible all at once to realize it. For the present we have a great multitude of defective, abnormal members of society on our hands. We cannot kill them. We cannot, as Dean Swift suggested, fatten and eat them. We are not cannibals. The past has left us this heritage of misery, along with better things. And the real problem of charity is to let this entire degenerate stock die out as quietly as possible, and meantime replenish the earth with human beings of a higher type. Every measure we adopt should move steadily and consciously in this direction, because mercy and humanity set this goal before us. We owe it to the coming generations not to burden them with a load bequeathed to us from ignorance, if we can in any measure diminish it.

In the paragraphs of this chapter a system of charity and penology will not be presented. All that is possible in the space is to state in aphoristic form the outlines of a comprehensive method of dealing with degenerate members of society. A fish-net must not have a hole in it anywhere or it is useless. If the fence is down at one angle the cows will soon go from lean pastures to feed in the fat corn. A system of charity and correction must be a cordon absolutely complete at every point; and to the present chaos and disorder of our methods is due a great part of existing evils. The system of charity and correction must be one organic whole in which every part has place and every action tends to a common goal. *Completeness essential.*

First of all, the entire nation must be led to adopt methods of life which will not deprave human life. It is not necessary to repeat here all that has been said in previous chapters on this subject. All that the social spirit is doing to promote health, intelligence, beauty, friendliness, morality, integrity, and faith in the Heavenly Father is a preventive measure. Much of the best charity is never conscious of working for the pauper. Mutual benefit societies, schools, insurance, savings banks, athletic clubs, art museums contribute to that vigor and energy which leave no room for theft and vice and beggary. He who builds a wall for a road along a dangerous cliff performs a higher service than the man who merely watches and waits at the bottom with an ambulance. There are bacterial diseases which never hurt a man so long as he has good digestion. *Preventive measures.*

Causes.

Pauperism and crime appear in their worst forms where the alleys are foul with stench; where food is scant and badly cooked; where human beings are crowded together like swine in a pen; where sunshine rarely falls; where schools do not give training for life duties and efficiency; where family customs are communistic; where women toil in factories and home is deprived of their presence and ministry; where wages are low and labor is irregular; where political leaders are corrupt and venal; where amusements are vile and sensual; where music and all higher elements are wanting; and where the rich and the educated set an example of skepticism, materialism, and egoism.

So long as we tolerate such conditions we shall have sickly, deformed, stunted, depraved people. We begin too late when we introduce reforms in out-door relief, in prisons and almshouses. The environment of a man is his school. The slum shapes and bends people to its character.

Environment.

The only way to reach men is by changing their environment. We are not pure ghosts. No spirit ever changed another spirit save by modifying the environment. By environment is meant here the material objects, the language, the pictures, the entertainments, the customs, the treatment of man by man, the habitual appeals of speech and books and papers.

Christ himself became incarnate so as to teach souls through the body.

> And so the Word had breath and wrought
> With human hands the creed of creeds,
> In loveliness of perfect deeds,
> More strong than all poetic thought.

God reveals himself in the forces and objects of nature and human life. No short path to abolition of pauperism is discoverable ; it must be attacked from all sides. Mr. Arnold White has attempted a summary program :

Emigrate four per cent of the fit among them, stop the immigration of the incurable paupers, take the children out of the guilt gardens, give relief work to the adults, restrict charities to the sick, aged, and young, encourage the growth of trades unions, discourage improvident marriage.

Here are hints of a system which needs to be worked out in detail and adapted to American conditions.

The story of Helen Keller, blind and deaf, reads like a tale of the Arabian Nights. Out from a night that knew no stars or moon she was led into intellectual day ; out from the gloom of speechless isolation she was, by the patient wisdom of skilful instructors, transformed into an inspirer and companion of mankind. Beautifully has she spoken for such wise charity armed with the weapons of science : *Helen Keller.*

Remember, no effort that we make to attain something beautiful is ever lost. Sometime, somewhere, somehow, we shall find that which we seek. We shall speak, yes, and sing, too, as God intended we should speak and sing.

We may distinguish among the children whose conditions and perils require social care the following classes : the slow, the truant, the toilers, the juvenile offenders, and the feeble-minded. *Dependent children.*

In every large school there are a few dull children who cannot keep up in the race and at last cease to compete. They require special care and sometimes separate rooms. The wiser teachers permit them to drop part of their studies rather than crush their hopes and bewilder their minds. Unless these little ones are very tenderly and tactfully helped they are in danger of becoming helpless or rebellious, paupers or criminals. *Dull children.*

Truants.

Truant children are cases of "reversion"; that is, they have a strain of an ancestral wandering instinct. All children are naturally travelers. And when the domestic environment is cramped, the air depressing, the light dim, the mother nervous and irritable with toil and hunger, there the centrifugal forces are strong. Our juvenile prisons are filled with these truant children. The parents cannot govern them. Principals of schools sweep them out of their sight and send up the report "incorrigible." The label sticks to the forehead and the boy tries to deserve his bad name by appropriate conduct. For the first time in his career the boy finds in the bridewell or reformatory compulsory education and a chance to train his hands to useful industry. We sow the wind and foolishly hope to reap a soft zephyr. We plant a briar and curse the ground for not growing us a fig. Crime is not a necessity; it is only a natural product of neglect.

None of us ever learned to speak or sing or pray without help of teachers. Truants do not acquire heroic virtues by intuition.

Parental schools.

The social spirit is at work nearer the foundations. Cities are providing "ungraded schools" and "parental schools" to correct these incorrigibles and make good men of them. Workingmen are away from home before dawn and after dark. Frequently their wives must help to earn the living. It is impossible for them to administer discipline. The tenement house is a Babel. The street is a theater of vicious influences, and at night a city is an unspeakable tempter. To ascend the stairs to his home the boy must often go through a saloon. See the Hull House Maps and cease to wonder that there are so many truants. It is amazing that there are so few. It is a hopeful sign that in these dull, noisome quarters blossom so many lovely characters, affectionate mothers, sober and industrious fathers, ambitious students. But the weaker ones need help.

With "labor-saving" machinery so powerful that it gluts the markets with goods, with armies of men seeking employment in vain, there is no excuse for putting school children into factories before their bones and muscles are developed, and before their brains have been disciplined for continuous and effective thinking. Machinery is doing nearly all the rough work now, and muscles without intelligence have low price. Mr. Depew says that the world is full of misfits, and that misfits are always cheap. A great and rich people cannot afford to rob a whole generation of the mental equipment which is essential to social adjustments in modern life. Compulsory education is social defense against crime and vagrancy. We must follow the better examples and remove the little girls from the streets. There is no social need for their service there, and the innocent daughter in such an environment soon becomes a plague and a sorceress. The retail shops are leading others to the dark and dolorous path of sin and shame. When mothers begin to investigate the histories of these toiling children, ever grazing the occupations of vagabonds, their hearts will cry out against the evil. Follow the telegraph messenger boy to his home. Talk with the match-seller, the bouquet-seller, the news-vending girl on the corner. See how ignorant these are of much that we think necessary for our children. Discover how precocious they are in knowledge of evil. Yonder are the "free" schools, but barred to these. Is it any wonder that we furnish recruits for the nameless haunts of vice? Here also is a

Working children.

Right of the state to compel school attendance.

task for the social spirit—to take the toiling children from factory, sweat-shop, street, and saloon and bring them into schools, and adapt the schools to their needs.

Orphans and deserted children.

Motherless children must have a real home. Temporarily they may be detained in an institution. But no woman can care properly for a great brood. There is need of a paternal as well as a maternal discipline. Dependent children should be carefully adopted in kind families. If it is impossible to find people to adopt them they should be apprenticed or boarded—never heaped up in orphanages as for "cold storage."

But when thus placed in homes there must be constant supervision. Children are not always easily fitted to a home. There are disappointments and must be changes. Oversight by correspondence is not adequate. The supervisor must actually visit the homes where children have been placed, and the visits must be without notice.

Duty of the state.

As the state must bear the burden of failures it should have a system, like that in Michigan, for caring for all dependent children. This does not prevent churches and charitable societies from caring for orphans and other homeless children, but it brings them all to safe methods. No state, city, town, or county should subsidize private or church institutions. No money raised by taxation should be expended or used by any persons who are not appointed and directed by the governments. A society which professes to be charitable should raise its own funds by voluntary contributions. It is hypocrisy to call that a gift to the community which is partly provided by taxes. Sectarian and other politically irresponsible institutions should have no grants from public treasuries. The subsidy system is wrong in principle, unfair to a part of the people, deceptive in form, tends to crowd institutions, increases the number of dependents, causes financial scandal, turns professed philanthropists into tricky lobbyists.

The feeble-minded persons number, perhaps, 90,000 in the United States. It is difficult to discover all of them by any process of census-taking. They are beings of arrested or unnatural development, dwarfs or monsters by heredity. Only a few states have provided for their custody. The girls grow up in many parts of the land without protectors and become unmarried mothers of weak, helpless, deformed creatures like themselves. In Mr. Dugdale's "Jukes" and in Mr. McCulloch's "Tribe of Ishmael" the reader can see what costly and sorrowful consequences follow this shameful neglect. Probably more than eighty per cent of the feeble-minded had such parents. In one generation it would be possible to cut off many thousands of these streams of vicious heredity. How? By the simple and comparatively inexpensive process of confining them in special institutions where they could work for themselves on farms and gardens and die without offspring. This is the only merciful and religious way to deal with this class, one of the most prolific sources of vice and crime. Fortunately, public opinion during the past few years has been directed to this evil and a great advance has already been made in some of the states. *Defectives.*

Education has been idolized among us. Almost unlimited virtue has been ascribed to it. But education has its limits of efficacy. Social selection is necessary. Education accomplishes very little with imbeciles and instinctive criminals; it cannot make them fit to be parents; it cannot take vice out of the blood. Religion itself does not consist altogether in sermons. A high *Limits of education.*

stone wall, with sharp spikes on top, is as necessary a means of grace to defectives as hymns are for normal people. A microcephalous idiot is not converted into a good mother by exhortations or by Froebel's gifts. Unscientific philanthropy in this field is cruel and antisocial.

The insane. In almost every state one of the first public institutions to be established by taxation is an asylum for the insane. These refuges of the mentally unsound are demanded by considerations of safety as well as of humanity. Our century has witnessed remarkable advance in the skill and gentleness of their treatment. The ancient superstitions which ascribed insanity to evil spirits have fled before the light of science which shows that some specific disease of nerves and brain is the sole and direct cause of every unusual disturbance of mental activity. The asylum is simply a hospital for treating nervous diseases. There is no more mystery about it than there is about a hospital for treating the eye and the ear.

Religious consolation. As mental states react upon the body, all quieting and cheering influences may be employed, under the physician's control, as remedial agencies. But fanaticism and excitement must be positively excluded from the hospital, and all æsthetic, educational, and religious exercises must be regulated by expert physicians. This principle is not always understood by zealous religious teachers and evangelists who have never studied nervous disease, and such misrepresentations of religion have provoked the deserved suspicion and hostility of eminent alienists who have seen the careful work of months utterly ruined in an hour of indiscreet excitement.

The public should understand that the prospect of permanent cure is much greater in earlier stages of disease than after it has made deep inroads. Therefore public sentiment should favor placing those who are mentally unbalanced under the care and direction of special experts as soon as the unpleasant symptoms are apparent. All of us should cultivate a mental habit of regarding the insane as ill, and should avoid whispering in their presence and making them feel that they are peculiar. *Early treatment.*

Luther edited a book of beggars. Vagrancy is not a modern pest. Centuries ago sturdy and valiant beggars moved in troops over Europe, levied on the stores of peasants, and demanded help at the gates of convents. There are fluctuations in the numbers of these wanderers at various periods. Times of business depression naturally increase their number. After a "crisis" for several months or years there are multitudes of the unemployed, and we are compelled to provide emergency relief. The following maxims, curtly stated, must be the present contribution to the discussion of method : *Tramps.*

We must distinguish the unemployed from the professional vagrant. In times of emergency neighbor should help neighbor, friend help friend. Those who are prosperous should extend their calling list and make new acquaintances among the poor. Manufacturers often make agreements with their employees to keep the factories running at reduced cost because wares can be marketed only at lower rates. It is a good time to make improvements which will some day be necessary. Cities, without opening public works, can undertake enterprises which can be done earlier and more cheaply when labor is abundant. It seems probable that a system of insurance against loss by non-employment will in the future help to tide over evil days. If forty millions of people are thinking of little ways of helping in months *Emergency relief.*

of emergency then as many millions of acts of aid will be done. In fact, it is in these unrecorded ways that many people have been kept alive during the past few years. Charity organizations assist this process by bringing many kind people into personal relations with those who are in want.

Vagabonds. Discrimination between honest workingmen and tramps is as necessary as it is sometimes difficult, because the tramp professes to be seeking work as the hypocrite professes to be seeking religion. In the chain of agencies developed in older countries we find the following, each one performing a part of the social duty.

Labor bureaus. The first step is to provide information by means of labor bureaus. Trades unions have organized one of the most exact and efficient agencies of this species. Mutual benefit societies are sometimes able to inform members of their fraternities where remunerative employment may be found. Charity organization societies always assist dependents as far as possible in cities, but skilled workmen avoid them and employers find that the grade of ability is frequently low. No very efficient system has yet been devised, and the best system will not find places for skilled workmen when the manufactories are closed all over the country.

Labor tests. Investigations and catechisms are of little value in discriminating between honest and dishonest wanderers. A very hungry man is greatly tempted to profess almost any creed which promises a mess of pottage. Free soup attracts to missions the same class of men who are drawn to saloons by free lunches. The labor test is necessary to separate, in a general way, the sheep from the goats. It does not tell who is "worthy" and who is "unworthy." These ancient distinctions have no practical value. When a man may be in danger of freezing or starving inquiry into his pedigree and religious biography is mockery. Investigation may do him harm. What if it should reveal that he is an ex-convict! The only question to ask of an able-bodied man is, Will you work? And the only evidence he can give, without a certificate from his pastor, is—that he actually does some work.

But such temporary work tests as sawing wood and wheeling sand are mere makeshifts. Tramps are often willing to earn a meal or two but are not willing to persevere in well-doing. They have no habits of industry, and a single work test cannot reveal this defect.

In order to take hold of a large body of dependent and homeless men associations or municipalities must have ready regular places of productive industry. In the cold climates of the North there is a great difficulty in providing work in winter. The county poorhouses are crowded with men who in summer live by begging, odd earnings, and theft. It is these men who frighten farmers into feeding them by threats of burning barns and ricks. It is these men who are voted in blocks of fifty by low politicians. It is these men, perhaps 50,000 or more in our country, who are venal voters, who are physically diseased, and who increase enormously the expenses of police and courts and prisons. *Voluntary farm colonies and shops.*

It is therefore imperative that work should be offered to this entire crowd in winter. A stone pile will empty a poorhouse or a wayfarers' lodge like magic. Breaking stone for roads within inclosures is ennobling exercise. Free soup-houses and free shelters simply attract men to the city and confirm young vagabonds in their habits.

The work test in poorhouses and city shelters and the voluntary farm colony will reveal the fact that some *Revelations of the work test.*

of the unemployed are strong and willing but have never learned any useful art. Perhaps they were newsboys, bootblacks, or telegraph messengers during the age when a trade might have been learned. When they became too big for such occupations they were turned adrift by parents to shift for themselves. Perhaps they left home to escape restraint and after a brief job in a factory were discharged and soon brought to beggary or theft. Once arrested they lost care for respectable people and abandoned themselves to the company of men and women who would not put them to shame. If they are ever to get back into society they must be taught some trade according to their nature and history. It may be difficult to accomplish this, but it is the only path to their salvation.

The "potato patch."

The educational value of the suburban garden scheme seems to be its chief recommendation. People learn how to get their food out of the soil, how to follow an art and reap the fruit of their own industry. Many families have thus been prepared for the transition to country life or to horticulture. Experiments made in Europe and in this country prove that it is a method worth trying on a larger scale. Small towns can assist some of their poor by lending them patches of ground for cultivation in the summer. In many cases some members of the family can thus raise so many vegetables that it is unnecessary to appeal to charity for relief in the winter.

The incompetent residuum.

After the labor test has selected out those who are capable and willing there will remain in the sinks of cities another mixed multitude who require further discrimination and varied treatment. Some of these will be found quite able and ready to work under the direction of managers, but incompetent to find a manager.

They require some one set over them to direct and arrange their work and show them just what to do. These futile, feeble people at present are now about half supported by charity. They throng the labor market and help to lower the wages of competent men, and reduce these to pauperism along with themselves. The best method of dealing with these is the farm colony, under county or city management, or under the care of benevolent and religious associations.

Still another institution will be found necessary if we are to deal effectually with vagrants. Some of them are criminals or at least confirmed beggars. It is useless to invite these men to a voluntary colony, for they will not come. Yet they are not fit to live in society and they are dangerous in the community. For these a compulsory residence of years on an inclosed tract of land seems the only method which promises restoration of the more hopeful cases, and guarantees the public defense. *The rebellious residuum.*

This last measure can be closely connected with a system of progressive sentences in the criminal courts. When it is thought safe to release regular offenders they should first be permitted to go abroad on parole and under guardianship. The present custom of giving short sentences is worse than useless; it discourages the reformable and confirms the incorrigible.

We have multitudes of independent, separated associations for distributing relief, and many kind-hearted individuals ready to bestow alms. But we have no organized system of charities. Our several pieces of benevolence are like short railroads cut off from trunk lines, or like a telephone which has no connection with the network of wires. Not only in cities but in county towns is there a necessity for voluntary associations of all benevolent persons, societies, and poor relief *Charity organization.*

officials for the purpose of systematizing philanthropic enterprises.

Objects and methods.

A charity organization society is charged with the duty of collecting and recording full information in regard to all dependent persons within its district, be it town, county, or city. Its secretary should be able on the instant to tell exactly what person or institution is ready to give help to a wanderer, an orphan, an aged and helpless dependent, a sick stranger, a friendless widow, a demented or insane charge.

Friendly visitors.

Such a society would have a conference or several conferences of "friendly visitors," of men and women who are willing to make acquaintances with needy persons or families and do the part of a kind neighbor. These conferences hear the reports of these visitors on each case, once a fortnight or once a month, and tell them what should be done until the next meeting. If a hired agent or an individual visitor is permitted to conduct the case, save in an hour of pressing danger, the conference will dissolve, will talk itself to death. If the conference is made to feel that it must reach decisions and determine treatment it will feel a sense of responsibility and the members will take pains to attend the meetings. These conferences can be organized in churches or in neighborhoods or in women's clubs, and each one should be related to the central office.

Public institutions.

A charity organization society will have committees to visit all public institutions, as jails, lock-ups, poor-houses, orphanages, and asylums; to study the conditions of the houses and the methods of treatment; to see that no children are kept under the same roof with adult paupers or criminals. A committee should act with the overseer of the poor, watch the effect of public relief on dependent persons, and devise means of helping them to support themselves. A committee of ladies or a circle of King's Daughters could visit the poorhouse, furnish concerts and entertainments, conduct musical religious services, plan suitable occupation for sick and aged women, and help them to live a useful and contented life. A committee of men should see to it that tramps are not sent on from place to place and confirmed in migratory habits, but held to task work and sent away to the place where there is some reasonable prospect of their finding employment.

A charity organization society in a small town can study the social causes of personal degeneration: the saloon, the coarse amusements, the idle groups for gossip, the rude practical jokes, the low and depraving entertainments furnished by strolling players. The character of entertainments can be raised; musical classes and concerts substituted for the demoralizing shows; debates and discussions planned to awaken the intellect and prepare for citizenship; common enterprises of sanitation and village improvement set on foot to kindle local pride and public spirit as antidote for animalism and selfish indulgence. The Raiffeisen credit banks could be organized for renters and small shopkeepers. Provident loan societies might provide small loans to honest men who would otherwise enroll themselves and their children as public paupers and take the first step downward. *Study of causes.*

Thus in all ways the conferences of friendly visitors would go from external symptoms to the deep, underlying causes of pauperism and crime, from the study of particular instances of misery to the large social forces which press upon the helpless individual and drive him to despair. *From individual to social.*

Every benevolent person is under moral obligations

to work in harmony with others engaged in similar service. The egoistic methods are dissolvents of society. Courtesy, coöperation, the use of a common registration of wants and resources are among the most solemn duties of churches and individual benefactors. The progress of the movement has been impeded by ignorance and misunderstanding, by sectarian animosity and suspicion, by the superstitions of tradition, by the jealousy of relief societies working by antiquated methods, and by the mistakes of inexperienced representatives. But charity organization principles have been tested in the history of this century, and with growing intelligence and fellowship will in due time command the respect and secure the devotion of all philanthropists.

Duty of coöperation.

Mr. George Duruy wrote :

When Dr. Roux began his fight against diphtheria, did he know the remedy for it? No. He said : "Here is a misfortune ; let us seek the means of combating it." Let us do the same with poverty, even while knowing that this old social evil, brother of disease and death, is, like them, eternal. It is no longer possible to accept as an axiom that the fatality of hard economic laws cannot be softened, when other fatalities, such as those of disease and suffering, are receding before the advance of science. . . . Minds suffer more than bodies nowadays. There are no asylums, workhouses, hospitals to appease the torments of envy that rack them nor the thirst for justice that burns them.

Help for the soul.

The charity organization society stands for instant and tender relief of passing need, of kindly and neighborly relations of mutual understanding between rich and poor, and for study of the large social conditions and forces which make for want and sin or for education, purity, health, happiness, and power.

Once each year there meets a national body of charity workers from all fields : members of state boards, state secretaries, friendly visitors, residents of social settlements, pastors, missionaries, trustees of benevolent institutions, and all the noble army of those who toil for the suffering. Their discussions are collected in a volume, and constitute a valuable library for every social student and practical worker for the poor. Not only philanthropists of the United States and Canada, but eminent persons from Europe are heard in these conventions. It is highly desirable that more pastors and other church leaders should become members of this organization whose thoughts and purposes are inspired by the Author of the Glad Tidings, and whose labors illustrate the "program of Christianity."

The National Conference of Charities and Correction.

CHAPTER XVI.

THE SOCIAL SPIRIT IN CONFLICT WITH ANTI-SOCIAL INSTITUTIONS.

HITHERTO we have dealt almost entirely with constructive methods. The best agencies of reform are those which make reformation needless. Right formation is the organic process of giving happiness the field. Medicine and surgery have a small place in the life of normal infants compared with milk, light, fresh air, and room for play. And yet there are evils to fight and there is a call for heroic adventurers and bold pioneers. There is a function even for fanatics and hobby-riders. If they are sane, honest, and pure of life they do disagreeable tasks which fastidious critics will not touch with their little fingers, gloved as they are.

There are so many anti-social customs, traditions, associations, corporations, and institutions that a mere list of them might fill a chapter. Therefore we may select a few contemporary enemies and use them as illustrations of the detestable. Life without healthy hate would be as insipid as fruits without acid. The meekness which the New Testament commends was not embodied in Uriah Heep, but rather in the whip of cords and the invectives against robbers of widows. Oliver Cromwell was a good soldier because he was humble before God. Bismarck declared that the Germans fear God—therefore none other.

We shall not imitate the big poltroon who always selected a dwarf for his attacks and challenges; but we

Food vs. surgery.

Healthy hate.

cast our glove in the face of a giant, the drink evil. What has the social spirit to say and do in presence of this monster? *The drink evil.*

First in order of duty is a study of the history and causes of the drink evil. Impatient declaimers protest against this scientific procedure, and say it is too slow. But there is an increasing number of citizens who are willing to join the sappers and miners since the open assault on the walls has met with indifferent success.

History tells us that we are dealing with an old foe. One of the most conspicuous acts of Saint Noah after the Deluge was to get drunk. It is impossible to tell when men discovered the intoxicating properties of fermented liquids. The religious myths of Asiatic and European peoples ascribed the invention to their rascally gods. When food was coarse and unpalatable, the higher pleasures few and feeble, the nobler interests of life yet undeveloped, it was not strange that animal excitement—war, chase, and drunkenness—should be sought as relief from the monotony of existence.

The exhilaration of wine has been the theme of song and story. The blessings of the grape have been praised in sacred books because the purple fruit made glad the heart and helped the poor to forget for the hour their poverty. Luther lent the sanction of his great name to the moderate indulgence in the use of intoxicants, and the educated men of his race have generally followed him. To this day the medical profession is divided on the question of the physiological value of alcohol, and this division of expert opinion is naturally reflected in the world of the unlearned. Appetite casts its vote in favor of indulgence when doctors differ, and the opinion of a physician who is given to strong drink is open to suspicion. *The voice of antiquity.*

Antiquity has no casting vote.

But history shows not only that evils are old but also that they are evil and that many harmful usages have been overcome. Slavery was old, but not eternal. Despotism was old, but found its conqueror at last. Hoary antiquity cannot make a hurtful custom respectable. The names of saints cannot adorn a sin. Indeed, the very fact that a custom originated with savages excites the inquiry whether it should not be left to savages. The whole question must be decided by modern science and by modern morality. There may be room for dispute about "Bible wines," but we are in presence of a contemporary enemy and must arm ourselves with the latest kind of weapons.

In the shrieking multitude it is hard to make the voice heard above the tumult. Perhaps the best way for us is to turn aside into a quiet place and study what has been offered for consideration. No sane man doubts the evils of drunkenness. Statistics may be ever so exaggerated but, sifted thoroughly, they leave a terrible residuum of suffering and wrong. The tongue of Gough and Father Mathew, the pen of Dickens, the pencil of Hogarth, eloquent as they were, have not been able to set forth the inexpressible, endless tragedy of the drink traffic. Only those who have suffered from the enslaving appetite, or from the insane conduct of its thralls, can ever realize the horrors of rum. Tables of statistics present only commercial considerations, but back of them is the sea of wan faces of the miserable.

History of the temperance movement in America.

The attempt to reform the drinking customs of the people had its origin in the studies of a physician, a patriot, and a philanthropist, chairman of the Committee on Independence in the Continental Congress of 1776— Dr. Benjamin Rush, a name identified with the cause of freedom for white and black. In the year 1785 he published a pamphlet entitled "The Effects of Ardent Spirits on the Human Mind and Body." While the statistics of that early day may be questioned, there is no doubt that the custom of drinking ardent spirits was common, fashionable, and destructive. It was countenanced and practiced by the clergy, and it was the disgraceful exhibitions of hilarity at an ordination which roused the wrath of Dr. Lyman Beecher and moved him to life-long opposition to the evil. *Beginning at Jerusalem.*

The early advocates of temperance usually went no further than moderation in the use of distilled liquors, and the substitution of wine and beer for the more fiery stimulants.

In 1826, "The American Society for the Promotion of Temperance" was organized, which urged total abstinence by educational means, but left liberty of action to the individual and permitted the use of alcohol when advised by a physician.

It was not long before "moral suasion" introduced "legal suasion," since many people had come to believe that the use of alcohol is a violation of moral law, a wrong to society as well as to the individual. In 1838 Massachusetts enacted a law which prohibited the retail sale of spirituous liquors. In 1847 the Supreme Court rendered a decision which has been the foundation of all subsequent legislation. This decision was to the effect that any state which deems the retail and internal traffic in ardent spirits injurious to its citizens, and calculated to produce idleness, vice, or debauchery, may regulate or restrain or prohibit that traffic, if it thinks proper. Later decisions have made clear the right of a state to prohibit not only the retail traffic but even the manufacture of intoxicants, without compensation for loss to former dealers. All modern legislation goes upon the *Legal suasion.*

principle that the liquor traffic, if not absolutely wrong, is at least "extra-hazardous," and in need of exceptionally severe and rigorous regulation, and so not to be treated as a legitimate and honorable business. The Washingtonian Movement, based on moral suasion and the total abstinence pledge, without resort to legal action, swept over many communities after 1840.

Protestants. Gradually the teaching, influence, and practice of Protestant churches have become larger factors in the temperance cause. Sermons, discipline, pastoral advice, resolutions of local and national conventions and representative bodies have been powerful agencies in educating the public and in securing strong laws. It is true that the moderate use of wine and other milder beverages is not universally condemned as a sin, but total abstinence is the ideal, and the minister who "tipples" is apt to topple to his fall in social disgrace.

The Church Temperance Society of the Protestant Episcopal Church seeks to unite all friends of temperance, total abstinence, advocates of moderation, Prohibitionists, and friends of regulation, so far as they can agree upon methods of practical reform.

Roman Catholics. The Roman Catholic Church is in a position of extreme difficulty, owing to the nature of its terms of membership and the heterogeneous composition of its constituency. Many of its members are interested in the liquor business. But there is a respectable number of the clergy who keep alive the honorable fame of Father Mathew. In 1887 the pope wrote a letter to Bishop Ireland which must strengthen the hands of the clergymen and bishops and laymen who are honestly seeking to combat the evils of intemperance, so sore a scourge among the people of that large and influential body of Christians. The Catholic Total Abstinence Union of

America was founded in 1872, and while it refrains from political action it is a very important agency of education in the principles of temperance. The same may be said of the charitable Society of St. Vincent of Paul.

The National Temperance Society and Publication House was organized in 1865 and is pledged to promote "total abstinence for the individual and total prohibition for the state." It has issued papers and books by the million; sent missionaries among the freedmen; sought to urge inquiries and legislation at Washington and at state capitals; held conferences and conventions in all parts of the country; promoted the introduction of temperance publications in public schools and into prisons, jails, shops, hospitals, and needy localities; and has sent volumes of temperance information to colored pastors in the South. National Temperance Society.

The Independent Order of Good Templars started upon its career in 1851. Its members are pledged to practice total abstinence; to work for prohibition and for all suitable methods of restricting the evils of alcohol. Women are admitted to membership and office on equality with men. The order has enlisted millions of members and has started many youth in the path of a sober life, and with deep convictions upon the subject of the immorality of intemperance. Good Templars.

The Sons of Temperance was organized in 1842, and its purposes are expressed in the records: "To shield its members from the evils of intemperance; to afford mutual assistance in case of sickness, and to elevate their characters as men." "The Temple of Honor," with its ritual and symbolism, has made successful appeal to those whose imagination sought gratification in the mysteries and allegories of ceremony. Mention of other less conspicuous societies must be omitted. Sons of Temperance.

Enforcement of law.

Various societies for the enforcement of existing laws have been formed from time to time, of which the Citizens' Law and Order League may be taken as a type. It was found that the best laws are neglected unless the officials are steadily reminded and urged to do their duty. The dealers in intoxicants naturally resist the restrictive measures, and will violate the laws unless there is a steady pressure of public opinion. The motto of the league was "We ask only obedience to law" and the watchword was "Save the boys." The Anti-Saloon League has a similar object.

The W. C. T. U.

It is natural that women should be deeply interested in the temperance cause. If there are any physical or financial benefits in the drink traffic they get none of these. The burdens of misery are borne by the innocent. American women, as a rule, are total abstainers, but they are great sufferers from the drinking habits of the "lords of creation."

The Crusade.

The Temperance Crusade which spread over the Central States from Ohio was an outburst of woman's moral indignation against the destroyers of her peace and her hope, against the enemies of her home. Without a voice in the election of magistrates or in the making of laws these women appealed to God and to conscience. They entered saloons and drug stores, or watched, prayed, and sang hymns in the street. Some said they were inspired prophetesses; some called them fanatics and fools. The enthusiasm in that form could not last; but it gave birth to a permanent society of women whose doctrine was thus stated:

> Woman is ordained to lead the vanguard of this great movement, until the American public is borne across the abysmal transition from the superstitious notion that alcohol is food to the scientific fact that "alcohol is poison," from the pusillani-

mous concession that intemperance is a great evil to the responsible conviction that the liquor traffic is a crime.

The Woman's National Christian Temperance Union, at present the most conspicuous organization in the temperance movement, was organized in Cleveland, Ohio, in 1874. Its headquarters are in Chicago, where the society owns a splendid building, The Temple, which cost $1,200,000. This society has comprehended the many elements which enter into the problem, and has seen that the evil must be attacked in its causes. Because the leaders saw that ignorance of the physical effects of alcohol aggravated the danger they have persistently sought to introduce instruction on the subject in the public schools, in Sunday-schools, families, and in all kinds of publications. Having observed the deleterious effects of nicotine poison on growing boys, they have worked successfully to secure laws prohibiting the sale of cigarettes and other forms of tobacco to minors. They have established industrial homes for girls, and caused the "age of consent" to be raised. The titles of the heads of department will illustrate the breadth of the movement and the largeness of view of the founders: Preventive, Educational, Evangelistic, Social, Legal, Organization. *Aims and methods.*

Miss Frances E. Willard, founder and for five years president of the World's Woman's Christian Temperance Union, has been for fifteen years president of the general society for the United States. She is the author of the motto so characteristic of the motives of good women everywhere: "For God and Home and Native Land"—religion, maternal and sisterly devotion, and high patriotism. *Miss Willard.*

A great publishing house, the Woman's Temperance Publication Association, founded by Mrs. Matilda B.

Carse in 1880, prepares and issues all kinds of publications for the advancement of the objects of the society.

An interesting experiment in the treatment of disease without alcohol is found in the National Temperance Hospital. The work of oral teaching is organized by the Women's Lecture Bureau. An auxiliary of considerable influence is the Young Women's Branch, which seeks to acquire and disseminate information, to work for children and youth, and to turn social influence and custom in favor of temperance and purity.

Social purity. The social purity reform is carried out in organic connection with the crusade against alcohol, since these noble women are teaching in all its applications the fundamental religious view that the body is the temple of the Holy Spirit and should not be defiled by drunkenness, lust, poisons, drugs, or any uncleanness. The influence of an instructed multitude of mothers working by all means, and especially at home, is beyond calculation. It is claimed that "scientific temperance instruction" is given in all but four states and that 16,000,000 children have been brought under this instruction; 10,000 have been enrolled in Bands of Mercy, and thousands more in Loyal Temperance Legions and Anti-Cigarette Leagues. Millions of pages of temperance literature have been distributed and striking advance has been made in the suppression of obscene literature.

Woman suffrage and prohibition. The organization is committed to woman suffrage and to a prohibitory legal policy. The most extravagant language of eulogy cannot express the obligation of the world to these devoted and able women so well as a simple record of their achievements, whose story is told in the annual reports and occasional summaries.

A cable of many strands is far stronger than a rod of

the same diameter. We are not shut up to a single mode of attack; artillery, infantry, cavalry, and starvation are all military forces which a skilful general will use according to circumstances. The members of society who realize the perils of the use of alcohol as a beverage have as their allies education, transformation of customs, and governmental control. In fact, a reform must necessarily proceed to develop itself in this order, until all available troops move in a single mass.

Methods of dealing with the drink evil.

If we could only get the doctors and physiologists to move harmoniously there would be a shorter campaign. Some of the experts are pronounced abstainers and declare that even as medicine alcohol has no use. Many others assert that alcoholic beverages may be used as medicines in sickness or with advantage even in health. All recognize the dangers of excessive use of stimulants, and it is only on this statement that we can honestly and truthfully claim a consensus of medical authority.

Education.

Certain it is that educational methods have made immense progress during the century. It is desirable to apprehend clearly just what "moral suasion" has achieved, because there is a strong tendency among many temperance advocates to lose faith in it, to undervalue appeals to reason and experience, in order to prove the necessity of legislation. Moral suasion first raised up a company of reformers and changed beliefs and family customs for hundreds of thousands of people. Reason, instruction, and persuasion induced multitudes of people to become more careful and moderate in their use of stimulants; then followed the total abstinence movement, and later still the effort to restrict or prohibit the traffic in liquors. Beliefs are the primary social forces, and so long as the people had no con-

Success of educational methods.

victions as to the physical and moral perils of alcoholic beverages they would not modify either custom or law. And beliefs must always sustain a reform after it has been once accepted. Teaching goes deeper than law and human penalties.

The public schools. For this reason it is wise to introduce instruction in the public schools, in connection with the teaching of human anatomy, physiology, hygiene, and sanitation, in respect to the effect of alcohol, tobacco, and other poisons, upon the various tissues and organs of the body. Moral and religious sanctions enforce the laws of health. Ethics learns of physiology and then issues commands to conscience.

Allies of the temperance reform. Perhaps legislation will be found to be only a subordinate factor in the promotion of temperance. Economic changes are going forward in connection with machine industry, the factory system, and modern transportation which will make drunkenness simply impossible. So long as a man worked by himself, at his own bench, with his own tools, he might get drunk without serious disturbance of industry. That condition belongs to the past. We are not under the reign of individualism, but of increasing collectivism.

Steady brains wanted. One of the chief railroad corporations in the world, the Pennsylvania, carries out, with great strictness, its regulation as to the use of intoxicating drinks by its employees. Every one violating the rule is dismissed. This is a matter not of sentiment but of pure, hard business. The company dare not intrust its great property and its daily freight of human lives to men who are liable to be deprived of their reason, the steadiness of whose nerves has been unsettled. A drink of whisky or a glass of beer may bring on a catastrophe costing enormously in life and money. In all this the company acts with that wise business judgment which has brought its success. Our great employers of labor have learned the same lesson. The proprietor of a shipbuilding yard said, "Many of our men are worth little for an hour or two of the afternoon, because of the beer which they have taken at their lunch." Another employer said, "That man used to earn $5 a day. He was richly worth it, we were glad to pay it; but drink gradually impaired the accuracy of his eye, the steadiness of his nerves, the delicacy of his touch; and now we can give him only a dollar a day, and he is hardly worth that." Not even to moderate drinkers can safely be intrusted the building of ships, on whose exact and faithful construction will depend the safety of the ship in the hour of storm and the honor of the nation in the hour of battle.

Most men want life insurance. But the insurance companies require medical examinations and these examinations tend to grow more careful and thorough. The "tobacco heart," the alcoholic pulse and skin, and the beery bloat stand in the way of securing a policy. Mutual benefit societies, trades unions, and all such organizations are learning to enforce sobriety whenever common interests suffer from the unreliable conduct of the drunkard. *Life insurance.*

Fashion has changed. Wine is used by many people "in society," but not by all, and intoxication is a social disgrace. Total abstinence is no longer regarded anywhere as a bar to good-fellowship. Woman's influence is steadily rising all over the civilized world, and it is usually favorable to temperance, if not always to total abstinence. *Fashion.*

Prohibition in actual practice, and apart from pure theory, is simply another method of regulating drinking

Legislation; prohibitory laws.

customs. The appetite for stimulants, the organic cravings for excitement, remain and they manifest themselves. The passion for stimulants is so imperious and general in all European people that it demands satisfaction and calls into existence a body of dealers interested in the business of selling alcoholic drinks. The physical craving thus forms a partnership or a conspiracy with motives of gain, and these two forces enlist all the resources of craving to evade the provisions of law. In many communities, where the use of beer and wine is believed to be innocent, there is a moral revolt against what the people sincerely regard an infringement of freedom. Under such conditions prohibition does not destroy the business but modifies and restricts it in various degrees, not without some undesirable consequences.

On one side it may fairly be claimed that where the great majority of the population have long lived in America, where cities are few and small, and where agitation has led the majority to regard the use of ardent spirits as a moral evil, a prohibitory law may be so enforced as to keep the traffic actually away from some districts and to compel it to hide in large towns. Whether the law really diminishes drunkenness is difficult to affirm because the law is only one of the educative agencies at work in such states. The dark side of the picture ought not to be concealed in our reformatory zeal. Many candid and well-informed witnesses declare that prohibition intensifies the vices of deception, fraud, perjury, social animosity, contempt for legal authority, corruption of courts and juries.

Local option.

One way of introducing prohibition is through the local option law which prevails in some states. In favor of this system it is urged that when the commonwealth cannot be brought to enact and enforce a prohibitory policy it ought to permit a community which desires to do so to protect itself against an institution which is hateful to the majority of the people. The best traditions of our national history are favorable to town democracy. But this method has a narrow field of usefulness. A town may vote "no license" and yet be abundantly supplied by a city just over a bridge. Some policy at least as wide as a state is demanded, for the evil is national in extent and power.

In some states the fundamental law or the public opinion will not tolerate legal recognition of the drink traffic so far as to give a license; but when a citizen actually ventures to set up his shop the state compels him to pay an annual fine. The motives for this legislation are mixed, but the central and avowed purpose is to hamper and restrict trade which the people cannot at once extinguish. *Mulct laws.*

Assuming that the license system is accepted by a commonwealth as, on the whole, the most satisfactory legal system of regulating a traffic which it is thought impossible to suppress, the problem of specific measures still remains. In the conclusions of an important recent study President Eliot makes several practical suggestions. Licenses should not be granted for more than one year. Under favorable circumstances the law which restricts the number of saloons by the population, as one saloon to 500 or 1,000 inhabitants, has been found to limit the open places of temptation. He commends the law which forbids the presence of a saloon within 500 feet of a public park, or within a short distance of a schoolhouse. In some cities the saloons are confined to the business portion and thus kept at a distance from the residences. All this educates the people to regard *License laws.*

the saloon as a menace of all good and to become accustomed to the idea of abolishing it altogether.

Desirable restrictions.

President Eliot summarizes the general restrictions which should be sought as follows : There should be no selling to minors, intoxicated persons, or habitual drunkards. There should be no selling on holidays, when multitudes are idle. Places of entertainment must not be permitted to sell liquor, and no games or sport of any sort should be tolerated in saloons. The place of sale should be open to inspection from the street, so that the force of public opinion may be fully felt by customers and dealers.

Government ownership.

The experiment with the "dispensary" system in South Carolina compels public study of the principle of direct government control of the liquor traffic. The results of the study of the "Committee of Fifty," however, do not indicate that the principle has yet had a fair trial in the Southern States, or in any other in this country. The chief reason for direct control of the traffic by the government is that this will remove the motive of private gain. But so long as the salaries of agents rise and fall with the amount of patronage, so long this principal object will be defeated.

Growth of the liquor traffic in America.

All these plans have been tried and the custom of drinking has, apparently, grown in America. The influence of immigrants from beer-drinking countries has had its effect. In 1850 the consumption of all kinds of liquors averaged 4.08 gallons per inhabitant ; in 1892 it was 17.04 gallons. During this period the consumption of spirits diminished from 2¼ to 1½ gallons per head, but beer-drinking advanced from 1.58 to 15.10 gallons per head of population. Wine-drinking increased slightly, from 0.27 to 0.44 gallons per head. (Professor Gould.)

In sheer despair of enforcing a prohibitory law, and in moral revolt against license system, many friends of temperance are considering the Scandinavian system, not with the expectation of imitating it, but in hope of learning something from it. The essential elements of this system have been carefully studied and stated by Professor E. R. L. Gould, Mr. J. G. Brooks, Mr. John Koren, and others, and they have strongly urged it for adoption. The Gothenburg system.

A few years ago a bill was introduced into the legislature of Massachusetts authorizing towns to adopt the "Norwegian System," and the measure was defeated chiefly by the liquor interest, by a single vote. It provided that a town might vote to license companies, not more than one to each city or town, under certain regulations. All hope of profits is cut off by the provision that after five per cent interest has been paid on capital the profits shall go to the aid of objects of general public benefit and utility, as industrial education, coffee-houses and reading rooms, parks, hospitals, public baths, and sanitary improvements.

On the basis of Scandinavian experience it is claimed that such a measure would work educationally in the direction of the extinction of the traffic. No individual is interested in the profits of the business. The state or the town does not, as in the South Carolina law, have a direct profit from the sale. Civil service rules govern the employees and the entire affair is kept out of politics. No liquor is sold to minors and drunkards, because there is no motive to push the sale. It is easy to enforce the restrictions as to hours of closing. It is an essential part of the plan that in evenings halls must be provided for the resort of working people, places for labor exchange and entertainment, where alcoholic Its elements.

drinks are unknown. Gambling, loafing, impure literature, and immoral exhibitions are excluded. Distillers and brewers no longer control the saloon as they do in America, and powerful whisky rings, with corruption funds and lobbyists working upon the electorate and upon legislatures, are banished.

Mrs. Mary A. Livermore represents the rational attitude of Prohibitionists toward this reform :

Testimonies.

First, last, and always, I am a Prohibitionist, and I favor the Norwegian Bill, because, if rightly understood, its tendency will be toward prohibition, and if our good temperance people would carefully study the bill I think their objections would disappear.

And the testimony of Mr. Gould will have weight with all who know him and his valuable studies of social conditions in Europe and America :

I undertook a mission for the United States Department of Labor to Sweden and Norway, for the purpose of studying and reporting upon the methods of controlling the liquor traffic adopted by those countries. I went there absolutely without prejudice of any sort; I came away a convert to the system. . . . It is a measure of progressive reform, sound in principle, operating harmoniously with well-defined laws of social advance. . . . Its trial will do more than anything else yet suggested to mitigate an intolerable social curse.

The Humane Society.

In the present imperfect condition of human nature the Humane Society for the protection of dumb animals and of little children from cruelty of thoughtless and unfeeling men is a social necessity. There remain in our civilized communities stray savages, "relics" of primitive man, who have not yet realized the meaning of the age, who have not learned that animals have rights and that sentient beings have nerves. We cannot permit these dwarfed natures to act out their impulses any more than we can open the tiger cages of menageries. Sympathy which does not defend the speechless lacks something of meeting the moral claims of this century. The law of the Pentateuch gave the beasts of burden a day of rest, and modern cities have not yet fully attained the level of the best humanity. The local society should secure suitable ordinances and regulations, have agents to prosecute persons guilty of cruelty, educate children in chivalry and kindness, and provide means of securing to horses, cattle, and pets reasonable treatment. The reactive influence of this social movement is seen in gentle manners in home and school, in kinder treatment of employees, and in more genial customs of street and assembly.

The most radical reforms are those which touch the domestic circle. In this connection it is a pleasure to mention one of the most efficient and praiseworthy organizations of our age—The National Divorce Reform League, of which Rev. S. W. Dike, D.D., Auburndale, Massachusetts, is permanent secretary. *The National Divorce Reform League.*

The moral disintegration of the family by conflict, strife, cruelty, and divorce is far more sad and ruinous than the sudden and premature dissolution by the death of parents. Divorces have been increasing in this country at an appalling rate. The statistical exhibit, although unfairly compared with European tables, is, on the best interpretation, enough to make us tremble for our country and our civilization. After all mitigating considerations are urged we must acknowledge that our nation is seriously in danger of general degradation of the marital relation.

The Divorce Reform League was formed to resist these demoralizing forces. It has proceeded upon these lines of work — investigation, publication, education, legislation, and watching the administration of laws *Its method.*

affecting the family. It was largely due to the efforts of this society that the United States government, through the Labor Bureau, compiled a monumental report on divorces and divorce legislation, and has passed uniform regulations on the subject for the territories. It is no longer thought wise to urge an amendment to the constitution authorizing Congress to pass a uniform law for all the states, since this would consume many years and, probably, not secure progress. The league is successfully urging the legislatures to raise the standards and improve the laws respecting marriage and divorce.

The secretary. The secretary has rendered a valuable national service by writing and lecturing, and directing public thought and action. He constantly urges the preparation of records and the collection of statistics of births, marriages, and divorces. He shows the connection between demoralized homes and the increase of juvenile crime. He makes an impressive statement of the fact that parents are the persons primarily responsible for habits of intemperance, and that the home must be made the chief organ of temperance reform. It is to the family more than to school or law that he must look for the most effective influences relating to the control and regulation of the physical appetites, and the conquest of the vices which attend their perversion. He concentrates public attention on the family as the primary institution for cultivating social impulses, for holding and distributing property, for training in good citizenship, for the most fundamental educational work, and for keeping alive the deepest interest in religious knowledge

Scope enlarged. and worship. The name of the society, as all agree, should be changed to correspond to the larger and more positive program of action. Every church should subscribe at least five dollars and make the pastor or some other person a local member of the league. The society could make excellent use of a much larger income than it now enjoys from all sources. The annual reports, which are sent to all members, are important contributions to the literature of divorce reform and domestic amelioration.

The most efficient instrument of reforms relating to chastity is the family. The newspaper, the lecture, the sermon cannot discuss the subject very far without doing more harm than good. All that can be said directly should be told youth, at the proper time, by the parents; and all that is necessary can be learned from such a book as Martin's "The Human Body," and, for younger minds, Margaret W. Morley's "A Song of Life." *Social purity.*

As there are mothers who have not the high ideals or the scientific knowledge which prepare them for this teaching function it has been found useful to hold "Mothers' Meetings" as normal schools of domestic morality. Pure-minded matrons have, in these assemblies, an opportunity to reach hundreds of children through the mothers.

The legislative measures for restricting the evils of impurity cannot be adequately treated here. But some elements of law must be mentioned: all pictures, gestures, exhibitions, and newspaper articles or advertisements which are unfit for children to see should be at least driven out of sight. Young girls exposed to danger should be at once removed from the vicious neighborhood. The corrupters of youth should be hunted down and punished to the utmost limit of severity. *Legislation.*

After all, there is no security save in a purity which is intelligent and not mere innocent ignorance; in lofty ideals, splendid ambitions, useful occupation, reverence for woman next to God, and a devotion to the welfare of society which makes the soul shrink from anti-social acts as from leprosy.

Gambling. The vice of gambling can boast antiquity as great as that of drunkenness. With multitudes of men it is a passion absolutely independent of the liquor habit, and pitilessly consumes them like a fever. Public gambling can be suppressed by the police, if there is a strong local demand for it. The laws are usually sufficient for this purpose. Happily the lottery is not intrenched in national law and custom in the United States as it is in France and Germany. The recent victories of reformers over the lottery companies ought to be remembered in hours of discouragement when temporary defeat has befallen the leaders of other reforms. Every such gain makes the next advance more promising. Slavery is dead. The lottery is dead. Next!

Sunday rest. All other reforms depend greatly on Sabbath customs. A general and profound change of belief has taken place in American thought on this subject during this century. The New England Sabbath is no longer possible or desirable. The legitimate interests of human life are too varied to justify the use of one day in seven precisely as our New England ancestors occupied its hours. The modern system of industry and transportation has compelled the town to feel daily the life of the nation and of the world. The tide of foreign immigration has brought among us millions of honest and religious people who hold with the cardinals and Luther, not with Calvin, in respect to the observance of the Lord's Day. To ignore these considerations is to waste life on a chimera.

Experience proves that we can secure a day of rest on the Lord's Day by law. Ordinary industry can be suspended, not absolutely but within reasonable limits, and all employees can be secured thirty-six hours some time in each week in all occupations. On this platform we can unite all parties.

Function of law.

But a day of rest from ordinary occupations is an opportunity, not an achievement. When the one demon of grinding toil has been expelled and the house swept and garnished, seven devils are waiting to enter, unless the good genius of the place has invited a house full of good company. Puritanism has much to answer for in diffusing abroad in this country a general impression that Sunday must be a day of boredom and misery, in which diversion is a sin.

Sunday reformers have not reached even the middle of their social task when they have released the city multitudes from the shop and closed the saloon. The question of what can be done with twelve hours of idle time once a week for 70,000,000 of people is one of the most tremendous problems of our age. Church-going cannot meet the need. The ministry cannot have the monopoly of Sunday. Culture requires many specialized agencies. If we assume merely a negative attitude, and are repressive and prohibitive in our methods, we shall appear to be the enemies of joy and health in the eyes of millions, and we shall misrepresent the Lord of the Sabbath.

Diversity of Sunday thoughts.

The English custom of having for weary people a "Pleasant Sunday Afternoon" has been introduced into this country, and it is an example of the positive and beneficent method of reform by displacement. Bright music is the chief element in these meetings. Pictures, cheerful talks, instructive addresses, readings

"Pleasant Sunday Afternoon."

from the best literature, social converse, a cup of tea, the sympathetic hearing of grievances and troubles and wrongs, hints of a practical way out—all within one glad and inspiring hour—that is a "Pleasant Sunday Afternoon." It is the Beatitudes of the Sermon on the Mount which makes the prohibition of Sinai unnecessary. A lamp will drive out darkness where a club of knotted oak would make no impression.

Needs of workingmen.

Jesus *vs.* the Pharisees.

The great masses of workingmen are honest and have good purposes. They crave recreation. They will have it and they ought to have it. Cramped muscles and repressed faculties cry out in agony for something different from the monotony of the bench and the furrow. We know what Jesus said of those Pharisaic religionists who were shocked at his doing good on the Sabbath day. His example is still before us. If our ministers and deacons would just leave their fine churches a few Sundays, and move around among the workingmen and rude boys whose homes are absolutely without attractions, they would often gain a new notion of the best way to spend Sunday. The "European Sunday" has many bad features, but the Puritan Sunday at the other extreme is from the standpoint of health, knowledge, beauty, and social order an ideal whose realization would bring national decay. What social welfare requires is neither the Puritan, the Pharisaic, nor the libertine's Sunday, but the Lord's Day, which was "made for man"; a day so sweet, so calm, so joyous, so full of all beauty in song and picture and story, that the weary millions who have known its pleasures will bless the Giver for its ever-welcome hours. Here and there we find the beginnings of some efforts to realize these dawning ideas. But the paralysis, the superstition, and the apathy of tradition and custom restrict our freedom of invention and experiment. Meantime to the multitudes who might be helped Sunday is an unmitigated curse, the occasion of all the debauchery which must go with idleness, and from revolt against a social order which presents many frowns but few smiles. We have as a Christian people yet to learn that joy and hope are better regenerative agencies than scolding and tears.

A redeemed Sunday.

CHAPTER XVII.

THE INSTITUTIONS OF IDEALS: THE ANCIENT CONFEDERACY OF VIRTUE.

J. R. LOWELL not only explained the interior impulses of the anti-slavery movement, but the inspiration of all life-giving enterprises, when he wrote:

<small>Christianity the mainspring of progress.</small>

It is not partisanship, it is not fanaticism, that has forced this matter of anti-slavery upon this American people, it is the spirit of Christianity, which appeals from prejudices and predilections to the moral consciousness of the individual man; that spirit as elastic as air, penetrative as heat, invulnerable as sunshine, against which creed after creed and institution after institution have measured their strength and been confounded; that restless spirit which refuses to crystallize in any sect or form, but persists, a divinely commissioned radical and reconstructor, in trying every generation with a new dilemma between ease and interest on the one hand, and duty on the other. . . . Shall it be said that its kingdom is not of this world? In one sense, and that the highest, it certainly is not; but just as certainly Christ never intended those words to be used as a subterfuge by which to escape our responsibilities of business and politics.

<small>Relation of the churches to Christianity.</small>

Christianity is the life of the Eternal Word in the souls of men, and it thrives and blossoms everywhere. Its clusters of fruit hang by all highways, its springs well up by every path. It can use any institution. Its sky arches over all peoples and kingdoms. It is the moral atmosphere of every living soul. It is the light of every man that cometh into the world. But the church is that human institution whose avowed and conscious purpose it is to teach the highest truth, to keep alive the ethical conscience, to awaken the spiritual faculties, to be a living witness by word and deed of the indwelling Christ. The church is not to be identified with the perfected kingdom of God, but it is the chief instrument of establishing that blessed reign.

Assuming that man is naturally a religious being, as he is naturally a musical being, a social being, a reasoning creature—then the church is a legitimate institution. It is not imposed on man, but grows out of man's needs and cravings. It expresses, manifests, and cultivates faculties which are necessary to human completeness, to perfect joy, to rich life. Man is not entirely man till he is "born again," that is, until out of self-consciousness, æsthetic consciousness, moral consciousness, has developed a God-consciousness, a sense of dependence on and relation to the Invisible, an obligation to the Eternal Righteousness, a grateful and loving response to Infinite Goodness. The family exists because it expresses certain needs of human life, and it persists through the centuries because it is the most suitable institution for its purposes. The galleries and schools of art have come into being because there is in humanity a taste for beauty. Academies and colleges spring up because man has a divinely implanted desire to learn and comprehend. Court-houses and legal systems are developed out of the human sense of justice and social requirements of order. The church, in a similar way, has come to exist because man is a creature who holds commerce with the sky; because he has infinite wants and loves and hopes. All social institutions are human, since they manifest human desires, and all are divine because the universe is a manifestation of that mysterious will "we so much wish yet dread to learn."

The church a natural growth.

The manifestation of religious life.

The specific function of the church.

If the church did nothing else but minister to the religious wants of man its existence would be socially justifiable. Religion has created a magnificent literature of poetry, philosophy, oratory, sacred sentences of wisdom, maxims, and suggestions of unbounded realms of spiritual heritage. It is in the church that men discover a freedom, an expansion, an enfranchisement which are denied them amidst the petty cares and trivial occupations of street and shop. This "literature of power" lives long after the "literature of knowledge" has become antiquated. Scientific treatises are soon pushed aside by recent discoveries, but the Psalms, the orations of Isaiah, the Sermon on the Mount, the letters of Paul, have undying influence.

Religion has not only a literature, but an art. Its architecture is most sublime; its "storied windows richly dight" are glorious with color and sacred memories; its symbolism suggests ineffable themes; its rites bind centuries to eternity, and the living with the mighty dead; its poetry, heroic and lyric, carries on its broad current the aspirations of the race; its music of anthems, hymns, songs, psalms, and oratorios is, of itself, worth one day in seven to hear and enjoy.

Social works of the church.

But the church does not and cannot minister to the religious wants of men without affecting all life. When its bells chime out to summon the devout to prayer, a hush falls on wheels and hammers, and the solemn vibrations influence every calling. It is this "social work" of the church which is the particular theme of this closing chapter, and especially the forms taken by that work in the United States. When we raise trees for fruit we also, incidentally, have grateful shade and beautiful flowers. So the indirect influences of the church are inseparable from its direct work. These institutions thus created by the religious energies of benevolence and justice are too numerous to be tabulated or described. Some of the most significant forms must be selected as types of a remarkable and growing movement of our age.

If we make a survey of human misery and trouble, of social wrongs and evils, of aspirations and growing desires, we shall discover that the churches of America are already attempting to minister in every direction, either directly or by means of agencies which they control. *Analysis of social needs.*

In the United States the care of defectives is chiefly intrusted to the state. In all commonwealths may be found special institutions for the insane, and usually for the blind and for deaf mutes. With the growth of intelligent charity all feeble-minded children are being gathered in schools and farm-homes by public authorities. Counties and towns provide asylums for aged and imbecile persons. The churches occasionally hold services in these institutions, and the attitude of the officers to religious visitors is usually very friendly. For prisons chaplains are sometimes employed at the expense of the public. *Defectives.*

Hospitals, general and special, are established in many ways, sometimes by taxation, but often by associations which represent a denomination or the people of several denominations in coöperation. These associations receive contributions from citizens generally, and where they are not connected with a particular sect but little notice is taken of the creed of the governing body. It is generally understood, however, that the boards of directors or trustees are chosen from the various Christian societies in order to secure funds and to maintain an unsectarian control. *Care of the sick.*

Poor relief.

The same thing is true of other forms of relief. Day nurseries, benevolent societies for assisting poor families in their homes, lodging-houses for homeless men, emergency relief, districts of associated charities, are frequently sustained by united efforts of many churches.

Mutual benefit associations.

The fraternal societies of wage-earners who accumulate funds for assistance in case of sickness, accident, non-employment, and burials, are not usually connected with any denomination among Protestants. These friendly societies, however, almost uniformly have religious rituals, and the members call each other "brother," a custom which has become less common in the churches, especially of cities. The Roman Catholics, however, have mutual benefit societies entirely composed of communicants of that body, and those societies are very strong in numbers and income. Very powerful organizations for friendly help exist among the Jews.

The reform societies.

The associations for social reforms, mentioned in the preceding chapter, have no organic relation to the church except those specifically named as under the supervision of the Roman Catholic, the Lutheran, or Protestant Episcopal Church. And yet the advocates of temperance, of social purity, of protection of animals and children from cruelty, for the suppression of the lottery and gambling, and all unmoral customs, seek and find in the churches an audience and following. The pulpit and the denominational newspapers are the most independent and outspoken advocates of many reforms when political motives make the secular newspaper either dumb or antagonistic.

Modes of organization.

Perhaps the following are the most common and characteristic methods of organizing religious people for social service in the United States: the local church, the denominational mission society, the incorporated association composed of members of all churches, the national young people's societies, orders, or sisterhoods, and coördinating agencies of integration.

It has been found by experience that the work of a local church, planted in a community, should minister to the whole complex nature of human beings. It seems certain that the wonderful success of the Young Men's Christian Association has had much to do with the recent and remarkable modifications of local church service, especially in the crowded parts of cities, where home life is so meager and the conditions of existence are so trying. *The open or institutional church.*

Without any sort of agreement or general plan, simply in response to local demands, many pastors and churches have undertaken various forms of ministry to their neighbors and constituency. Within a few years the principal aims and motives of these churches have found distinct expression and formulation in the manifesto of the "Open and Institutional Church League."

The open and institutional church depends upon the development of a certain spirit, rather than upon the aggregation of special appliances and methods. *Platform of the Open and Institutional Church League.*

Inasmuch as Christ came not to be ministered unto, but to minister, the open and institutional church, filled and moved by his spirit of ministering love, seeks to become the center and source of all beneficent and philanthropic effort, and to take the leading part in every movement which has for its end the alleviation of human suffering, the elevation of man, and the betterment of the world.

Thus the open and institutional church is known by its spirit of ministration rather than by any specific methods of expressing that spirit; it stands for open church doors for every day and all the day, free seats, a plurality of Christian workers, the personal activity of all church members, a ministry to all the community through educational, reformatory, and philanthropic channels, to the end that men may be won to Christ and his service, that the church may be brought back to the simplicity and comprehensiveness of its primitive life, until it can be said of every community, "The Kingdom of Heaven is within you" and "Christ is all and in all."

Methods of the institutional church.

It is almost dangerous to describe the external machinery and appliances of a modern institutional church, because people are sorely tempted to copy the form while they miss the spirit and aim of the movement. This is fatal to genuine life, and all slavish imitation produces reaction and disgust. It should be remembered that all really useful churches of this type have slowly grown into their present forms; that they have carefully studied the physical, educational, moral, and religious needs of the parish and then sought the most direct and inexpensive method of meeting the demand. No two of these churches are alike. There is a wonderful variety in their plans. Let us select a few illustrations of devices and explain them by the social conditions surrounding the urban churches. In order to make a somewhat systematic presentation we must select and put together features of several well-known societies.

The ministry of health.

An intelligent and practical pastor finds his lot of duty cast in a neighborhood where the rate of mortality, especially among infants, is very high. As he visits the people and becomes intimate with their life and habits he discovers the causes. In college he was trained in modern physical science, and his powers of observation and reasoning are acute. Knowledge burdens him with a sense of responsibility. He dare not ascribe to "Providence" the disease, misery, and mourning which he knows are due to ignorance, crowding, bad cooking, decayed food, bacteria, filth, and darkness. A medieval monk, with a purely classical culture, would not have thought of these things; but a modern pastor has at least a smattering of chemistry and microscopy, and his conscience has modern contents.

If the city did its duty, perhaps, or the state, these evils would not exist. Meantime this knight of the nineteenth century must fight alone against darkness and disease. The babies are fed impure milk. He and his wife know about Pasteurized milk and they supply it. There are no bathrooms in the houses, and the stench of unwashed bodies and bedding is shocking to the visitors. What can be done? Wait for the slow action of a municipality? No. There is a room in the church basement which, with a little expense, can be fitted up with spray baths for ten or twenty persons at a time, and the pennies paid will almost meet the expense. The clerks and factory hands suffer from cramped positions and confinement. They need a gymnasium. They cannot afford to go to a swell club. It is easy to set the chairs aside in the prayer-meeting room and have dumb-bells and Indian clubs ready for use. Boxing and wrestling do not require much apparatus, and a room can soon be cleared for developing athletes. *Methods.*

The boys are in danger of physical and moral ruin unless they have suitable physical drill. There is a young man who has belonged to a military company, knows the manual of arms, and is pining for a field of usefulness. He will turn agnostic in six months if he merely listens to sermons and psalms. Give him the mission of saving twenty boys in a brigade and he works out his own salvation, even without fear and trembling.

This pastor discovers that poor women in his parish are begging because young children keep them all day from work. He has heard of the crêche, named origi- *Care of children.*

Bethlehem cradle.

nally from the Bethlehem manger crib, and he asks some of his well-to-do friends to rent a room, hire a nurse, and provide care for these infants whose mothers are obliged to go out to wash or weave during the day. Thus the baby's life is saved, the family is preserved from pauperism, and the mother is taught the scientific care of infants.

Some of the little fellows, between the ages of three and six years, are proper subjects for a kindergarten, but this is a luxury for rich folks. Not so. A wealthy lady is glad to furnish a room. A circle of King's Daughters in an uptown fashionable church will pay the salary of a teacher out of their pin-money. The thing is done. The poor children enjoy the luxury of the rich. Father Froebel comes to make them turn work into play and learning into song. Pianos are cheap, and the young souls are developed into musical critics. Harsh noises come to be disagreeable to them. They learn that a gentle voice is an excellent thing. Weary fathers are refreshed and delighted in the evening to hear the simple sweet melodies learned in the children's garden. Christian teachers have cunningly woven into the poetry a canticle of the glad tidings, and the midgets become missionaries to drinking fathers. Purgatory is driven back by song.

Industrial training.

The girls do not know how to sew and darn and mend. Will this pastor wait for an angel or a school board to instruct them? Rather will he bring an angel from some earthly mansion, some young people's society, to teach these eager girls the useful arts. And what does this signify? Garments are more tidy, habits of order prevail, the earnings of the father are doubled in purchasing power. At the same time the girls learn beautiful songs; they see the gracious and refined manners of the young ladies; they imitate the gentle ways; they discover that wealth is not heartless, that the good God has not forgotten them.

Then come the cooking schools. They are not a luxury, but rather a necessity. These people are fresh from Italy and do not know how to prepare American foods. There are some from Ireland, and many Americans who are in a similar plight. In a few years those same girls will respond to our advertisements for domestic help, for cooks, and they will come asking the wages of experts. Let us help them in their own neighborhoods, for their own sake and for ours. The institutional church, finding no provision for this social want, opens another room in the basement, employs a teacher, and she proclaims a gospel of healthy diet, with all other gospel which a wise Christian woman carries along with her, whatever she is doing.

Cooking schools.

The poor are like the rich—they will save if it is not too inconvenient. The pastor sees boys "shooting craps," making themselves gamblers. His daily walks and talks reveal a thousand wastes where waste means woe. There is no penny postal system in this country —more's the pity! Even if we had a postal savings bank these people would not form a habit of going to it without tuition. The institutional church opens a penny provident fund. It collects the pennies of the children. Its visitors go from house to house preaching the doctrine of Benjamin Franklin's "Poor Richard." New habits of thrift are formed, and the foundations of independence are laid.

Economic devices.

We may use an English example of what many pastors could do in America. In a small town like Berkhamsted, in Hertfordshire, a distributive union of 330 families already own, after a few years' effort, a joint

Popular banking.

capital of £3,000 ($15,000). At the village of Childe Okeford, in Dorset, the Rev. T. G. Beymer commenced in 1883 a coöperative village store. In two months it had repaid the loan of initial capital of £200 ($1,000). Debt has been gradually abolished. The stimulating principle of the nest-egg has been learned by the poor. Wages are being more wisely spent. A beneficial change is passing over the cottages. On the continent of Europe many similar examples could be found, where the pastors have set up Raiffeisen banks, driven out usury, and won back the dull, hopeless, discouraged peasants to thrift and religion.

<small>Labor conferences.</small>

Pastors, employers, and professional people cannot join trades unions, but they might extend friendly acquaintance among wage-workers by joining the fraternal lodges, coöperative banks, and mutual benefit clubs to which the working people belong. This is already done by many sagacious Christian leaders. Politicians know the value of such connections, and sometimes use them for selfish ends.

<small>Themes for discussion.</small>

There are many troublesome questions which ought to be discussed before religious people by representatives of the trades unions, in order that professional men may realize the sufferings and the aspirations of the unions. Such problems are the tenement-house reform, the sweating system, eviction laws and their harsh administration, the housing of janitors in apartment houses, conciliation and arbitration in trade disputes, the treatment of children and youth in factories, and the wages of women. It is often a great relief to pent-up feelings of sorrow or of wrong if they can find a sympathetic hearing, even if the hearer can do nothing but listen. On the other hand, benevolent and honorable employers would frequently mitigate evils if brought to their attention. The church parlor is a good place for such conferences ; but the officers of the church must know how to keep their tempers when the mouthpieces of the trades unions and of socialism vent their epithets of abuse. We should remember that this invective, however coarse, is not altogether without justification, and we must be patient till the noisy torrent runs clear.

Our open church believes in a complete manhood, in a full development of faculty. It is not blind to the craving for fellowship. Its minister does not stand in the street asking men to come out of the warm saloon and shiver with him on the pavement. He invites them to rooms where they will find a purer air, games, recreations, magic lantern shows, concerts, "soft drinks" rather than hard cider and bad whisky. If they must smoke, he has a room where they can go and choke to their hearts' content. He will chat with them there, a comrade and friend. He will make them feel at home and tell their story. Next Sunday they will get back their own vocabulary in a sermon, but it will be transfigured, glorified. *Sociability.*

The institutional church may find opportunities of ministering to the hunger for knowledge and beauty. It has a reading-room, rival of the public dramshop, and a good deal better. Not too fine, lest a hod carrier with lime on his shoes may not feel at home as he drops in on his way home. There are many illustrated papers. The place is still. Courtesy prevails. No policeman is called in, because there is a sense of gratitude and fair play in these rough, strong men. *Intellectual and æsthetic.*

They will listen to lectures, but the speaker must have a genius for illustration and humor, and he must have a stereopticon. These men will crowd the hall and follow you the world over and up among the stars, if you

Poetry in request.

lead them with pictures. But they cannot endure prose. They want poetry. Of plain, hard matter-of-fact they have enough all day, all the years. They will hear of religion, too, any night of the week, if it comes down into life, and is not separated from experience. All shams and pretense they detect, abhor, and punish on the spot. Noble sentiment will be applauded. Music will soothe or stir them. They can be made to see the difference between good drawing and caricature in painting. Catch them young and they will learn to render classic music. The open church has musical classes. It is a schoolhouse for those who have no other school. It has a library of choice books, if the public library is too far away or does not fully meet the requirements of the people. All things to all men that it may by all means save some—this is the principle of a divine pedagogy.

Worship and evangelism.

The open church has for its ideal daily services for prayer and teaching. On Sunday seats are free. Support comes from voluntary contributions, gifts, or endowments. In this kind of work rented pews are empty pews. A noble business man of Boston vowed when he was young and poor that, if he became rich, he would see to it that the poor had in at least one church as good music as the rich. He did become wealthy and did not forget his vow. In the institutional church of which he is a member and a benefactor may be heard some of the best voices of the city. Not all such churches can command equal income, but all aim to make the service of worship splendid, attractive, free, and sincere.

The evangelistic, missionary spirit is intense in these churches. It is not "secularized" by the numerous forms of ministry. On the contrary, these agencies tend to the supreme end of the church, all contribute to the highest good.

But the open church is more than an attraction, it is a mission. It goes out into the highways and byways of the city, and carries its message to the indifferent and the hostile. It multiplies pastors and visitors. Its corps of trained nurses or deaconesses has free access to humble rooms when sickness and sorrow prepare the heart for the heavenly call. Happily we are now introducing into America that method of woman's ministry which Pastor Fliedner made so famous at Kaiserswerth in the German Fatherland. In connection with the institutional church movement these trained nurses are having already an unlimited field of usefulness.

Perhaps one of the most characteristic social institutions of the American church is the Young Men's Christian Association. It is founded on a distinct and articulate recognition of the fact that man is a complex being, having many interdependent wants, and the fact that man is an organic unity. Every member of the body is connected by a muscular and nervous and bony system with every other member. Body and intellect act and react on each other. Morality and religion are influenced by the studies, the work, the recreations of men, and in turn react on all that one does and thinks and wills. It is a clear vision of this deep law of the organic unity of the individual which created the method of the Young Men's Christian Association, and the idea has become more clear and fixed with experience. *The Y. M. C. A.*

If we enter the building of a completely developed Y. M. C. A., where the central principles are fully expressed, we shall find three fairly distinct lines of work — the gymnasium and bath for the body, the night classes *Its apparatus.*

for the intellectual life, the Bible classes and evangelistic services for the religious nature.

The relation of these societies to the churches is very intimate. The voting members must be also members of some "evangelical" church, and the constitution requires that the officers shall represent the "evangelical" creeds. Associate members, who need not be church members, have all privileges except voting and control.

The "liberal" churches, having strong objections to these restrictions, have established similar associations of their own in some of the cities, and in connection with particular churches have developed "institutional" agencies which perform the same functions as those just described.

The Y.W.C.A. Recognizing the beneficial influence of the associations for young men, a strong effort has been made to furnish corresponding advantages for young women. The essential features of these institutions have been indicated in a previous chapter (Chapter III.).

The Salvation Army and the American Volunteers. The Salvation Army was established in 1861 by William Booth, and set up its banners in America in 1879. It presents, like all popular movements, many points for criticism. Artists declare that their music is intolerable; sermonizers insist that their exhortations violate the canons of sacred rhetoric; devotees of fashion are confident that the lassies show bad taste in bonnets; philosophers and theologians consider their teaching beneath contempt; people who boast of their humility dislike such a parade of religion; reverent worshipers are shocked at their parodies of sacred song and their rude familiarity with Deity; patriotism cries out against the despotic military policy which holds the officers in the grip of austere discipline—and yet the army moves on.

The unfortunate division of 1896 reminds one of the days when sects arose over doctrines or rules, and yet the two bodies move forward to the same end by somewhat different methods.

No one can foretell the issue; no mortal can predict the consequences of their sensational methods. But this much is certain: the Salvation Army has compelled the members of the churches to consider the problems of the "submerged twentieth," to see that the conventional ways and places are not adequate; that multitudes are alienated from the church who might be helped; that they who touch the soul must minister to the body, as Jesus did; that while many able ministers preach on Sunday evenings to almost empty houses, they might, by going to halls and theaters, speak to thousands. No man has a right to criticise these rude workmen so long as he makes no attempt in the same field.

In our cities there are men whose clothing, habits, speech, culture, and history exclude them from the regular churches. The "rescue mission" has a field for itself, but the more varied "institutional church" is far more hopeful. Experience soon shows us that a man may be sincerely "converted" and yet sink back into bad habits unless he is helped to work and higher companionship. *Evangelism among the wandering and isolated classes.*

The specialized forms of ministry demand specialized training schools. The Lutherans and Catholics have led the way in establishing schools for training deaconesses and sisters for the care of the sick. But other denominations are rapidly following their example. The Y. M. C. A. has established classes for training the "secretaries" who are charged with the multifarious duties of superintending the work for young men. *Training of workers for activities.*

Various institutes and training schools have been founded for discovering and developing the gifts of persons who will become assistants of pastors, evangelists, leaders of rescue missions, colporteurs, and Sunday-school superintendents.

Among unsectarian organizations few have had a more rapid growth or are doing a nobler work than the International Order of the King's Daughters and Sons. Started eleven years ago by ten women, in New York City, it has increased until its members are found all over the world. In 1891 "International" was legally added to its title. Its purposes are "to develop spiritual life and to stimulate Christian activities," and all who accept these aims and purposes, and who "hold themselves responsible to the King, our Lord and Savior Jesus Christ," are welcome to its membership.

As its name indicates, the order accepts and teaches the fatherhood of God and the brotherhood of man. Its first work is to strive to win the individual heart for Christ, so that the individual life may be governed and guided by his spirit. "Within its ranks are found not only the little child and the wayworn pilgrim, but some of the noblest men and women who, in the church, the state, the university, and the business world, to-day are shaping the policy and guiding the affairs of the nation." The King's Daughters and Sons, for the love of Christ, and "In His Name," are ministering to the souls and bodies of men; "building churches; paying mortgages on those already built; educating the young men and women for the ministry and for the foreign mission field; taking care of orphans and widows, of the old and the sick; building hospitals and infirmaries; sending trained nurses to the homes of the poor; and following the sailors with evidences of loving care." Nearly 400,000 have taken the silver cross as the outward symbol of their pledge of love and service, and more than one thousand different lines of work upon which they have entered are recorded at the headquarters of the order.

The remarkable growth of the church societies of young people, under the inspiration of the Young People's Society of Christian Endeavor, is a social factor of the first order. Its ministry to the religious life is its chief glory; but religion means to these hosts of educated youth a living out of the Golden Rule. Hence we see that those organizations are pushing the work of education, Sunday-schools, rational entertainments, industrial classes, temperance reforms, defense of the day of rest, political purity, and all the movements for social betterment. *Young people's societies.*

If one desires to see how general and real the devotion to religious life is in the United States he must study the Sunday-school. According to statistics published in 1896 we had 142,089 schools, 1,476,369 teachers, 11,556,806 pupils, and there had been a gain in three years of 1,337,967 in the grand total. In Canada there were 55,050 teachers and 467,292 pupils. This institution is absolutely voluntary, and, with very few exceptions, all these teachers serve without pay. In no country in the world is the Sunday-school so well equipped and so enthusiastically supported as in America. The general organization of this movement includes a committee in each township, a county committee, a state convention, a national and international convention, and, to crown all, a world's Sunday-school convention. Who can measure the social importance of this vast army of students of righteousness, banded together by common beliefs, hopes, and affections? *The Sunday-school.*

The church and the family.

It has long been felt that the church ought to return moral inspiration to the institution out of which all other institutions grow—the family. Dr. Dike has made this idea central in the league of which he is secretary. About 1881 a movement was promoted by Dr. W. A. Duncan which deserves the attention of all philanthropists—"The Home Department of the Sunday-school." Many persons are not church-goers, the invalid, the aged, those too poor to provide suitable clothing, and those who are indifferent. Such persons are visited by an agent of the church school and invited to sign a card which pledges them to study the lesson at home, unless prevented by some good cause. They are furnished with lesson helps and enrolled as members. Traveling men in this way keep up their connection with the school while on their journeys. A family in the far West, on prairie or deep in the forest, is a living member of the old church in Connecticut. A domestic servant saw boys stealing fruit in a garden, invited them to her kitchen, and formed them into a class. Thus the two most ancient institutions of society, family and sanctuary, are closely united and are made reciprocally helpful. The home department is full of promise of further development of this prolific idea that the family is central in all educational work.

Coördinating agencies.

The disposition to subordinate self to social good, to make partisan and denominational interests serve human welfare, has created agencies of coördination and coöperation. In many communities there are local societies, ministers' meetings, civic federations, Christian citizenship leagues and others which act in various ways as organs for the religious and reforming convictions which are held in common.

Denominational societies on a voluntary basis are

formed for the prosecution of various kinds of missions and church extensions, as city mission societies, state conventions, national missionary societies, and publication houses. Each denomination provides for the enlargement of its Sunday-school work in new places, largely in connection with the organs of publication.

The Evangelical Alliance has no legislative powers and seeks no control over the churches. Its mission is to promote unity of feeling, thought, and action in that large field where differences of creed have no place. Its discussions, to which men of all churches have contributed, have helped to concentrate attention upon "practical Christianity," to show the church at large where its ministry was most needed, to organize the best thinking upon those problems, and so to promote economy of force and secure liberality of action and generosity of sacrifice. There seems to be a place for it like that of the central committee of the inner mission in the German state church. The time is approaching when at least all Protestants will unite in a systematic way to consolidate and direct their philanthropic endeavors. Unity of creed is out of the question, but real spiritual and practical union is already locally realized in a hundred ways. The Evangelical Alliance appears to be the best organization for advancing this desirable unification of all the church forces which make for charity and righteousness.

National union societies.

The Convention of Christian Workers is composed chiefly of persons who are deeply interested in rescue mission work in this country. Its members are in touch with the vagrant and unsteady classes of our cities, and they have offered many examples of heroic sacrifice.

Convention of Christian Workers.

The American Sunday-school Union was organized in 1824. Some conception of its work may be formed from the fact that in three years (1884–87) this old society brought 185,034 children into 4,947 new Sunday-schools ; aided 4,825 other schools ; visited 92,584 families ; supplied 45,019 destitute persons with the Scriptures ; and held 27,247 religious meetings.

Open Church League. The Open and Institutional Church League, already mentioned, has for its object a band of union between churches of this type and the extension of their principles.

It is impossible to name in this place all the institutions which the churches have, directly or indirectly, created for the amelioration of human life, for aiding to make man's life complete and perfect in body, mind, and spirit, to bring all men into fraternal and equitable relations. What has been mentioned is but an imperfect suggestion and illustration of the luxuriant and generous outgrowth of the social spirit at work in the churches. It is not claimed that these societies are doing their whole duty. They fall far short of it. But the springs of vitality are in them ; they produce foliage and fruit ; and they give promise of better things.

CONCLUSION.

Multiplication of organs. Many have complained that the societies auxiliary to the church are too numerous ; that too much time, energy, and money are expended upon them in proportion to the work accomplished ; that machinery consumes the power without corresponding product ; and that the church itself is lost out of sight. There is some ground for this criticism, and it suggests an explanation and a measure of relief.

The explanation of these societies lies chiefly in the following facts : that these improvements always begin with a devoted, self-sacrificing, and far-seeing minority which dares not wait for the majority before it launches its enterprise. Why did the anti-slavery societies organize outside the churches? Because the churches persecuted or misunderstood them, and clothed them in wet blankets. Why did the temperance societies organize separately? Because the churches could not be brought to support the movement, and because the combined membership of all workers of all denominations was necessary to success. Why did the foreign and home missionary societies develop independently of ecclesiastical machinery? Because, in some denominations at least, only a minority was favorable to missions, and the great majority was indifferent or hostile. In the same way the Sunday-school movement has been compelled to erect its own machinery and pursue its own path. The majority must be won to a new cause by examples of success more than by verbal arguments. Nearly all our charitable institutions depend on a comparatively small minority of members for support. There never was an age when there was not a social necessity for the organization of societies auxiliary to the church, friendly to its interests and aims, yet somewhat self-supporting and self-governing. When the prophetic minority has demonstrated the value of its work the church as a body may safely adopt it as its own. This seems to be the most practical method of forward movements. *[Pioneers of progress.]*

The church is not and cannot be exempt from the universal laws of organic and social evolution. Progress in life implies specialization and multiplication of organs and functions. The egg of a bird is at first a homogeneous mass and no particular organ is discoverable. During the process of brooding the various parts of the bird manifest themselves in special forms, *[Law of differentiation.]*

and when the shell is broken the creature is equipped for its various functions, marvelously complex. The low forms of life, as the jelly fish, have no particular hands or eyes, while the highest forms are endlessly diversified. Savage society is simple, while civilized society is complicated. The primitive church was a single cell, while the modern church has a thousand modes of manifesting its increasing life. "God fulfils himself in many ways." We can no more force the church back into its pioneer form than we can force a developed oak back into the narrow husk and undeveloped germ of the acorn. Life branches endlessly; death carries us back to the original monotony of dust. Sacred institutions if studied in the light of sociology will be seen to conform to the divine laws of development. The multiplication of agencies corresponds to the wealth of internal gifts and graces and to the multiform demands of a complex and advanced social environment. This variety should not frighten or annoy us, for it is a proof of abundant vitality.

Higher life multiplies machinery.

The measure of relief grows out of the social situation. Specialization must be accompanied by integration. As far as the local church or the denomination comes to approve a measure, after the experimental stage is passed, it can provide for its regulation. Take an example. The local church in a certain large town agrees by vote of its members or authorized officers that it should favor and support the following objects: foreign, home, state, and city missions; the religious education of the children and youth by appropriate graded methods; ten different forms of charity to the dependent poor; two forms of work for criminals; the temperance, social purity, and rest day reforms; municipal and electoral reform. This church appoints

Economy through better organization.

a committee for each of these interests; requires them to study a particular social work, to promote, to raise money for it, to secure assistants in its personal work, and to report all to the church. This would mean integration and regulation. It would not take the place of experimental efforts of the pioneers and pathfinders, and it would not suppress adventurous souls. In some such way the most worthy causes would receive official recognition and the wild schemes of eccentric sentimentalists who "mistake activity for usefulness" would be obliged to give good reasons for their claims. By coöperation with the Society for Organizing Charities, each church would come into an arrangement for the whole community. The ideal will be reached only when all Christians regard the community as a single parish, with one united plan of service. But this ideal can be realized only by tentative and gradual approach. We are under the most solemn obligations to work in this direction. We should seek to be one "that the world may believe." We must practice the divine economy even in working miracles: "Gather up the fragments, that nothing be lost." {.sidenote}Regulation.{/}

But economy is not synonymous with niggardliness. The Great Giver has enriched the people of the United States beyond all other nations of the earth. Our material and mechanical resources, our mercantile and agricultural wealth, surpass the fables of fairyland. We are called upon to develop our social institutions, to serve therewith our Maker and our fellowmen; to make them effective instruments of the perfection of our citizens; to offer them as a worthy contribution to the world-wide movement of human progress whose ideal and consummation is in that holy and happy society which Jesus called "The Kingdom of God." {.sidenote}The service asked of us.{/}

APPENDIX

APPENDIX
A

APPENDIX.

NOTES ON THE CHAPTERS.

THE object of these notes is to give brief hints for those who desire to follow the special subject of the chapter with further reading and investigation. A few titles of books and articles are given for reading, and these will frequently guide to full bibliographies, and will give the addresses of institutions.

A select list of typical institutions is added for those who wish to visit them or to secure their reports. It ought to be remembered that the people who are at work in these institutions are busy and often weary ; and no one should take their time or energy without serious reason. It is a shame and a sin to disturb and tax philanthropic workers in order to gratify an idle curiosity, the caprice of a mere sightseer.

CHAPTER I.—INTRODUCTION.

BIBLIOGRAPHY.

W. H. Tolman and W. I. Hull : *Handbook of Sociological Information.*
A. W. Small and G. E. Vincent : *An Introduction to the Study of Society.*
Arthur Fairbanks : *Introduction to Sociology.*
J. S. Mackenzie : *An Introduction to Social Philosophy.* Second edition.
F. H. Giddings : *The Principles of Sociology.*

Chapter II.—Home-Making as a Social Art.

BIBLIOGRAPHY.

C. F. and C. F. B. Thwing : *The Family.*
Helen Campbell : *Household Economics.*
Lucy Maynard Salmon : *Domestic Service.*
R. A. Woods and others : *The Poor in Great Cities.*
Marion Talbot and Ellen S. Richards : *Household Sanitation.*
The Le Play Method of Social Observation, translated by C. A. Ellwood, in *American Journal of Sociology*, March, 1897.
Hull House Maps and Papers, by Residents of Hull House.

Chapter III.—Friendly Circles of Women Wage-Earners.

BIBLIOGRAPHY.

C. D. Wright : *The Industrial Evolution of the United States* (Chap. XVI.).
J. A. Hobson : *Evolution of Modern Capitalism.*
Maude Stanley : *Clubs for Working Girls.*
Helen Campbell : *Prisoners of Poverty ; Women Wage-Earners.*
Anna Nathan Meyer : *Woman's Work in America.*
Working Women in Large Cities, Department of Labor Report, 1889.
Reports of State Factory Inspectors and Bureaus of Labor.
Reports of Working Women's Society, New York.
The Consumers' League, New York City, Mrs Josephine Shaw Lowell, President.

INSTITUTIONS.

In all cities may be found clubs for women and girls in connection with settlements, missions, institutional churches, kindergartens, and the Y. W. C. A.

CHAPTER IV.—BETTER HOUSES FOR THE PEOPLE.

BIBLIOGRAPHY.

E. R. L. Gould : *The Housing of the Working People; Eighth Special Report of the Commissioner of Labor*, Washington, 1895.

Review of Reviews, December, 1896, p. 693.

INSTITUTIONS.

City and Suburban Homes Co., New York City, E. R. L. Gould, President.

Improved Dwellings Co., of Brooklyn.

Boston Coöperative Building Co.

Local Building and Loan Associations in all parts of the United States.

CHAPTER V.—PUBLIC HEALTH.

BIBLIOGRAPHY.

G. E. Waring : *Sanitary Drainage of Houses and Towns*, and other works.

L. C. Parkes : *Hygiene of Public Health*.

J. F. J. Sykes : *Public Health Problems*.

W. H. Tolman : *Report on Public Baths and Public Comfort Stations*.

CHAPTER VI.—GOOD ROADS AND COMMUNICATION.

BIBLIOGRAPHY.

Roy Stone : *New Roads and Road Laws*.

Publications of League of American Wheelmen.
Bulletins of Wisconsin Farmers' Institutes, 1896.
Year Book of United States Department of Agriculture, 1894, pp. 501, 513.

Chapter VII.—The Socialized Citizen.

BIBLIOGRAPHY.

H. Spencer: *Principles of Sociology*, Vol. III., Part VIII.
"A Free Lance": *Toward Utopia*.
R. Grant: *The Art of Living*.
E. Kelley: *Evolution and Effort*.

Chapter VIII.—What Good Employers are Doing.

BIBLIOGRAPHY.

D. Pidgeon: *Old World Questions and New World Answers*.
N. P. Gilman: *Profit Sharing; Socialism and the American Spirit*.
Paul Monroe: "An American System of Labor Pensions and Insurance," in *American Journal of Sociology*, January, 1897.
O. D. Ashley: "Railways and Their Employees," *The Railway Age*, Chicago.
W. Gladden: *Working People and Their Employers*.

Chapter IX.—Organizations of Wage-Earners.

BIBLIOGRAPHY.

R. T. Ely: *The Labor Movement in America*.
A. T. Hadley: *Economics*.

F. J. Stimson : *Handbook of the Labor Laws of the United States.*
H. Myrick : *How to Coöperate.*
H. W. Wolff : *People's Banks.*
E. B. Andrews : *The Last Quarter Century in the United States.*
Beatrice Potter : *The Coöperative Movement in Great Britain.*
Articles on "Fraternal Insurance," *Johnson's Universal Cyclopædia.* Edition 1895.
Bulletins of Labor, No. 6.
Ninth Annual Report of the United States Commissioner of Labor, on the Building and Loan Associations of the United States.
Reports of Provident Loan Associations in Boston and New York.

CHAPTER X.—ECONOMIC COÖPERATION OF THE COMMUNITY.

BIBLIOGRAPHY.

R. T. Ely : *Socialism and Social Reform.*
A. Shaw : *Municipal Government in Continental Europe; Municipal Government in Great Britain.*

CHAPTER XI.—POLITICAL REFORMS.

BIBLIOGRAPHY.

J. Fiske : *Civil Government.*
W. Wilson : *The State.*
W. H. Tolman : *Municipal Reform Movements.*
J. R. Commons : *Proportional Representation.*
National Conference for Good City Government. (Report for 1894 has bibliography.)

Publications of National Civil Service Reform League.
Reports of Civil Service Commissioners.

INSTITUTIONS.

National Civil Service Reform League, National Municipal League.

American Proportional Representation League, Stoughton Cooley, Chicago, Secretary.

Civic Federation, of Chicago, and many similar local societies.

CHAPTER XII.—THE SOCIAL SPIRIT IN THE STATE SCHOOL SYSTEM.

BIBLIOGRAPHY.

G. S. Hall : *Bibliography of Education.*
C. H. Ham and C. M. Woodward : *Works on Manual Training.*

Reports of United States Commissioner of Education, Washington (very valuable).

INSTITUTIONS.

Small parties of citizens may visit public schools with advantage if they are prepared by reading and experience, and if they are accompanied by a competent teacher or superintendent.

Manual training schools in Philadelphia, Cleveland, Toledo, Chicago, and other cities.

CHAPTER XIII.—VOLUNTARY ORGANIZATION OF EDUCATION.

BIBLIOGRAPHY.

Miss Jane Addams and others : *Philanthropy and Social Progress.*

J. H. Vincent : *The Chautauqua Movement.*

M. Katharine Jones : *Bibliography of Settlements.*

Report of the United States Commissioner of Education, 1894–5, on Chautauqua, article by H. B. Adams.

National Conference of Charities and Correction, 1896 (Social settlements).

INSTITUTIONS.

Chautauqua : Office of Bishop John H. Vincent, Buffalo, N. Y.

Vacation Schools : Office, Room 105 E. Twenty-second Street, New York ; Superintendent of Schools, Chicago.

Social settlements are found in all the large cities.

National Household Economic Association, Dr. Mary E. Green, Charlotte, Mich., President.

CHAPTER XIV.—SOCIALIZED BEAUTY AND RECREATIONS.

BIBLIOGRAPHY.

N. H. Eggleston : *Home and Its Surroundings.*

Atlantic Monthly, 1896–7, articles by Miss Mary C. Robins.

Leaflets published by the Civic Club, Philadelphia.

CHAPTER XV.—CHARITY AND CORRECTION.

BIBLIOGRAPHY.

A. G. Warner : *American Charities.*
F. H. Wines : *Punishment and Reformation.*
C. R. Henderson : *Dependents, Defectives, and Delinquents.*
W. D. Morrison : *Juvenile Offenders.*

Reports of National Conference of Charities and Correction, G. H. Ellis, Boston.

INSTITUTIONS.

In each city is published a list of all charitable institutions, in the directory or in a special volume.

CHAPTER XVI.—THE SOCIAL SPIRIT IN CONFLICT WITH ANTI-SOCIAL INSTITUTIONS.

BIBLIOGRAPHY.

F. H. Wines and J. Koren : *The Liquor Problem*, 1897.
H. W. Blair : *The Temperance Movement*, 1888.
W. F. Crafts : *Practical Christian Sociology* (many interesting notes and references).

Temperance : *Cyclopædia of Temperance*.
Report of Commissioner of Education, 1894-5, on Scientific Temperance Instruction in the Public Schools, p. 1829.
Divorce Reform : *Reports of National Divorce Reform League*.
Report of Commissioner of Labor, 1889, on Marriage and Divorce.
Society for the Suppression of Vice (Anthony Comstock); the *Times* Building, New York.
Social Purity : *Publications of White Cross League and W. C. T. U.*
The American Purity Alliance.

CHAPTER XVII.—THE INSTITUTIONS OF IDEALS.

BIBLIOGRAPHY.

B. G. W. Mead : *Modern Methods of Church Work*, 1897.

J. Strong : *The New Era.*
W. Gladden : *Ruling Ideas of the Present Age.*
J. R. Commons : *Social Reform and the Church.*
W. DeWitt Hyde : *Outlines of Social Theology.*
G. Hodges : *Faith and Social Service.*
Lyman Abbott : *Christianity and Social Problems.*
H. K. Carroll : *Religious Forces in the United States.*
D. Dorchester: *Christianity in the United States.* Edition 1895.
H. S. Ninde and others : *Young Men's Christian Association, A Handbook.*
E. W. Donald : *The Expansion of Religion.*
Christianity Practically Applied; being reports of the Evangelical Alliance, 1893. See other volumes of these proceedings.
The Open Church, quarterly ; 50 cents a year ; organ of the Institutional Church Movement.
The Year Books and Reports of Institutional Churches; see lists in *Open Church* and in *Forward Movements;* the latter published at 4 cents by *The Congregationalist,* Boston.
Reports of Conventions of Christian Workers, Rev. J. C. Collins, New Haven, Conn.
The World's Parliament of Religions; edited by J. H. Barrows.
Salvation Army. List of publications and reports sent on request by Staff Captain James Burrows, 558 W. Madison Street, Chicago, Ill.
The National Christian Citizenship League, 153 La Salle Street, Chicago. Organ, *The Christian Citizen.*

INSTITUTIONS.

All local religious institutions can be found from a city directory.

NOTES TO CHAPTER II., PAGE 32.

HOUSEKEEPING RECORDS OF EXPENSES.

FORM A.

Form of an Account Book to be kept by the Housekeeper: the Day Book.

DAY BOOK.

On Hand.	Date.	ITEMS.	Receipts.	Expenditures.

DIRECTIONS.—1. Give quantity as exactly as possible with the "Items." 2. Under "Receipts" state the source of income; as wages, rent, interest, gifts.

FORM B.

This Form Analyzes the Items set down by the Family in the Day Book.

I. Food.

Bread.	Flour and Crackers.	Other Cereals.	Butter.	Lard Drippings.	Meat.	Bacon.	Fish and Poultry.	Milk.	Eggs.	Cheese.

I. Food (Continued).

Potatoes.	Other Vegetables.	Fresh Fruit.	Sugar.	Jam and Syrup.	Condiments.	Meals out.	Tea.	Coffee, Cocoa, etc.	Alcoholic Drinks.

FORM B.

II. Dwelling.

Rent, actual or estimated.	Furniture.	Heat.	Light.

III. Clothing.

For Men.	For Women.	Laundry.

IV. Moral Needs, Recreation, and Health.

Worship.	Instruction of Children.	Alms.	Recreations and Festivals.	Health.

V. Industries, Debts, Taxes, Insurance.

Industries.	Interest on Debt.	Taxes.	Insurance.

FORM C.
THE POSSESSIONS OF THE FAMILY.

DATE,..............................

PROPERTY.

I. *List of Securities, Stocks, Bonds, Notes, etc.* . . . .

II. *Furniture, Silverware, Ornaments, Books, Musical Instruments, and Music Books* . . . .

III. *Bedding and Clothing.*
   Bedding . . . .
   White Goods . . . .
   Clothing . . . .

IV. *Supplies.*
   Household Supplies . . . . . .
   Fuel . . . .

V. *Amounts Due on Open Accounts* . . .

VI. *Cash on Hand, or Equivalent* . . . .

DEBTS AND LIABILITIES.

VII. *Debts.*
   On Open Accounts . . . .
   On Interest . . . .

VIII. *Liabilities.*
   Taxes . . . .
   Insurance . . . .

NOTE.—By subtracting the sum of VII. and VIII. from the sum of I.-VI., one has the actual value of property over debts and liabilities.

For further explanations of the use of these accounts, see *American Journal of Sociology*, March, 1897, page 662.

NOTE TO CHAPTER IX., PAGE 152.

Membership of New England Coöperative Societies.

Name of Society.	Location.	Membership.
Sovereigns' Trading Co. . . .	New Britain, Conn. . .	200
Lewiston Coöperative Society .	Lewiston, Maine . . .	125
Lisbon Falls Coöperative Ass'n	Lisbon Falls, Maine. .	275
Sabattus Coöperative Ass'n. .	Sabattus, Maine. . . .	125
Farmers' and Mechanics' Exchange.	Brattleboro, Vt.	509
Woodlawn Coöperative Ass'n	Pawtucket, R. I. . . .	174
First Swedish Coöperative Store Co.	Quinsigamond, Worcester, Mass.	262
Harvard Coöperative Society .	Cambridge, Mass. . . .	1909
Cambridge Coöperative Society	Cambridge, Mass. . . .	185
Riverside Coöperative Ass'n .	Maynard, Mass.	398
Hampden County Coöperative Ass'n	Springfield, Mass	184
Knights of Labor Coöperative Boot and Shoe Ass'n . . .	Worcester, Mass. . . .	201
Coöperative Store Co.	Silver Lake, Kingston, Mass.	123
Plymouth Rock Coöperative Co.	Plymouth, Mass. . . .	82
Arlington Coöperative Ass'n .	Lawrence, Mass. . . .	2850
Lawrence Equitable Coöperative Society	Lawrence, Mass. . . .	732
German Coöperative Ass'n . .	Lawrence, Mass. . . .	169
Industrial Coöperative Ass'n .	New Bedford, Mass. . .	410
Beverly Coöperative Ass'n . .	Beverly, Mass.	188
Dorchester Coöperative Ass'n	Dorchester, Mass. . . .	20
Lowell Coöperative Ass'n . . .	Lowell, Mass.	1130
West Warren Coöperative Ass'n	West Warren, Mass. . .	196
Haverhill Coöperative Society	Haverhill, Mass. . . .	45
Lynn Coöperative Society. . .	Lynn, Mass.	60
Rockland Coöperative Society	Rockland, Mass. . . .	60
The Hub Coöperative Emporium.	Boston, Mass.	80
Total membership		10692

NOTE TO CHAPTER IX., PAGE 152.

MEMBERSHIP OF COÖPERATIVE SOCIETIES OUTSIDE OF NEW ENGLAND.

Name of Society.	Location.	Membership.
Trenton Coöperative Society	Trenton, N. J.	465
Hammonton Fruit Growers' Union and Coöperative Society	Hammonton, N. J.	646
Vineland Fruit Growers' Union and Coöperative Society	Vineland, N. J.	54
Sovereigns' Coöperative Ass'n	Dover, N. J.	253
Raritan Coöperative Ass'n	Raritan, N. J.	175
Coöperative Association No. 1	Phillipsburg, N. J.	114
Jamestown Coöperative Supply Co.	Jamestown, N. J.	217
Integral Coöperative Ass'n	Pittsburg, Pa.	300
Allegan Coöperative Ass'n	Allegan, Mich.	150
Ishpeming Coöperative Society	Ishpeming, Mich.	350
Zumbrota Mercantile and Elevator Co.	Zumbrota, Minn.	294
Texas Coöperative Ass'n	Galveston, Texas	300
Greenwood County Coöperative Ass'n	Eureka, Kans.	165
Lyon County Alliance Exchange Co.	Emporia, Kans.	378
Johnson County Coöperative Ass'n	Olathe, Kans.	900
Osage County Coöperative Ass'n	Overbrook, Kans.	108
The Alliance Coöperative Ass'n	Green, Kans.	97
Wakefield Coöperative Ass'n	Wakefield, Kans.	154
Patrons' Coöperative Ass'n	Cadmus, Kans.	217
Zion's Coöperative Mercantile Institution	Salt Lake City, Utah.	600
Socialists' Coöperative Store and Productive Ass'n	Los Angeles, Cal.	102
Santa Paula Coöperative Ass'n	Santa Paula, Cal.	50
Poplar Coöperative Ass'n	Poplar, Cal.	26
Total membership		6115

INDEX.

Absentee, landlords, 65.
Accounts, family, 32, appendix.
Addams, Jane, 234.
Æsthetic element of welfare, 37, 199, 240, 315.
Air, foul and pure, 77.
American Sunday-school Union, 323.
American Volunteers, 318.
Amusements, 244.
Arbitration, 159.
Arnold, T., 205, 232.
Art, 240, 247.
Ashley, O. D., 130.
Association of Working Girls' Societies, 53.
Associations, voluntary, 19.
Australian ballot, 186.
Baths, 83.
Beauty, 241.
Beliefs, a social force, 9.
Bemis, E. W., 152.
Boarding-houses, 46.
Body, the, its dignity, 79.
Booth-Tucker, Commander, 260.
Broadus, J. A., 195.
Brooks, J. G., 295.
Building societies, 67, 153.
Cairnes, J. E., 257.
Calling lists, 39.
Carnegie, Andrew, 121.
Carse, Matilda B., 287.
Catholic Total Abstinence Union, 284.
Chadwick, E., 126, 243.
Chandler, Senator, 253.
Channing, W. E., 132, 158.
Character, 112.
Charity, methods, 271, 275, 308, 327.
Chautauqua, 220.
Chicago, water, 76.
Child labor, 126.
Children, working, 162, 267; dependent, 265, 268.
Christianity, 304.

Church Temperance Society, 284.
Churches, 304.
Citizens' Law and Order League, 286.
City and Suburban Homes Company, 67.
Civil service reform, 179.
Civilization, its nature, 20.
Clubs, 38, 143, 226.
Commons, J. R., 188.
Communication, 96.
Compulsory education, 164, 213, 267.
Conciliation, 159.
Conduct and theory, 9.
Consumers' League, 49.
Convention of Christian Workers, 323.
Cooking, 32.
Coöperation in housekeeping, 33.
Coöperation, Rochdale type, 147; in banking, 153.
Corrupt Practices Act, 184.
County fairs, 37.
Culture, 132.
Death-rate, the, 60.
Debatable questions, 19.
Decorative Art Society, 37.
Defective children, 203, 265.
Degenerates, 30.
Democracy, 192.
Development of family, 24; of industry, 103.
Dike, S. W., 201, 297.
Disease, cost of, 72.
Divorce, 31.
Dodge, Grace H., 51, 57.
Dolge, Alfred, 131.
Domestic science, 203.
Drama, the, 246.
Dress, 33.
Drink evil, the, 281.
Duncan, W. A., 322.
Duruy, George, 278.
Dwellings, defects of, 27, 59.

Index.

Education, voluntary organization of, 207; higher state of, 214; missionary, 237.
Electoral reform, 182.
Electric roads, 95.
Eliot, President, 294.
Emerson, R. W., 191.
Employers, 117.
Employment bureaus, 167.
Environments, 264.
Ethical teaching, 214.
Evangelical Alliance, 323.
Evangelism, 319.
Evans, Margaret J., 255.
Extension, High School, 208.
Factory laws, 162.
Fairchild, C. G., 63.
Fairs, county, 37.
Family, the, 23.
Farm colonies, 273.
Farmers' reading circles, 227.
Findlay, J. J., 193.
Fiske, John, 186, 189, 225.
Fitch, J. G., 225.
Food, 76.
Franchises, 168.
Friendly visitors, 81, 276.
Gambling, 300.
Garfield, President, 193.
Giddings, F. H., 256.
Gilman, N. P., 102.
"Ginx's Baby," 105.
Girls' Friendly Society, 47; clubs, 52.
Godkin, E. L., 108.
Good roads, 88.
Gothenburg system, the, 295.
Gould, E. R. L., 79, 80, 295.
Government, ministrant functions of, 170, 176.
"Grubb, Mrs.," 40.
Hale, E. E., 225.
Harland, Marion, 58.
Harris, W. T., 196.
Health, public, 72.
Hegeman, President, 221.
Heredity, 74.
High School Extension, 208.
Hill, Octavia, 35, 62.
Home Department of the Sunday-school, 322.

Home, essentials of, 29; and school, 195; libraries, 233.
Hospital, the, 231.
Household economics, 227.
Housekeeping, coöperative, 33.
Houses on farms, 69.
Housing of the poor, 26, 59.
Howe, Julia Ward, 58.
Humane Society, 296.
Ideals, 191.
Improvements, how they begin, 18.
Independent Order of Good Templars, 285.
Independent, The, 238.
Individualism, 104.
Initiative, the, 187.
Insane, the, 270.
Institutional churches, 309.
Institutions a growth, 15.
Insurance, 73, 144, 291.
Intemperance, 30.
Interests of society, 12.
"Jane Club," the, 56.
Jenks, J. W., 185.
Jevons, W. S., 244, 250.
Johnson, G. E., 244.
Juvenile offenders, 29.
Keller, Helen, 265.
Kindergartens, 211.
King's Daughters and Sons, 46, 320.
Koren, John, 295.
Labor bureaus, 272.
Labor conferences, 314.
Labor movement, 137.
Landlord missionaries, 62.
Landscape gardening, 248.
Lanier, Sidney, 243.
Laundries, public, 84.
Lavatories, public, 84.
Lecky, W. H., 187, 257.
Lecture courses, 209.
Libraries, 215, 233.
License laws, 293.
Little Mothers' Aid Association, 47.
Local option, 292.
Lodges, 143.
Lowell, J. R., 240, 245, 304.
Luxury, 34, 114, 256.
MacAlister, James, 201.
Machinery, social effects, 228.
MacVeagh, Franklin, 183.

Index. 349

Malthus, 111.
Mann, Horace, 125.
Manny, F. A., 208.
Manual training, 210.
Martin's "Human Body," 299.
Meliorism, 105.
Milk, 85.
Mill, J. S., 110.
Morals, teaching, 214.
More, T. (Utopia), 229.
Morley, Margaret W., 299.
Morris, W., 259.
Mothers, in factories, 28; duties, 34.
Mothers' Union, the, 42.
Motives, of action, 12.
Mott, A. J., 204.
Mount, J. A., 229.
Municipal institutions, 172.
Municipal reforms, 182.
Music, 245.
Mutual benefit societies, 143.
National Conference of Charities and Corrections, 279.
National Divorce Reform League, 297.
National Household Economic Association, 227.
National League for Good Roads, 253.
National Temperance Society, 285.
Natural laws in economic world, 100.
Nelson, N. O., 120.
New England manufactory, 124.
Newspapers, 175.
Noon rest for girls, 46.
Open and Institutional Church League, 309, 324.
Open church, the, 309.
Orphans, 268.
Parker, Superintendent, 205.
Parks, 250.
Parochial schools, 219.
Parties, political, 176.
Pauperism, 261.
Pawnshops, 172.
Peabody, George, 238.
People's Banks, 158.
Picot, George, 229.
Pidgeon, D., 124.
Plays, 244.
"Pleasant Sunday Afternoon," 301.

Political economy, 101.
Political reforms, 174.
Politics and health, 82, 86.
Popularizing science, 231.
Population, problems of, 110.
Postal saving banks, 171.
Post-office, 97.
"Potato patch," 274.
Prairie scenery, 251.
Preventive charity, 263.
Prisoners, to work roads, 92.
Problems, 19.
Profit-sharing, 131, 133.
Progress, 86.
Prohibition, 292.
Proportional representation, 187.
Protective agencies, 48, 161.
Provident measures, 129.
Public opinion, 129.
Public schools, 196, 296.
Pullman, 66, 252.
Raiffeisen banks, 155, 314.
Referendum, the, 187.
Reforms, 17.
Religion, a social force, 9; at home, 42; in schools, 213; teaching, 220, 304.
Rent, collecting, 64.
Roads, 88, 253.
Robins, Mary C., 248.
Roosevelt, Theodore, 140.
Rural schools, 206.
Rural villages, 70.
Rush, Benjamin, 282.
Rusk, Jerry, 229.
Ruskin, John, 62, 116.
Salvation Army, 318.
Sanitary aid societies, 72.
Schäffle, 9.
Schools, 191.
Schurz, Carl, 180.
Self-interest, 14.
Sellers, Edith, 48.
Shaftesbury, Earl of, 198.
Sidewalks, 91.
Slater, J. F., 237.
Sloyd, 211.
Slums, the, 60.
Smith, Goldwin, 115, 257.
Social purity, 288, 299.
Social selection, 78.
Social settlements, 234.

Socialists, 104, 173.
Sociologists, duty to society, 9.
Sociology, relation to theology, 11.
Sons of Temperance, 285.
South, R., 191.
Spahr, C. B., 169.
Specialization in philanthropy, 21.
Spencer, Herbert, 100.
Spendthrifts, 258.
Spoils system, 82.
Standards of conduct, 25.
Starr, Ellen, 199.
Strikes, 140.
Struggle, value of, 15.
Suburban homes, 65.
Sunday rest, 300.
Sunday-school, the, 321.
Sweating, 166.
Taxing power, 170.
Telegraph, the, 96.
Temperance movement, the, 282.
Theater, 246.
Theory and conduct, 9.
Thrift, 109.
Towns, plans for, 66, 250.
Trade schools, 209.
Trades unions, 138.
Tramps, 83, 271.
Transportation, 95.
Trusts, 167.

Twain, Mark, 240.
Unemployed, the, 107.
University Extension, 229.
University settlements, 234.
Unsocial Club of Women, the, 38.
Vacation schools, 238.
Variety of wants, 12.
Village improvement societies. 254.
Wages, 123, 127, 134.
Ward, L. F., 260.
Washington, B. T., 237.
Water supply, 75, 81.
Wealth, duties of, 113, 117.
White, A. D., 115.
White, Henry, 166.
Wiggin, Mrs. Kate, 40, 47.
Willard, Frances E., 287.
Woman's National Christian Temperance Union, 287.
Women of leisure, 41; wage-earners, 44; clubs, 255, 266.
Women workers, 164.
Woodward, C. M., 211.
Working Women's Social Club, 55.
Wright, C. D., 44, 154.
Young Men's Christian Association, 309, 317.
Young people, societies of, 321.
Young Woman's Christian Association, 45, 318.